Knowledge Management
Initiatives in Singapore

Series on Innovation and Knowledge Management

Series Editor: Suliman Hawamdeh   **ISSN: 1793-1533**
(University of North Texas)

Published*

Vol. 5   Creating Collaborative Advantage Through Knowledge and Innovation
edited by Suliman Hawamdeh *(University of Oklahoma)*

Vol. 6   Knowledge Management: Innovation, Technology and Cultures
edited by Christian Stary *(Johannes Kepler University, Austria)*,
Franz Barachini *(Vienna University of Technology, Austria)* and
Suliman Hawamdeh *(University of Oklahoma, USA)*

Vol. 7   Knowledge Management: Competencies and Professionalism
edited by Suliman Hawamdeh *(University of Oklahoma, USA)*,
Kimberly Stauss *(University of Arkansas, USA)* and
Franz Barachini *(Vienna University of Technology, Austria)*

Vol. 8   Managing Knowledge for Global and Collaborative Innovations
edited by Samuel Chu *(The University of Hong Kong)*,
Waltraut Ritter *(Knowledge Dialogues, Hong Kong)* and
Suliman Hawamdeh *(University of Oklahoma, USA)*

Vol. 9   Governing and Managing Knowledge in Asia (2nd Edition)
edited by Thomas Menkhoff *(Singapore Management University,
Singapore)*, Hans-Dieter Evers *(University of Bonn, Germany)* and
Chay Yue Wah *(SIM University, Singapore)*

Vol. 10   The Dynamics of Regional Innovation: Policy Challenges in
Europe and Japan
edited by Yveline Lecler *(University of Lyon, France)*,
Tetsuo Yoshimoto *(Ritsumeikan University, Japan)* and
Takahiro Fujimoto *(University of Tokyo, Japan)*

Vol. 11   Knowledge Management: An Interdisciplinary Perspective
by Sajjad M. Jasimuddin *(Aberystwyth University, UK)*

Vol. 12   Knowledge Management Initiatives in Singapore
by Margaret Tan *(Nanyang Technological University, Singapore)*
and Madanmohan Rao *(The KM Chronicles, India)*

**The complete list of the published volumes in the series can be found at
http://www.worldscibooks.com/series/sikm_series.shtml.*

Series on Innovation and Knowledge Management – Vol. 12

Knowledge Management Initiatives in Singapore

Margaret Tan

Nanyang Technological University, Singapore

Madanmohan Rao

The KM Chronicles, India

World Scientific

NEW JERSEY · LONDON · SINGAPORE · BEIJING · SHANGHAI · HONG KONG · TAIPEI · CHENNAI

Published by

World Scientific Publishing Co. Pte. Ltd.

5 Toh Tuck Link, Singapore 596224

USA office: 27 Warren Street, Suite 401-402, Hackensack, NJ 07601

UK office: 57 Shelton Street, Covent Garden, London WC2H 9HE

Library of Congress Cataloging-in-Publication Data
Tan, Margaret, author.
    Knowledge management initiatives in Singapore / by Margaret Tan (Nanyang Technological University, Singapore) and Madanmohan Rao (The KM Chronicles, India).
        pages cm. -- (Series on innovation and knowledge management, ISSN 1793-1533 ; vol. 12)
        Includes bibliographical references and index.
        ISBN 978-9814467803 (hardcover : alk. paper)
        1. Knowledge management--Singapore--Case studies. 2. Information technology--Singapore--Case studies. 3. Strategic planning--Singapore--Case studies. I. Rao, Madanmohan, author.
II. Title.
    HD30.2.T358 2013
    658.4'038--dc23
                                                            2013009941

British Library Cataloguing-in-Publication Data
A catalogue record for this book is available from the British Library.

In-house Editor: Lee Xin Ying

Typeset by Stallion Press
Email: enquiries@stallionpress.com

Printed in Singapore by World Scientific Printers.

Foreword

This is a timely book in that it situates a range of pragmatic projects within a wider conceptual and historical setting. The competitive value of knowledge at a country level opens the book, contrasting Korea with Ghana, both of which started with similar GDPs but then diverged significantly. Singapore can claim a similar success; charting the knowledge management practice of its various ministries and agencies is thus of significant value to anyone concerned about the development of government in times of increasing resource scarcity. Of course, we need to understand the context in which this takes place.

Singapore is arguably a modern *Polis* — the re-incarnation of the Greek city state in a modern age. Its two major universities are constantly in the world's top 100 rankings and its economic success comes from a unique blending of state and private enterprises. Its various government organisations were among the early adopters of knowledge management practices the best part of two decades ago, but it has also sustained these practices over time. In particular, the Singapore Armed Forces have, to quote the citation for the Platinum award from the Information & Knowledge Management Society, seen "sustained and pervasive impact of its KM initiatives". This is in part due to both continuity and change; some personnel have directed and guided the initiative throughout that period while encouraging and enabling wider participation. They have focused on both operational needs and back office functions. As a result, they are still perceived as strategic while in other countries, knowledge management has been progressively shifted away from the centre to a peripheral aspect of IT. This is also true of the 11 other governmental organisations detailed in this book — each brings a distinct perspective reflecting their organisational context.

This is a unique book, in that it does not seek to generalise partially understood practice into naive simplified recipes, something all too common in the literature. The introduction provides an overview of the history of knowledge management which recognises that the discipline existed before it was known by that name. Its claim that knowledge management is at the core of management movements today is controversial, although the suggested application to innovation is surely not, neither is the value of knowledge or the cost of ignoring it.

Knowledge management is that rare beast in management science, a movement with many origins which may explain its resilience. Its origins are frequently attributed to Nonaka's 1991 HBR article "The Knowledge Creating Company", but in the same period we see the Intellectual Capital movement with Leif Edvinsson and Tom Stewart from Buckman Labs pioneering work on distributed computing, as well as developments of information theory by Prusak, Davenport and many others. In the modern era, Peter Drucker coined the phrase "The Knowledge Worker" in 1959, but the major growth of knowledge management as a distinct function within companies coincided with the advent of scalable technology, the shift from mainframe to micro-computer and the rapid development of collaboration software and email (especially Lotus Notes), but more recently various products from Microsoft such as the ubiquitous SharePoint, a plethora of search engines, community software and the like.

The focus on technology was the making of knowledge management, but may also be its nemesis. Focusing on knowledge as information contrasts with older models of knowledge development such as the apprentice model in which knowledge is transferred by experiments, tolerated failure and teaching. Taught by Journeymen, apprentices observe the master, and share stories with each other. As they gain knowledge, they are called to walk the tables of the craft hall to assume the status of Journeyman, after which their masterworks are accepted by their peers. The body of knowledge develops; it is not simply codified and transferred. Narrative is a critical aspect of that process, as it is in any professional community. Engineers tell stories around the water cooler and the knowledge transfer thus engendered is as important as any drawing or document.

To date technology has not been able to replicate that model, and the focus on codification and machine-based search is limited compared to the power and capability of a human network. This may now be changing with the rapid growth and use of social computing. This is of its nature messy, just as all human exchange is messy, yet coherent. A tweet or a blog linked to a book is a better reference than a search as it includes the validation of a human you've chosen to follow. Humans in social computing are augmented by information flow, not replaced by it. I remember tweeting a request for information in the early hours of morning and my own Twitter network responded quickly not only to solve the issue, but to do some of the critical work to get a new project up and running within hours. That network extended across three continents and was not designed — it evolved. Access to the network was not achieved by formal position, but by publishing and linking interesting material. It's not who you are, but what you say that gives you access to sense-making networks.

If knowledge management is to survive, it has to embrace *mess* and create a symbiosis of human intelligence with the scalability of open computing platforms. IT departments seeking to control networks and information (besides truly confidential data) will simply be left behind in this new, dynamic ecology. The challenge for knowledge management is using technology to augment, but not replace, human intelligence. It is to focus on supporting decision-making at both a strategic and operational level and to enable an environment which encourages innovation by accident as well as by design. During World War II, a Raytheon engineer noticed that a candy bar in his pocket melted when he was standing in front of an active radar set. That accidental act of *noticing* resulted in the microwave oven. Over-structured, over-codified approaches to knowledge management would not have permitted that intervention, just as over control through excessive measurement can destroy innovation. Knowledge management needs to use technology to augment and scale the natural processes of the apprentice model rather than the needs of taxonomists and database managers. If it does that, and the technology now permits it, then, and only then, it has a future.

So take the examples in this book, see them in context, learn from them, but do not slavishly copy them. Each case has created something appropriate to its context, some mundane, some strategic, but all valuable. Any knowledge management project has to constantly adapt and shift to accommodate changing contexts. To date, Singapore has achieved something that has escaped other countries and this is recorded in this book; but it is the start of a journey that others can share, not the end point.

Dave Snowden
Founder and Chief Scientific Officer
Cognitive Edge Pte Ltd

Preface

The emergence of the knowledge-based economy has highlighted the need for effective exploitation of knowledge, making knowledge management an important function in organisations. Addressing its importance, the Division of Information Studies at the Wee Kim Wee School of Communication and Information (WKWSCI) at the Nanyang Technological University launched the Master of Science degree in Knowledge Management in 2002. The programme provides graduates with professional education in knowledge management to meet the demands of the knowledge-intensive organisations.

The book focuses on the 12 organisations that won the knowledge management excellence awards in 2008, 2009, and 2010 constituted by the Information and Knowledge Management Society of Singapore. Thus, the objective of the book is to share the extensive knowledge, various experiences, diverse perspectives and practical learning of the organisations that initiated their knowledge management projects. The book provides in-depth descriptions of the organisations' knowledge management journeys, origins, destinations, roadmaps, speed bumps and compasses.

The book therefore makes a good read for a wide spectrum of the knowledge management community who is contemplating similar journeys. Although there are many publications on knowledge management from consultants and scholars, most of these are about private sector organisations, largely in the United States of America and Europe, reflecting the origins of the discipline. This book, however, brings in the perspectives from Asia, especially the award-winning public sector organisations from Singapore.

Margaret Tan and Madanmohan Rao
February 2013

About the Authors

 **Margaret Tan** is Associate Professor at the Wee Kim Wee School of Communication and Information and Deputy Director at the Singapore Internet Research Centre, both at the Nanyang Technological University in Singapore. She has published widely in scholarly academic journals and co-authored the following books: *The Virtual Workplace, e-Payment: The Digital Exchange* and *Understanding the Interactive Digital Media Marketplace: Framework, Platforms, Communities and Issues.* She has published over 100 academic papers, spoken at various international conferences and seminars, and served as program chairs and organising committee for over 60 international conferences. She also sits on numerous editorial and review boards of international journals and publications.

Her research and teaching interests include understanding the organisational impact on the strategic deployment of internet technologies, particularly on electronic security, data protection and privacy policies, e-Government and digital societies, and the implications of interactive digital media on knowledge management.

 **Madanmohan Rao** is a KM author and consultant based in Bangalore. He is the editor of *The Knowledge Management Chronicles, The Asia Pacific Internet Handbook, AfricaDotEdu, Global Citizen,* and *World of Proverbs*; and was on the international editorial board of the book *Transforming e-Knowledge.* He is also the co-founder of the Bangalore K-Community, a network of KM professionals. He was formerly the

communications director at the United Nations Inter Press Service Bureau in New York, vice president at IndiaWorld Communications in Bombay, group consultant at Microland in Bangalore, and research director at the Asian Media Information and Communication Centre in Singapore.

Madan has given talks in over 80 countries, including conferences such as KM World in California, KM Russia in Moscow, KM Asia in Singapore, and KM Challenge Australia. A graduate with a MS in computer science from the Indian Institute of Technology at Bombay and a PhD in communications from the University of Massachusetts at Amherst, he is an adjunct faculty at the International School of Information Management, where he teaches KM courses at the master's level. He is also an active blogger and Tweeter on KM (http://km.techsparks.com/; http://twitter.com/MadanRao).

Acknowledgements

We are very grateful to the Wee Kim Wee School of Communication and Information for providing the funding to support the Knowledge Management cluster research. We would also like to thank our colleagues in the Division of Information Studies for their support in the project. A very special gratitude is extended to Dr Lee Chu Keong who has contributed his thoughts and works in the book.

As the idea of documenting the cases came from the Knowledge Management awards conferred by the Information & Knowledge Management Society of Singapore (iKMS), we are very appreciative of the support from its two past presidents, namely, Mr Ng Kok Chuan and Mr Patrick Lambe, who have shared and given us access to the organisations to conduct our interviews for the book.

Most important, we are especially grateful to the knowledge management teams and leaders of the 12 public organisations who have patiently and generously given us their precious time, sharing with us their experiences and insights during our many interviews and site visits.

Without doubt, the team at World Scientific Publishing deserves a lot of credit in the publication of this book. We are most grateful to Ms Lee Xin Ying for her conscientious efforts and patience in editing the final proof of the manuscript.

Margaret Tan and Madanmohan Rao
February 2013

Contents

List of Figures

List of Tables

CHAPTER ONE

Introduction

*"In the end, the location of the New Economy is not in the technology,
be it the microchip or the global telecommunications network. It is in
the human mind."*

(Webber, 1993, p. 27)

1.1. Knowledge Management: The Road Thus Far

The journey began on September 1992, during the Non-Aligned Nations
Heads of State Meeting which was hosted in Jakarta. At the meeting,
Ghanaian Prime Minister Paul Victor Obeng requested Singapore's
Prime Minister Goh Chok Tong to aid Ghana by providing development advice. Prime Minister Goh agreed, and the Economic Development Board of Singapore set out to work immediately, researching the
Ghanaian economy. In the process of their research, the team encountered a startling fact. Although South Korea and Ghana started developing their economies from about the same time (Ghana from 1957, after
gaining independence from the British; and South Korea from 1953,
after the Korean War), and from about the same starting point (from
approximately US$250 GDP per capita), by 1990, the South Korean
economy had surpassed the Ghanaian economy by almost eightfold.
When asked about this large discrepancy, the World Bank explained
that South Korea's ability to acquire and use knowledge was responsible for at least half of that difference.[1]

It is clear that some countries are more aware of their need to
continually acquire new knowledge to reinvent their economies. Of

[1]Story adapted from Chan's (2002) Heart Work (pp. 240–241).

these countries, some are more adept at doing it, and some less. One example of a country that has successfully transformed itself economically is Finland, whose economy in the 1960s was based on forestry and paper production (Powell & Snellman, 2004, pp. 203–204). By the year 2000, Finland had reached a level of 137.6 high tech patent applications per million inhabitants, the highest number within the European Union (Zoppè, 2002). Finland is now known more for Nokia and its innovations in mobile and wireless communications than for its paper products.

Through their policies, countries can choose to acquire and use knowledge more effectively. At the national level, Singapore's then Acting Minister for Manpower, Dr Ng Eng Hen, explained in parliament that the government's 'foreign talent policy', a policy that allows companies in Singapore to hire foreign manpower, is a strategic asset as companies can then bring in workers with the specific experience and skills they require.[2] He gave the example of IBM Singapore, which hired people from 25 countries who had valuable experience and in-depth expertise in esoteric areas.

On the other hand, countries can also choose to reject knowledge through their policies. The best example of the conscious rejection of knowledge is the actions of Adolf Hitler. In the early decades of the 20th century, Germany was probably the foremost scientific nation in the world. When Hitler came into power in 1933, he single-handedly destroyed the tradition of scholarship in Germany and dismantled her institutes of higher learning by dismissing approximately 2,000 academics and scholars of non-Aryan descent (Marks, 1983). The move was followed by the public burning of books that were 'un-German' on May 10, 1933 to purify the German language. Among those who left were 20 professors who were either Nobel laureates, or would be Nobel laureates. Germany's brain drain was Britain's and the United States's brain gain.[3] The exodus of scientists from Germany enabled the United States to surpass Germany as the world's leading scientific nation after World War II.

---

[2] *Source*: http://www.mom.gov.sg/publish/momportal/en/press_room/mom_speeches/2004/20040319-attractingforeigntalenttoworkpasssystem.html.

[3] The two thousand included four categories of people: (1) those who were Jews, which formed the majority; (2) those whose wife was a Jew; (3) those who left to protest the way in which their colleagues were being treated; and (4) those who disagreed with the National Socialist attitude to science and scientific objectivity (Marks, 1983, p. 372).

Such policies are the same at the organisational level — companies differ in their ability to acquire and use knowledge. Those able to do so innovate and thrive; those unable to do so wither and perish. Many industries are faced with an uncertain and rapidly changing environment. Industry deregulations, new and disruptive technologies, and changing cultural trends, demographics and economic realities are posing challenges for many organisations. Some examples are listed below.

In many countries deregulation of the aviation sector has caused 'legacy carriers' (airlines founded before the deregulation) to face stiff competition from the newly formed 'low-cost' or 'budget' carriers. Travellers now have a choice, and many of them choose budget carriers when travelling shorter distances. The impact of 'budget' carriers is not limited to vacation travels, even business travels have been affected. Due to the economic downturn, many organisations introduced austerity measures and as a result, on the short-haul routes, their employees have to take budget carriers! The 'budget' carrier model is so successful that it is being adapted for long distances. AirAsia X started daily flights from Kuala Lumpur to London. Besides offering lower ticket prices, budget carriers are also innovative. An example of their willingness to experiment is AirAsia's SMS ticket reservation service launched in 2003 — the first in the world — to reach the ten million mobile phone users in Malaysia.

Voice over IP telecommunications providers, such as Skype,[4] TokBox,[5] VZOchat[6] and Google Voice[7] and Talk[8] offer free unlimited worldwide PC-to-PC calls and PC-to-PC video chats, are having a major impact on telecommunications companies, whose profitability is likely to be hit significantly and permanently due to reduced fixed line and mobile revenues, especially revenue from long distance calls. At CeBIT Technology Industry Summit in 2005, Niklas Zennström, CEO and co-founder of Skype Technologies SA, announced that people should not be charged for making phone calls. Skype users use their computers to call other Skype users free anywhere in the world regardless of distance or service provider. Suddenly, geography is

---

[4]http://www.skype.com/ (accessed 30 June 2012).
[5]http://www.tokbox.com/ (accessed 30 June 2012).
[6]http://www.vzochat.com/ (accessed 30 June 2012).
[7]http://www.google.com/googlevoice/about.html (accessed 30 June 2012).
[8]http://www.google.com/talk/ (accessed 30 June 2012).

rendered meaningless, and this is significant because traditional phone companies have based their charges on the distance a call travels. In 2005, Skype was sold to eBay for US$2.6 billion.

E-books represent the fastest growing segment of the book publishing industry. While traditional publishers are still coming to grips on how best to alter their business model to take advantage of e-books, new publishers like Smashwords[9] have already given authors free services that help them publish, promote, distribute and sell their books as a multi-format e-book, ready for immediate sale online at a price they determine. The traditional publishing model is encumbered by intermediaries, e.g. literary agents, editors, publishers, printers, distributors and bookstores, which stand between the author and their prospective readers. Smashwords' social publishing model removes the middlemen and allows readers to decide what's worth reading, and vote for it with their purchase.

Higher education has not been spared. In countries where the birthrate has been low, the survival of universities has been threatened because of declining enrolments. For instance, in Taiwan, some 60 universities (out of about 160) may have to close in the next 12 years (Taipei Times, 2009). In addition to demographic challenges, several Ivy League universities have started to offer free, online, college-level courses. Calling theirs edX, Harvard and MIT have leveraged on their reputation (MIT even offers 'MITx', certificates of mastery for individual courses for a small fee) to attract students online. What is to become of the less well-known universities, now that the Ivy League universities can offer courses to hundreds of thousands of students at any one time?

Caterpillar is faced with an aging workforce, and a large proportion of their existing workforce will retire in the near future. They are trying to collect the knowledge of their retiring workers and make it available to those who need it. Caterpillar is not alone in its predicament. Organisations in countries that have a rapidly ageing demographic profile have to think of how to retain and capture the knowledge of their employees before they retire.

Similarly, the survivability of organisations is dependent on their ability to adapt to new challenges; and the critical issue lies with the

---

[9]http://www.smashwords.com/ (accessed 30 June 2012).

acquisition and usage of knowledge. Organisations that succeed will be the South Korea or Finland of their respective industry. Organisations that merely manage to do this will have to be contented to be the Ghana in their industry. Organisations that fail (e.g. Kodak) will cease to exist in the years ahead. Indeed, organisations need to have a constant stream of ideas, and the ability to convert these ideas to novel products and services.

1.1.1. *The Field of Knowledge Management*

To survive, many of these organisations have turned to knowledge management (KM), but what is knowledge management? Universities have started postgraduate programs on KM, publishers have started journals with KM as its focus, professional bodies with KM practitioners as its main members were founded, and conferences organised with KM as its theme. But what is KM, really? Many researchers have defined the term knowledge management, and several definitions will be reviewed.

Definition I

Liebowitz (1999) defines knowledge management as the process of creating value from an organisation's intangible assets. It deals with the conceptualisation, review, consolidation, and action phases of creating, securing, combining, coordinating, and retrieving knowledge. It is an amalgamation of concepts borrowed from the fields of artificial intelligence/knowledge-based systems, software engineering, business process re-engineering, human resource management, and organisational behavior. Kaplan and Norton (2004) classify an organisation's success in creating value out of its intangible assets into three categories:

- Human capital: employees' skills, talent and knowledge;
- Information capital: databases, information systems, networks, and technology infrastructure; and
- Organisation capital: culture, leadership, employee alignment, teamwork, and commitment.

Considering that employees in an organisation have had different work and life experiences, and possess different knowledge bases, the important question to address is — how can an organisation deploy the knowledge of its diverse workforce to further its goals? How can an organisation use its employees' skills, talent and knowledge to bear on the problems it faces, and the opportunities it encounters? Some organisations encourage their employees to contribute what they know into KM systems; others offer rewards to employees that make the effort to document what they know. The following examples illustrate how organisations encourage their workers to contribute towards the organisation's knowledge base.

At 3M, Spencer Silver invented a 'failed' (not-sticky-enough) adhesive. Arthur Fry sang in his church choir during weekends, and used slips of paper to mark the pages of his hymnal. One day, it occurred to him that Silver's 'failed' adhesive could be put to use to create a better bookmark. The result is the Post-it notes that can be found today in almost every office. 3M managed to tap on its human capital (even knowledge related to singing in a choir, an activity completely unrelated to work at 3M!).

Buckman Labs developed a system called K'Netix which included an electronic forum to facilitate the exchange and cross-fertilisation of ideas. As CEO, Robert Buckman took the lead when he announced that "those individuals who have something intelligent to say now have a forum in which to say it". In stating that "management can no longer hold them back", Buckman attempted to remove fear so long as they had "something intelligent" to say. He was deeply involved with the development of K'Netix, and wrote the Code of Ethics that would govern the use of K'Netix. As Buckman Labs was an international company, Buckman ensured that the most important messages were translated into different languages within 48 hours.

Daimler Chrysler developed the Engineering Book of Knowledge (EBoK), a knowledge database containing the best practices contributed by its employees. Before its inclusion, a best practice is identified, refined, and verified. Any engineer may propose a best practice, and Tech Club members responsible for that area of knowledge comment on the knowledge. As the Book Owner is ultimately responsible for approving new entries and changes to the EBoK, he joins in the discussion. The proposer then considers the inputs given by the Tech Club members and uses the comments to build a more refined practice. Finally, the Tech Club decides on the new knowledge to be entered into the EBoK.

Definition II

Rumizen (2002) defines knowledge management as: "The [set of] systematic processes by which the knowledge needed for an organisation to succeed is created, captured, shared and leveraged. Knowledge management focuses on how an organisation identifies, creates, captures, acquires, shares, and leverages knowledge. Systematic processes support these activities, also enabling the replication of successes. All of these are specific actions organisations take to manage their knowledge." Many scholars have taken this approach, and have proposed different sets of processes that make up KM. Such 'stage models' for KM are very common, and they vary according to the granularity of the processes proposed. The simplest, by Davenport and Prusak (1998), divides knowledge management into three processes:

- Knowledge Generation;
- Knowledge Codification; and
- Knowledge Transfer.

On the other hand, Schwartz (2007) proposed a more comprehensive model with twelve processes:

- Knowledge Creation;
- Knowledge Discovery;
- Knowledge Acquisition;
- Knowledge Classification;
- Knowledge Verification and Validation;
- Knowledge Codification;
- Knowledge Calibration;
- Modelling Knowledge;
- Knowledge Integration;
- Knowledge Sharing;
- Knowledge Dissemination; and
- Knowledge Maintenance.

These stage models are useful in that they identify the different activities that are part of the KM processes. Although the processes give an impression that they are carried out linearly, this is usually not the case. In fact, the processes may overlap with each other, and often more than one process is involved.

1.1.2. *Knowledge Management: The Seventh Era of Management*

The 20th century saw tremendous progress in management theories and insights, and there are general trends guiding business in different periods throughout this time. Hickman and Silva (1988) summarised six eras of management, the first three related to rational and scientific management, the rest to qualitative and humanistic management. They are described below.

Era 1 (1910–1935): Structure building

In this era, the world economy was boosted by World War I, and many companies took advantage of the opportunity to expand their enterprises. Multiple operating units and management hierarchies were established; new educational training on business skills started in universities and colleges; business and management journals published articles on organisational structures; professional consulting firms emerged, all dedicated to serve the increasing business volume and activities. Adjusting, refining, improving, and perfecting organisational structures became the first priority for business leaders. For those companies that took actions in making structural changes, they enjoyed a head start for the next era of management: to enhance efficiency and productivity.

Era 2 (1935–1955): Productivity enhancement

In this era, the worldwide economy experienced fluctuations due to the Great Depression and World War II. With rising demand for consumer goods during and after the war, even the smallest companies employed scientific management methods to push for operational efficiency. Technological techniques were explored to meet the needs of the exploding market. Many companies adopted a diversification strategy to maximise their asset and resource utility rate, combining technology into products and production lines. Among those scientific managing methods, Taylorism gained momentum, leading to significant increases in output through specification of workers' job tasks. Some business leaders started to realise the importance of employee morale, but this trend did not gain enough attention until the next few decades. The focus for managers was to redesign their lagged organisational systems to ensure and sustain the increased productivity.

Era 3 (1955–1970): Systems design

Businesses entered the period of 'golden economic era' during this period, with a large scale of merger and acquisition, especially with those in unrelated product areas, and overseas market expansion. To better control and manage their financial investments and operational resources, business leaders turned to advanced management systems to standardise, simplify and streamline their workflow. Indeed, the development of computers resulted in advancing automation with effective tracking of business data and processes. However, the business environment became more complex and managers began to work under pressure, tightening up control over employees and operations, and minimising cost incurrence. After three eras of internal improvement on structure, productivity and systems, the business communities resorted to a more qualitative and humanistic approach for further organisational development.

Era 4 (1970–1980): Strategic planning

The American way of scientific and rational management was challenged in face of dynamic market changes, intensified global competition and constant need for innovation in the early 1970s. Business leaders realised that internally efficient structures, high productivity and effective systems alone could not guarantee promising results because they were insufficient to address problems in overall planning. Thus, managers shifted their attention to the external environment and to the building of corporate strategies for guidance. Companies proactively collaborated with consulting firms to reorganise for long-term success. Strategic business units were set up; new management concepts were brought in; and strategic movements were initiated. The business world found advantages of this management technique over the previous rational management styles, in gaining a competitive position in the market.

Era 5 (1980–1985): Culture shaping

For business strategies to be implemented successfully, they need to be carried out by the right people with the right culture. To provide an illustration, it appeared that the Japanese companies upstage their American counterparts because of their successful internal corporate cultures, which includes having a common purpose, committed employees, consistent corporate behaviors, harmonious interpersonal relations, and so on. These organisational cultures tried to provide a sense of belonging, recognition, and satisfaction in work. They also found significant increases in productivity achieved through matching and balancing employees' personal goals and corporate missions. The culture movement pushed for stronger and more distinct organisation cultures, bringing about superior performance.

Era 6 (1985–1990): Innovation management

In the late 1980s, most business leaders agreed on innovation as the key driver to the next stage of success. Words such as innovation, creativity, entrepreneurship, intra-preneurship, personal breakthroughs, and adaptation became popular. Companies that succeeded in innovations experienced greater advantages such as reduced cost, expanded markets, and satisfied customers, thus motivating economic and social progress.

Era 7 (1990–): Knowledge management

The publication of Nonaka and Takeuchi's book, *The Knowledge Creating Company: How Japanese Companies Create the Dynamics of Innovation* in 1995, can be conveniently taken to be the starting point of the era of knowledge management. They advocated that the single sure source of sustainable advantage in the uncertain economy is knowledge. Yet, few managers knew exactly how to manage knowledge or organisations that depended on knowledge for their survival. Using mainly Japanese companies as examples, Nonaka provided evidence that the creation of new knowledge involved more than the processing of information, but more importantly, tapping into the subjective insights, intuitions, and even hunches of one's employees.

In a sense, the seventh era of management incorporates the ideas and concerns of the last six eras. Today, organisations are also rethinking the structure of their organisation (the preoccupation of Era 1), and how it is being transformed by technology. Employees, on the other hand, are rethinking their relationship with their work, which has been transformed by technology. Where previously work ended when they left the office, now it continues when they reach home — all because

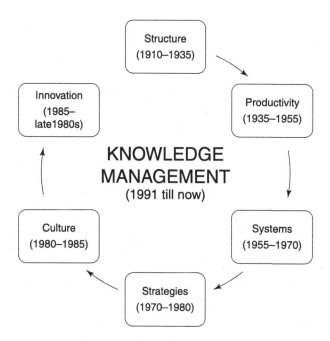

Figure 1.1 The Management Eras.

technology makes it possible. Managers are also rethinking productivity (the preoccupation of Era 2). With Facebook, GTalk and various means of communication, how does the organisation maintain productivity? Innovation (the preoccupation of Era 7) is often discussed by CEOs; it is even more important with global competitions. Apple is one of the most admired companies because of its ability to innovate. Its stream of best-selling products, iPod, iPad, and iPhone, is the envy of its competitors.

Figure 1.1 shows KM being the core in the management movement today incorporating the different aspects of previous six management eras.

1.1.3. *The Knowledge Movement*

The knowledge movement, addressing the centrality of knowledge factors in performance and innovation, is spreading beyond organisations and industries to cities and countries as units of analysis. In cities around the world, this has been taking place through communities of KM practitioners across industrial sectors, who regularly meet to share knowledge, benchmark their KM initiatives, hold seminars and conferences to confer awards and publish research. The Information & Knowledge Management Society of Singapore (iKMS) is an example of a community movement of KM professionals in Singapore.

Malhotra (2001) offers broader insights into the range of this knowledge movement by showcasing KM practices across a variety of organisations. He classifies these as project-based (e.g. construction industry), umbrella corporations (e.g. GE), virtual business communities (e.g. the Linux movement on the internet), and the multi-directional network (e.g. lobbies of small and medium enterprises in Taiwan).

Wimmer (2002) charts new territory at the KM frontier in public sector and government agencies, in areas like smart citizen services and better administrative decision-making. Knowledge assets can be assessed at the organisational as well as national economic levels, while planning for growth and performance for the entire country. National prowess can be measured in terms of financial capital (productivity, exports), market capital (diffusion of new products, participation in international events, openness to different cultures, language skills), process capital (computerisation and communications infrastructure, internet usage), and renewal and development capital (research expenditures, scientific publications, patents, startups, entrepreneurship).

Top-down (government-led) and/or bottom-up (practitioner-led) clusters of knowledge industries are emerging in Cambridge, Bangalore, Singapore, Helsinki, Tel Aviv and Hsinchu (Rosenberg, 2002). Many success factors of knowledge hubs such as Silicon Valley are being replicated in these cities to nurture knowledge industries: business webs, IT-savvy workers, local 'living laboratories', activities and organisations for communities of interest, organisational mergers for flow of skilled labour and intellectual property, local academic and research institutes, and commercial partnerships between academia and the industry.

In sum, recent literature and studies on KM reinforce the importance of a knowledge strategy driven by a combination of technology, people and process considerations, while keeping in mind the complex nature of organisational behaviour and the uncharted terrain of business, national economic indicators, and competition, with regards to the global economy. A number of books have focused explicitly on organisational KM case studies (e.g. the experience of Buckman Labs, Siemens). Most of these are from private sector organisations in western countries; this book makes a valuable contribution in two ways: by focusing on public sector agencies, and by bringing in KM perspectives from the Asian region.

1.2. KM in Singapore: iKMS Award Winners

This book builds on the trends in the knowledge movement identified in Section 1.1, and addresses how Singapore organisations are meeting the KM challenge. For the research conducted in this book, the target case studies were winners of KM awards in Singapore: the annual KM Excellence Awards conferred by iKMS. As described on its website (www.ikms.org), it is a non-profit organisation aimed at serving information and knowledge management professionals.

Founded by the Division of Information Studies in the School of Communication and Information at Nanyang Technological University, iKMS started as a KM interest group, meeting and discussing KM matters within Singapore since 1999. It now serves its members by making information on KM easily available through a wide array of resources such as evening talks, seminars, conferences, networking opportunities, journal, newsletters, special interest groups, collaboration forums, and group discussions. Its goals include creating awareness of KM and information processing, and promoting research and development in these fields. Its membership extends to 200 members in 8 countries, with an interest group of over 1,000 professionals.

iKMS holds its annual KM Singapore conference and publishes the annual book *Knowledge Management: Singapore Perspectives*. The annual KM Excellence Awards were launched, and aimed at recognising KM efforts in Singapore that have positive business impacts on their host organisations. The first KM Excellence Awards process was launched at iKMS's conference on 9 October 2008. Participating organisations were evaluated by an international panel of experts representing different areas of KM practice and expertise.

The KM Excellence Awards are intended to illustrate examples of good KM practices within Singapore, for the learning benefit of the professional KM community; to promote knowledge exchange among organisations that are already on a KM journey; and to build the confidence of organisations that are considering a KM journey.

Good KM practice for the awards means any KM effort that results in helpful learning on how to implement knowledge strategies effectively, and that delivers some kind of value to the organisation. Such examples can come from organisation-wide KM or from smaller KM projects within a part of the organisation. The iKMS KM Excellence Awards are much more about professional peer evaluation, dialogue, and feedback, and not so much about benchmarking to a prescribed standard. They do not measure or compare progress with other organisations in the industry or field, nationally or internationally. They are intended simply to make good KM practice visible and to support the collective learning of the KM community in Singapore by finding and highlighting useful examples of positive KM impact.

The process starts with participating organisations submitting an application to iKMS according to a prescribed format, giving the background and purpose of their KM programmes/projects, and any business benefits and lessons learned that they have achieved. The panel evaluates the submissions, discusses them, as well as requests for more detailed clarification to get a clearer understanding of the applicants' KM efforts. The panel then shortlists the applications and seeks consensus on their award recommendations. In some cases where consensus is difficult to achieve, a site visit was held to provide further clarification. The panel also provides feedback in the form of a citation.

Applications are evaluated in two categories: whether they are making innovative and productive use of technology and infrastructure to support knowledge and information management; and whether they are successfully introducing change in culture and processes to support the knowledge and information management goals. The types of awards are as follows:

- Platinum — where an organisation has closely aligned its efforts in both technology and culture categories, and is judged to merit a Gold in both categories;
- Gold — where a KM initiative is judged to have a pervasive, positive business impact in all parts of the organisation;
- Silver — where a KM initiative is judged to be having a real business impact in parts of the organisation, but this impact is not yet pervasive across the organisation;
- Bronze — where a KM initiative is judged to be starting to make some positive impact; and

- Merit — where a KM initiative is judged to show great promise but have yet to demonstrate a clear business impact.

The first set of government organisations to win the KM Excellence Awards in 2008 were Defence Science and Technology Agency (DSTA), Singapore Police Force: Police Technology Department (SPF-PTD), Urban Redevelopment Authority (URA) — Silver Awards, and National Library Board (NLB) — Bronze Award. The second set of winners in 2009 was Inland Revenue Authority of Singapore (IRAS) and Jurong Town Corporation (JTC) — Silver Awards, as well as Ministry of Finance (MOF) and NLB — Bronze Awards. The third set of awards in 2010 went to Singapore Armed Forces (SAF) — Platinum Award, Singapore Youth Olympic Games Organising Committee (SYOGOC) — Silver Award, Attorney-General's Chambers (AGC) and the Supreme Court (SC) — Bronze Award, as well as Intellectual Property Office Of Singapore (IPOS) — Merit Award. These winners, along with a summary of their citations from iKMS, are listed in Table 1.1.

In 2011, the KM heads of organisations that had won these KM Excellence Awards were approached by the book's authors to share the story of their KM practices. The materials were augmented by interviews covering factors such as understanding their evolutionary trends, infrastructure, knowledge assets, communities of practice (CoPs), return on investment, cultural issues, capacity building, and incentive schemes. This section covers the key highlights of the KM practices of the organisations based on the commonalities and differences of their rationale, implementation, and impacts.

1.2.1. Attorney-General's Chambers (AGC)

The Attorney-General's Chambers (AGC) commenced its KM journey with the Singapore Government's KM Experimentation Programme in 2002. An external consultant conducted the KM audit and designed the KM initiative. AGC's KM vision was to provide quality legal services through effective, swift and thorough application of knowledge and experience. To drive this, AGC created posts for Divisional KM Champions and a KM Director. A contest was conducted for the logo design and portal name (SA-GE; KM Central). Supporting tools included a wiki. A mentoring programme consisting of a buddy system was put in place. KM was promoted via an annual Innovation Day.

Table 1.1   iKMS KM Excellence Award Winners in 2008, 2009, and 2010.

Organisation	Award	Citation
2008		
Defence Science and Technology Agency (DSTA)	Silver Award: for clear business impact in parts of the organisation	Successfully integrated KM and knowledge sharing efforts with core capabilities of the organisation, the competency development of its staff, and provided a strong supporting infrastructure.
Singapore Police Force: Police Technology Department (SPF-PTD)	Silver Award: for clear business impact in parts of the organisation	An exemplary case of strong commitment to changing the knowledge-sharing culture of a workgroup to achieve strong business benefits.
Urban Redevelopment Authority (URA)	Silver Award: for clear business impact in parts of the organisation	A strong example of a mature KM initiative with strong, consistent management support over several years, where KM efforts have been brought together under a common framework and roadmap, and aligned with the core business of the organisation.
National Library Board (NLB)	Bronze Award: for the beginnings of a positive impact in a part of the organisation	The initiative to establish a knowledge-sharing platform to help reference librarians improve their service excellence in addressing customer reference enquiries. A good collaborative platform allied with culture change and innovations in work processes to achieve improvements in customer service.
2009		
Inland Revenue Authority of Singapore (IRAS)	Silver Award: Culture category	Building a knowledge-sharing culture leading to improved performance, and integrated into its organisational processes the creation of clear roles and expectations for knowledge sharing, career development and training, amongst others.

(Continued)

Table 1.1 (*Continued*)

Organisation	Award	Citation
Jurong Town Corporation (JTC)	Silver Award: Technology and Infrastructure categories Bronze Award: Culture category	Sustained commitment to improving and developing its platforms for accessing and sharing key information and knowledge across the agency, which is a critical lever to support the effectiveness of its key operations. Promising work in improving collaboration, developing knowledge activists and the sharing of expertise.
Ministry of Finance (MOF)	Bronze Award: Technology and Infrastructure categories	Innovative implementation of an email repository and supporting taxonomy to improve information access and corporate memory in the organisation — the initiative is showing promise of a strong positive impact on the ability of staff to work effectively and efficiently.
National Library Board (NLB)	Bronze Award: Culture category	Promising signs of impact in building cross-organisation knowledge sharing from the Knowledge Champions Programme — an innovative approach to moving the champions' role beyond advocacy to modelling and deploying knowledge-sharing techniques through a structured training programme, clearly defined roles and support through a community of practice.
2010		
Singapore Armed Forces (SAF)	Platinum Award	Sustained and pervasive impact of its KM initiatives, encompassing both culture change and technology deployment, to enhance their capabilities across a very wide range of operational contexts.

(*Continued*)

Table 1.1 *(Continued)*

Organisation	Award	Citation
Singapore Youth Olympic Games Organising Committee (SYOGOC)	Silver Award: Culture category	Disciplined approach to knowledge capture, knowledge transfer and 'learning on the go' to ensure success in an extremely fast-moving and high stakes event for Singapore.
Attorney-General's Chambers (AGC)	Bronze Award: Technology and Culture categories	Strong mentoring culture, stress on collaboration and knowledge transfer to retain institutional knowledge, the openness to learning from the best practices of law firms, significant impact on the consistency and quality of legal opinions.
Supreme Court of Singapore (SC)	Bronze Award: Technology and Culture categories	KM efforts to support the work of Judicial Officers and the Legal Registry, in support of their key performance indicator: the timely and effective determination of cases filed.
Intellectual Property Office Of Singapore (IPOS)	Merit Award: Technology category	KM-friendly SharePoint implementation.

1.2.2. *Defence Science and Technology Agency (DSTA)*

Singapore's Defence Science and Technology Agency (DSTA) was established in 2000 as the first statutory board of Singapore's Ministry of Defence (MINDEF). Its ten-year KM plan focuses on knowledge retention, release, and reuse in three phases: exploration, foundation and growth. Its KM vision was to create an effective work environment by leveraging collective wisdom, knowledge sharing, and promoting innovation. A comprehensive framework via eight competency centres is used to sustain existing capabilities as well as for building new expertise. Employees have personal pages that formed the foundation of an expertise locator. KM tools implemented include the eHabitat portal and Ask@eHabitat query system. Key priorities focus on the creation of 'vibrant' communities and promoting a 'wow' experience.

1.2.3. Intellectual Property Office of Singapore (IPOS)

The Intellectual Property Office of Singapore (IPOS) first conducted a detailed KM case study with the assistance of an external consultant in 2007. It adopted the Singapore's governmental portal solution — KEN. In a popular vote, 95 percent of the employees approved the new portal named KENNY (Knowledge ENterprise 'N You). A KM Steering Committee was formed, and positions for both the KM Director and KM Representatives were created. An early challenge was that KM was seen as additional work; this was later embedded into routine workflow. A three-year plan was drawn up, to nurture a knowledge-sharing culture. In terms of tools, IPOS migrated from Lotus Notes towards SharePoint.

1.2.4. Inland Revenue Authority of Singapore (IRAS)

The Inland Revenue Authority of Singapore (IRAS) focused its KM initiative on creating a knowledge-sharing culture. To initiate its KM initiatives, it sought inputs from economic development agencies and other KM experts. A set of cultural KM archetypes were drawn up after extensive surveys. Regular knowledge-sharing sessions were instituted. Video recordings were made accessible via the intranet. Informal 'Learning Bites' lunch sessions were also conducted. Comprehensive Branch Knowledge Maps provided overviews of domain expertise. Organisational Climate Surveys were regularly conducted, and the portal called iNex was the IT platform for knowledge activities.

1.2.5. Jurong Town Corporation (JTC)

Jurong Town Corporation (JTC) was an early player in KM. It created its KM Department in 2001, and in 2002, CoPs were formed, followed by Workspaces in 2003. Roles for knowledge activists were created in 2008, and an updated taxonomy was launched in 2010. The portal was called CRISP (Corporate Reporting Information Services Portal). Knowledge captures were embedded in workflows, and a balanced scorecard helped track and record knowledge activities of employees. Early challenges included content governance as knowledge assets proliferated.

1.2.6. *Ministry of Finance (MOF)*

The Ministry of Finance (MOF) started its KM initiative with the appointment of Directorate Knowledge Activists in 2007, focusing on email as a communication and documentation tool. A vendor (Third Sight) assisted with the designing and training for its KM tool roll-out. The taxonomy was finalised in 2008, and in 2010 the MOF intranet portal, MoFi, was launched. Next steps include a systematic way of soliciting suggestions and innovations and the use of social media.

1.2.7. *National Library Board (NLB)*

The National Library Board (NLB) had an expertise-centric KM approach to harness its network of specialists. Surveys of expected knowledge behaviours were conducted, and it was decided to create a layered presentation of knowledge in digestible chunks. Internal and external metrics were designed to measure KM's impact. Some internal metrics were quantitative (e.g. number of threads and reads; number of man-days to answer an enquiry); while others were qualitative, e.g. anecdotes. External metrics included feedback, assessments and compliments from customers.

1.2.8. *Singapore Armed Forces (SAF)*

Singapore Armed Forces (SAF) launched its KM initiative in 2002, to support its leadership mandate. The KM vision was to nurture first class people within a world class organisation, strengthen professionalism, promote open learning, and create deep specialisation. To nurture a learning culture, SAF moved away from the traditional regimented culture towards a fresh one which was receptive to new ideas and tolerant of mistakes. Numerous CoPs were set up, and knowledge capital was built up through military domain experts and professional military education. A unified IT system consolidated disparate systems ranging from portals and wikis to blogs and workspaces. Knowledge hubs and branches facilitated cross-organisational learning.

1.2.9. *Singapore Police Force: Police Technology Department (SPF-PTD)*

The Singapore Police Force (SPF) was cited as a learning organisation by Peter Senge in 2006, focusing on the Five Disciplines: personal mastery, mental models, shared vision, team learning, and systems thinking. The Chief Knowledge Officer is the Deputy Commissioner of Police himself, thus reflecting a top-level commitment to KM. A broad spectrum of KM activities was rolled out, ranging from annual competitions, site visits to e-learning and social media forums. KM was promoted via activities such as Leadership Moments, KM Day, and Learning Festivals, which included skits and storytelling competitions. Blogs and a communications team helped promote dialogues and narratives about KM. Its impacts have been analysed in terms of productivity, employee satisfaction, and innovation.

1.2.10. *Singapore Youth Olympic Games Organising Committee (SYOGOC)*

The Singapore Youth Olympic Games Organising Committee (SYO-GOC) is the most international case study in this book, in terms of the number of cultures, nationalities and languages involved in the organisation. Its activities were conducted under full media glare. The deadline of the Youth Olympics served as a key driver for undertaking and completing various KM activities. The after-action review processes in SYOGOC's KM initiative helped formalise the learning culture, shorten learning curves, and left behind a valuable legacy both for Singapore and for international sporting organisations such as the World Cup, Asian Games, Commonwealth Games and other similar international activities.

1.2.11. *Supreme Court of Singapore (SC)*

Singapore's Supreme Court set a lofty KM vision: providing knowledge support for disposing cases through timely judicial decisions of the highest quality. The CEO is also designated as the Chief Knowledge Officer; KM Champions are located in functional groups, and KM Activists manage key functions and domains. In 2006, the KM Justice Portal was launched. In 2008, Web 2.0 enhancements such as a wiki were layered on. A 'Creanovator' room for Innovation Activists was instituted. The Supreme Court has won a range of honours, including awards for Business Excellence, the Public Service Milestone Award, and the Singapore Quality Class Star Award. It is also one of the world's first Supreme Court to participate in a KM competition.

1.2.12. *Urban Redevelopment Authority (URA)*

The Urban Redevelopment Authority (URA) aligned its KM vision with its overall goal of creating a 'city in a garden' and to transform Singapore into one of the most liveable cities in Asia. In 2002, the American Productivity and Quality Center's KM framework was utilised to draft its KM strategy. The intranet termed URANIUM was created, along with the portal eKRIS (electronic Knowledge Repository Information System). Annual 'Learning Days' were instituted. A strong focus was placed on external knowledge inputs via intelligence management, environmental scanning, and benchmarking.

1.3. Outline of the Book

This section provides the outline of the book, which is broadly structured in three parts that provide the KM plans, implementations, and finally the impacts on the organisations.

1.3.1. *KM Rationale, Plans, and Roles*

Part I consists of the first three chapters of the book that focus on the 'Why', 'How' and 'Who' of knowledge management. Why do organisations launch KM initiatives? How do they plan the KM journeys? Who are the leaders and managers who design and implement the KM initiatives? Each organisation has its own context for KM, described in terms of its history, founding values, growth, operational ethics, competitive or regulatory pressures, and workforce demographics. These factors tend to shape the organisation's KM initiatives in a number of ways: which department or leader decides to launch the KM initiative, what kinds of phases are launched initially and which ones later, and what the scale or scope of the KM initiative is.

Chapter 2, Rationale and Drivers, focuses on the driving force for launching KM initiatives of the organisations profiled in the book. It addresses how organisations view knowledge, and the role it plays in the context of their structure and strategy, and why they choose to launch KM initiatives. It also analyses the drivers of the knowledge strategies.

Chapter 3, Plans, Phases and Frameworks, covers the various knowledge planning approaches and roadmaps. It focuses on how organisations develop a plan for their KM initiatives, how they chart out near, medium and long-term phases in the plan by developing a framework to evolve their KM initiatives.

Chapter 4, Leadership and Governance, addresses the 'who' of KM in the organisation, that is, the key knowledge leaders and managers, who plan, execute, assess, and refine the KM initiatives in the organisations. It also discusses the attributes, skills, and aspirations of the KM team, and who takes on the governance roles in various KM committees.

1.3.2. KM Initiatives: People, Process and Technology

Part II consists of three chapters that address the type and format of KM practices, such as what kinds of knowledge cultures are defined to shape the organisations, what were the workflow processes connected with knowledge activities, and what KM tools and technologies were deployed to provide the foundation for knowledge assets and flows.

Chapter 5, Cultivating Cultures, covers people strategies and incentives with regards to promoting a dynamic knowledge-sharing culture. People aspects of a KM strategy include culture, community activities and organisational attitudes. Does the organisation have a culture of learning where its employees thirst for knowledge, trust one another, and have visible support from their management? What core communities are aligned with the organisation's activities, and what support is there for identifying, nurturing and harnessing these communities?

Chapter 6, Processes and Techniques, focuses on the kinds of workflow connected with activities, and new processes designed and embedded for knowledge generation, validation, sharing and dissemination. It analyses effective processes for knowledge co-creation and codification of knowledge (e.g. via after-action reviews, repositories and taxonomies) and connecting knowledge workers.

Chapter 7, Tools and Technologies, focuses on practical technological applications along with considerations of usability and training for effective knowledge activities. The chapter also addresses the types of connectivity interfaces, portal, devices, and tools that knowledge workers deploy for digital content management, search, visualisation, authoring, expertise directories, and social networking.

1.3.3. *KM Outcomes and Futures*

Part III consists of the last three chapters that focus on the 'so what' and 'what next' questions. What kinds of quantitative and qualitative impacts did the KM initiatives have? What are the learnings and recommendations from these experiences for other KM practitioners? What is next for the KM initiatives in the featured case studies, and for the knowledge industry?

Chapter 8, Measures and Impacts, focuses on the outputs and outcomes of the KM initiatives in the case studies. It covers metrics being used by practitioners and researchers, the effectiveness of these measures, and how they guide future actions and policies of KM. It discusses how services were improved, how employees were better able to locate experts, and how KM aided in the retention of critical knowledge leading to improved employee satisfaction.

Chapter 9, Learnings and Recommendations, provides useful perspectives from the reflections, learnings and recommendations of the KM practitioners. It discusses how the KM launch must be preceded by a thorough understanding of the organisation's culture, strategy and context and that top management support is particularly critical at the early stages.

Chapter 10, The Road Ahead, addresses the reassessments and new directions being explored by KM practitioners. This concluding chapter focuses on the 'what next' perspective, analysing the next step after the KM initiatives. Depending on the phase of the organisation's knowledge journey, there are three stages — mature, intermediate and early — and each of these phases have different implications and outcomes with respect to building the knowledge culture, establishing the structures or even responding to the external environments.

In summary, the book analyses the core aspects of a KM initiative and its implementation: rationale, planning, governance, culture, process, technology, impacts, learnings, and evolution. While earlier KM literature has focused extensively on the people, process and technology aspects of KM, this book provides valuable analysis of the 'pre-launch' and 'post-launch' phases of KM as well. The learnings will be useful for other organisations in the early stages of assessing their KM strategies, as well as mature organisations looking for validation and future evolution of their KM initiatives.

CHAPTER TWO

Rationales and Drivers

"It isn't what you know that counts; it's what you think of in time."
— Benjamin Franklin

This chapter focuses on the rationales and the driving forces for organisations initiating KM projects. It addresses how organisations view knowledge, and the role it plays in the context of their overall structure and strategy, and why they should choose to launch KM initiatives.

Due to globalisation, organisations constantly face increasing workforce diversity and mobility. Compounding the above with shorter employment contracts and increasingly transient workers, it is a challenge for organisations to retain their organisational memory, as well as intellectual capital. Thus, with a reduction in the loss of intellectual assets due to employee turnover or attrition, and a constantly changing workforce; there is a demand for employees to engage in lifelong learning, but the most crucial strategy involves the capturing and retention of intellectual assets within organisations.

The increased flux of complexities within a working environment is primarily caused by rapid innovations and technological advances. Hence, it is critical for managements to adopt KM at strategic levels rather than merely from tactical practices. Natarajan and Shekhar (2000) aptly suggested that the "conscious capture, storage, and archiving of knowledge can lead to the creation of invaluable intellectual property that has both tactical and long-term strategic value for the organisation".

Although most of the driving forces for an organisation to launch KM are often internally tied to reducing risks and meeting challenges of increasing shareholders' value, in recent times we are observing various organisations rationalising external forces that are related to exploiting new opportunities to launch their KM initiatives.

2.1. KM Rationales

Rationales can be defined as catalysts or factors which influence decisions to accomplish certain goals, such as the pressures to achieve defined outcomes, to minimise emerging risks and vulnerabilities, to adopt new technologies for process efficiencies, or to sustain competitiveness in the shifts of globalisation. The rationale and priority for undertaking KM initiatives may differ depending on the types of organisation, whether they are commercial, or government and public sector agencies. For instance, the rationale for KM in the consumer-focused private sector companies differs from that of the citizen-focused public sector agencies and government bodies, though there may be some overlaps; indeed, there are occasions where both sectors can learn from each other, as well as those from initiatives stemming from academia and civil societies. Organisations typically launch KM because they would like to create an attractive work environment, improve existing processes and reduce costs, develop new products and services, or improve the organisation's strategic position (Owen, 1999).

Contextually, KM is more organic and humanistic as compared to other business strategy paradigms, such as total quality management (TQM), business process re-engineering (BPR), portfolio management and core competencies (Gamble & Blackwell, 2001). The human factor was downplayed in BPR, as the focus on process efficiencies often ignored opportunities for knowledge sharing and exchange via employees' and customers' feedback. One of the major shortcomings of the TQM and quality control philosophy was also the narrow focus with regards to problem solving, and not on other organisational issues such as long-term innovations and sustainability. Although it has been emphasised that KM can bring many organisational benefits, the study of cooperative behaviours shows that some social dilemmas could result from the 'tragedy of the commons' (where beneficiaries overuse shared resources, leading to ultimate depletion), and 'leeching' behaviours. These dilemmas also plagued the philosophy of KM where knowledge sharing is of great significance. Ekbia and Hara (2006) provided three views of KM incentives to overcome these dilemmas, namely, the techno-centric, human-centric, and socio-technical as follows:

- The techno-centric view (product-oriented) emphasises the importance of knowledge capture. It regards knowledge as something that can be codified, organised, stored and accessed, and that Information Technology (IT) is vital as it enables faster codification and wider access to organisational knowledge. However, not all knowledge can be codified, especially the tacit knowledge that has been accumulated over decades of experiences. This view neglects the fact that employees need incentives and motivations to share.
- The human-centric view (process-oriented) emphasises the trust and interpersonal relationships during social interactions among employees. Communities of practice and interpersonal communication are more important to successful KM, since social recognition, reputation, status and reciprocity become motivations for their sharing behaviours. Knowledge sharing often emerges from the bottom up, once trust is built. This approach draws lessons from the human-capital view of an organisation.
- The socio-technical view is by far the most comprehensive view of KM, combining the previous two schools of thought. It regards IT as a catalyst to facilitate KM (but not the most critical element), and puts KM in contextual frames rather than isolated practices. With the help of both top-down intervention and bottom-up engagement, employees would be better involved in the knowledge-sharing processes.

2.1.1. Understanding the Tiers of KM

Due to the existence of the differences in volume and actionability of knowledge, it is important to understand the five tiers of knowledge as shown in Figure 2.1 to guide the organisations' KM efforts so as to alleviate possible confusion and support a KM life cycle such as planning and managing the knowledge assets in the firm (Hicks *et al.*, 2006). Fundamentally, the five tiers of knowledge are briefly described

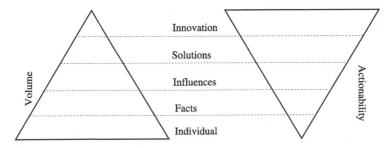

Figure 2.1 Five Tiers of KM on the Dimensions of Volume and Actionability.
Source: Adapted from Hicks *et al.* (2006).

as follows:

- 'Individual' refers to the 'knowledge contained only in the mind of a person'. Such knowledge exists in huge volumes in the organisations, but in most cases, they are tacit in the individual's mind, not articulated or not even articulable, thus such knowledge is low in actionability.
- 'Facts' refer to the 'atomic attribute values about the domain'. Such knowledge is actionable, since facts can be explicitly explained and proactively analysed by organisations.
- 'Influence' refers to the 'data in context that have been processed and/or prepared for presentation'. Such knowledge is extracted from facts, and can have a greater impact on organisations.
- 'Solutions' refer to the 'instructions and authority to perform a task'. Typically, most companies would have solutions, be it standard working procedures or employee handbooks. Such knowledge is highly actionable as they have been accumulated for a long time and exist to guide the organisations' strategies.
- 'Innovation' refers to the 'exploitation of knowledge-based resources'. Since innovative ideas are supposed to be highly actionable, those who have such knowledge could build up the organisations' competitive advantage and become industry leaders.

2.1.2. *Categories of KM Drivers*

Various scholars have identified different types of KM drivers; depending on the context of the KM efforts, some drivers tend to be more strategic, while others are more operational and tactical in their approach. As

KM can be applied to a wide range of tasks or activities in routine, logical, complex, unexpected or unusual situations, it is important that management thinks through how to effectively direct their resources on utilising the knowledge assets to enhance the strategic performances of the organisations, and to steer the organisations towards desired goals across the range of processes and procedures.

Mathew (2011) identified a range of more operational motivations or drivers for organisations to launch KM initiatives that include the following: to improve decision-making, to increase collaboration, to create a learning environment, to increase productivity, and to raise motivation and retention of employees. Alstete and Halpern (2008), however, identified five broad categories of drivers ranging from economic, process, structure, and technology to knowledge. Table 2.1 summarises the drivers as follows:

- As economic drivers focus on increasing return, it is important that customer services are improved continuously to contribute to its return. Adequate customer services not only bring loyal customers but also help to attract and establish aggressive channel partners.
- In terms of process drivers, KM can impact the reduction of mistakes, as well as increase responsiveness to customers and employees. Two key processes include collaboration, such as establishing

Table 2.1   KM Drivers.

Category	Drivers
Economic	To achieve increasing returns
	To maximise cost savings
Process	To avoid repeated mistakes and reinvention of solution
	To be proactive and responsive
Structure	To respond to deregulation and globalisation
	To react to functional convergence of products and services
Technology	To capitalise on technology to provide advantages
	To compress the life cycles of products and processes
Knowledge	To provide rapid knowledge dissemination and application
	To prevent tacit knowledge walkouts or hoarding

Source: Adapted from Alstete and Halpern (2008).

communities of practice; and content management, such as taxonomies and navigation.

- Convergence of products and services can lead to structural readjustments in an organisation (e.g. mergers or regulatory bodies). Measuring the value of knowledge can be challenging, since the most compelling values are derived from intangible benefits, which are difficult to quantify.
- Technology as a driver often leads to changes in workflow habits. It is important to integrate and plan the appropriate tools to enhance the delivery of accurate information to the appropriate people on time with minimum costs to improve the effectiveness of the business strategy.
- Knowledge loss in the organisations due to high employee turnover is a challenge that affects the management. It is therefore important that the organisation ensures that it is able to capture the knowledge base of the different roles such as knowledge broker, information collector, user, analyst, or decision-maker before it is too late to do so.

Nair (2010) has a different approach to classifying drivers for KM into two types: the demand drivers (e.g. based on organisational needs) and the supply drivers (e.g. based on newly available tools). On the demand side there are several structural, demographic and economic factors that have driven the heightened interest in KM (e.g. organisational restructuring, employee attrition). On the supply side, new communication and knowledge-sharing applications drive new kinds of KM opportunities. For instance, the rise of social media is one of the new supply-side drivers of KM in organisations. Plessis (2005) also identified five related drivers of KM: geographically dispersed work environments, the increased volume of knowledge, the advent of new technologies including the internet and new media, the need for quick and efficient decision-making, and finally, the need to stop knowledge attrition.

Applying Al-Hawamdeh's (2002) key drivers for KM to help organisations achieve efficiency, maximise organisational potential, preserve organisational memory, and manage intellectual capital, KM should be practised by all organisations. Indeed, it can also help to create organisation cultures where 'learning from mistakes' can help the management to understand critical organisational knowledge.

2.1.3. KM Drivers in the Public Sector

The management of knowledge is of increasing importance for governments in dealing with the challenges of the knowledge economy (OECD, 2003). Governments are starting to realise the importance of KM for policy-making and service delivery to the public, and some governmental departments are beginning to place KM high on their agendas (Cong & Pandya, 2003). Indeed, many governments see KM as inseparable from strategy, planning, consultation and implementation.

In Singapore, most public sectors have strong interests in KM with some agencies having full-fledged KM departments. Also most public sector organisations have started to embrace KM to serve the public more effectively especially when citizens are increasingly more knowledgeable and tech-savvy in the digital world. It is therefore not surprising that most citizens expect their governments to offer higher service quality especially in the context of the knowledge economy. Indeed, Zhou and Gao (2007) identified the drivers of KM in e-government to include enhancing government competence, raising government service quality and promoting the constant development of e-government.

However, the public sector faces various challenges, the more obvious include having compartmentalised structures, silo organisational culture, and static culture mindsets of 'knowledge is power', 'what's in it for me', and the 'not invented here' syndrome (Cong & Pandya, 2003). For the public sector to deliver quality services, it has to improve accountability, make informed decisions, enhance partnerships with stakeholders, and improve overall performance (Jain, 2009). To deal with these challenges, several progressive public sector and government agencies have introduced reforms and measures including KM to combat some of the more common issues such as the loss of institutional knowledge with the retirement of older employees, challenges for the retention and transfer of knowledge by retaining vibrant staff, demands for higher returns on taxpayers' money, and the push to implement e-government.

Dinca (2011) identified the avoidance of duplicating resources as a good reason why institutions adopt KM, particularly in the public sectors; indeed, excessive duplication leads to a waste of institutional resources. Various institutions launched KM initiatives to better understand their operating context, to promote creative thinking and support idea generation, and to create an atmosphere of learning from errors (error-friendliness rather than error prevention) in order to prevent unnecessary duplications. In other words, an important driver of KM is the need to reduce risks, such as the costs of ignorance. Learning should derive not just from best practices but also from understanding flawed and erroneous practices. Costly mistakes should not be replicated and new lessons need to be learned quickly. There may also be delays in responsiveness if employees are spending too much time searching for resources and experts, or if the information they received are outdated, unauthorised or unvalidated. In hospitals, the practice of Morbidity and Mortality (M&M) allows medical staff at all levels to review their mistakes, summarise lessons learned and figure out what to do next time to avoid the mistakes.

The rationale for an organisation's KM initiative will also frame the context of its strategy and eventually shape the outcomes and impacts. KM is a "core company value and management philosophy" (Conway & Sligar, 2002). The goals of a KM program should not be based solely on its performance indicators such as productivity, efficiency and knowledge asset growth; in fact, a key driver of KM should be the creation of value through collaboration and connection to knowledge sources.

In essence, KM blends perspectives from cognitive science, motivational studies, business strategy, and behavioural science, thus, it is most valuable when tied to an enterprise-wide strategy, encompassing workflow and organisational objectives and goals. Its plans and strategy must take into account the unique knowledge typology in the organisational domain and the knowledge approaches best suited to the organisational culture (Natarajan & Shekhar, 2000).

2.2. Perspectives from Case Studies

This section explores the KM rationale and drivers in each of the case studies. Each profile covers the internal and external drivers, along with the perceived opportunities and threats.

2.2.1. Attorney-General's Chambers (AGC)

Singapore's Attorney-General's Chambers is an organ of state with a pivotal role in enhancing the rule of law and constitutional government in Singapore. Under the constitution, the Attorney-General (AG) is the government's chief legal advisor whose duty is to advise the government upon such legal matters and to perform other such duties of a legal character which may from time to time be referred to the AGC by the government. The AGC thus provides a vast array of legal expertise for the good governance of Singapore. The AG is also the Public Prosecutor and the AGC promotes a just criminal justice system through its prosecutorial functions. It has over 400 employees in six legal divisions (Civil Division, International Affairs Division, Legislation and Law Reform Division and the Crime Cluster comprising the Criminal Justice Division, State Prosecution Division, and Economic Crimes and Governance Division) and two support divisions (Corporate Services Division and Information Division).

AGC had to deal with duplication of information, incomplete documentation in the context of decision-making, and knowledge attrition due to staff rotation and turnover. Originally, information in AGC resided in physical files. With different waves of computerisation efforts since the 1980s, information has been captured in multiple repositories and in different formats. Operational 'silos' developed where divisions may not be fully aware of initiatives and developments in other divisions. Delays often occurred when trying to find relevant information and expertise with some degree of reliance on 'personal' repositories of institutional knowledge. Further, while information would be available in work files regarding the decision made on specific matters, details as to the reasoning processes and the alternatives that were considered might not be as readily available. Some lessons learned had to be re-learned over the passage of time. There was also a danger that inconsistent advice might be rendered to client agencies. KM was the natural choice to address such issues as AGC is essentially a knowledge-based organisation. With growth in organisational size and increasing complexity of legal issues, the implementation of an enterprise-wide KM platform was seen as a critical factor for communication, collaboration and coordination with specialists within the organisation.

AGC's role is heavily knowledge-intensive and its intellectual capital resides in the work output that is produced when its best legal minds collaborate and engage in robust discussion and thorough research on important legal issues and opinions. To ensure that advice given is consistent, that the knowledge can be reused to avoid duplication of work, and to encourage the sharing of tacit knowledge, AGC has a strong need to focus on putting organisational knowledge into a form that is easily accessible to those who need it. Thus, it was important to codify its internal knowledge in addition to leveraging external sources like Lexis.com and Westlaw to conduct research.

To ensure systematic management of information that is easily accessed and searchable, AGC realised that it would have to promote collaboration amongst the divisions. In fact, many projects in AGC require cross-divisional sharing. For example, the drafting of the Smoking Act (Control of Advertisements and Sale of Tobacco) required the Legislation and Law Reform Division to consult the International Affairs Division to ensure that the Act complies with international treaties that are binding on Singapore. Cross-divisional advice would need to be archived for future reference. It was also seen as important that the AGC Gazette, a bi-monthly publication, includes contributions on reviews of problematic or noteworthy cases that the officers have handled. In sum, coping with knowledge attrition, duplication of information, incomplete documentation, a limited talent pool and lack of easy access to information were key drivers for KM at AGC.

2.2.2. Defence Science and Technology Agency (DSTA)

The Defence Science and Technology Agency was established in 2000 as the first statutory board of Singapore's Ministry of Defence (MINDEF). Its mission is to harness science and technology to provide leading-edge technological solutions for the Singapore Armed Forces (SAF), enhancing Singapore's defence capabilities. DSTA's work encompasses four areas of expertise: Acquisition Management (e.g. weapon systems), Systems Management (e.g. engineering support, weapons systems), Systems Development (e.g. IT systems, command and control systems) and Technology Management (e.g. advanced defence systems). DSTA employs about 3,000 staff, comprising engineers and scientists who manage complex defence science and technology programmes, and conduct research and development in multi-disciplinary fields ranging from engineering, IT to biomedical sciences. The organisation also helps to promote a strong community of scientists and engineers from the universities, research institutes, government and the industry.

Over the years, DSTA's operations environment continued to grow in complexity and unpredictability with new threats stemming from global terrorism and emerging pandemic situations. In order to deliver value-added solutions and services in the complex and turbulent environment, DSTA is required to stay relevant with new knowledge and intelligence. This included the build-up of new knowledge capabilities and steps to encourage staff to take ownership of their learning and competency development.

As one of its strategies is to ensure build-up and sustenance of its multi-disciplinary expertise in defence science and technology, it is therefore critical for DSTA to create value for its primary stakeholders. The benefits are to optimise the existing knowledge and to shorten the project delivery life cycle. To do so, a practical framework is needed to allow DSTA staff to tap onto the existing knowledge and reservoir of past experiences. DSTA mapped this practice onto three crucial areas: knowledge retention, knowledge release and knowledge reuse. Thus, its KM practice focuses on creating a knowledge-filled workplace where the community of knowledge workers can effectively and efficiently create, capture, share and reuse the organisational knowledge.

Its KM initiative is geared at retaining valuable experience, and technical and institutional knowledge at every step of the process. To fulfil the requirement, it needs to effectively manage its information assets as resources by creating a common repository for proper storage of documents and records. In other words, its information resources has to be well organised to facilitate sharing and retrieval knowledge. In brief, the key internal drivers for KM include the need for leading-edge solutions, increasing workforce creativity and expertise, improving organisational innovation, and the retention and reuse of knowledge.

2.2.3. Intellectual Property Office of Singapore (IPOS)

The Intellectual Property Office of Singapore is a statutory board under Singapore's Ministry of Law and is the lead government agency advising on and administering intellectual property (IP) laws, promoting IP awareness and providing the infrastructure to facilitate the development of IP in Singapore. Acting as an IP regulator and policy advisor, IPOS is committed to maintaining a robust and pro-business IP regime for its protection and commercial exploitation. IPOS currently employs close to 170 staff.

After IPOS became a statutory board in April 2001, its role moved from being a regulatory body of IP into other areas such as promotion of IP, international collaboration on IP-related issues and to help raise IP capabilities and awareness in Singapore. The enhanced role created an increased demand for knowledge acquisition and knowledge sharing. The key issue was that there was no central location for archiving and retrieving information. Information was captured and resided in multiple platforms and locations such as the Lotus Notes database, email database and Windows shared drive. Although information was kept in Microsoft and Lotus Notes documents, there was no standardised method of capturing and categorising information to facilitate search. Such a chaotic approach caused much information overload and duplication.

IPOS also lacked key processes to retain valuable work-related history, especially for handover processes and new staff training. In positions that have encountered periods of continuous low staff retention or high staff turnover, a significant portion of work scope history became disjointed and this was problematic. There was clearly a lack of mechanism to retain knowledge to enable increased productivity of new hires.

IPOS therefore launched its KM initiative based on a range of internal and external challenges and opportunities. Internally, IPOS faced various problems, for instance, the processes were chaotic and there was no central location for storing information and no standardised methods for knowledge acquisition and sharing. Exasperated with a high staff attrition rate, IPOS faced challenges in raising the organisation's capabilities. In addition, the need to form international collaborations caused IPOS to realise that it needed a more structured approach to managing its information and knowledge.

Its KM effort is to leverage on technology as an enabler to manage information in order to maintain the operation-wide efficiency and effectiveness of IPOS that spanned 6 divisions and 19 departments. Thus, its imperatives are to help staff in the creation, capture, storage, sharing and dissemination of knowledge to ensure efficiency in their tasks.

2.2.4. Inland Revenue Authority of Singapore (IRAS)

The Inland Revenue Authority of Singapore is a statutory board under the Ministry of Finance (MOF) and is the main taxation administration with about 1,700 staff. IRAS acts as an agent of the government and provides services in administering, assessing, collecting and enforcing payment of taxes. It also advises the government and represents Singapore internationally on matters relating to taxation. The performance of IRAS is dependent on preserving and growing high levels of technical tax knowledge, as well as constantly improving its capabilities.

Based on an organisational assessment and an understanding of its knowledge culture, IRAS realised that it needed to inculcate a knowledge mindset to deliver empowered performance, but would face challenges from a weak knowledge-sharing culture. Over time, the organisation also faced a loss of institutional knowledge.

Indeed, IRAS views knowledge as a strategic resource which should be made available to every member in the organisation. Its goal is to equip its people with the necessary information tools and knowledge mindset to deliver empowered performances. With this as the objective, the IRAS sharing session was introduced in 2003, with a mandate to make knowledge sharing a way of life for every officer who plays a part in helping to build up the stock of its organisational knowledge. The management notes that if its workers actively engage in the discussion of issues related to their work, the organisation will then benefit from the new knowledge that is created from these discussions to meet the challenges of the knowledge economy.

Prior to the introduction of the IRAS sharing session, sharing of knowledge was limited to colleagues within the same functional teams; an organisation-wide knowledge-sharing culture was not prevalent. Indeed, with the initiation of the sharing sessions held organisation-wide, a learning environment that nurtures earnest seekers and a sharing platform that encouraged generous sharers were created. Consequently, the accumulation of institutional memory became more efficient, thus minimising the loss of institutional knowledge over the passage of time.

2.2.5. *Jurong Town Corporation (JTC)*

Jurong Town Corporation is Singapore's leading industrial infrastructure specialist, spearheading the planning, promotion and development of a dynamic industrial landscape. For more than 40 years, JTC plays a crucial role in the growth of the economy by providing cutting-edge industrial estate solutions. It recognises that to fulfil its role as a key government agency supporting the nation's economic development in building its industrial real estates, it should enhance its resilience and sustain its business and organisational excellence.

With a heavy information-centric workflow, it required a better life cycle management of its information and the integration of information into its collaborative workflow. Increasing innovative capacity also became a performance objective. Thus, a key thrust in its pursuit of organisational excellence was the implementation of KM commencing more than a decade ago. Its KM mission is to "formulate and drive corporate strategies and implement initiatives to transform JTC into a knowledge-enabled organisation". Of course, true to its mantra, it also holds a vision to create "a knowledge-enabled organisation wherein the work culture and supporting infrastructure nurture collaboration and sharing of knowledge".

Fundamentally, JTC's KM efforts focus on ensuring that the organisation can better capture, use, reuse and leverage on information and knowledge as wisdom throughout the organisation, supported effectively by IT.

2.2.6. *Ministry of Finance (MOF)*

The Ministry of Finance is a civil service organisation with a staff strength of approximately 200 officers. Its mission is to create a better Singapore through finance, and with a vision of advancing leading ideas, driving synergies across the government and ensuring fiscal prudence. To establish Singapore as an international business and financial centre, the MOF works to ensure comparability with international standards and best practices in areas such as company law, accounting standards and corporate governance principles. Its activities include reserves management, fiscal sustainability and creating a conducive business environment. MOF deals with various financial levers in the formulation and implementation of social, economic, tax, fiscal, governance and investments as well as international policies. The ministry serves to uphold the Singapore economy through the effective planning and release of the Annual Budget.

The MOF's KM initiative was driven by a strong need to overcome internal challenges in the areas which were found wanting: the organisation of information, having a specialised system to manage large quantities of information, and building institutional memory. It faced various challenges in managing the information; for instance, there was no structured approach of organising its information, it lacked a mechanism to manage and search its large database, and it suffered a loss of institutional memory over time.

The lack of an organised policy with regards to filing and storing important emails and corresponding documents was a grave concern. Any filing or retention of such documents was left largely at the officers' discretion, which resulted in some documents being filed, and others not. To further intensify the problem, the softcopy filing did not follow any form of governance or structure. In addition to the paper files as one of the repositories, officers would also file the softcopies into system applications such as Lotus Notes within the intranet, shared network drives, or officers' hard disks and emails. The chaotic approach led to duplications and repetitions of information in various repositories. As a federated search feature was not available, any attempt at retrieving required documents was time-consuming and inefficient, as it required searching through several repositories.

Compounding the above issue was the lack of an integrated search engine that could search across the various repositories. Moreover, the search mechanism within each individual repository was slow and the effort to comb through thick paper files was tedious. Indeed, there was a need for a powerful search engine that could search through the various repositories.

Its KM initiative was thus to identify an IT system which gave the organisation the capability and capacity to access the required knowledge resource at the right place and the right time. Like most organisations without a proper KM approach, the loss of institutional memory posed a problem. In MOF, with a rate of staff turnover around 20 percent, it was a challenge trying to retain the explicit knowledge of the officers when they leave. With almost all communications done through email, the lack of institutional memory and retention becomes magnified as a significant problem that required vital action.

2.2.7. National Library Board (NLB)

The National Library Board is responsible for preserving and making accessible the nation's literary and publishing heritage, and intellectual memory. Its public library branches provide professional services to Singaporeans in their pursuit of lifelong learning and discovery. Using a range of traditional and digital media, NLB provides reference and advisory service for researchers, government officials, industry players, students and the general public. Reference librarians provide answers to queries, suggest search strategies and guide library customers to relevant and useful resources.

The National Library Board faced a range of internal challenges before it launched its KM initiative: Its librarians were functioning in an isolated manner, thus making it difficult and time-consuming to find the right subject experts. As a result the reuse of knowledge was limited, and KM was therefore seen as a way to increase collaboration and coordination of the various subject matter skills.

In the provision of reference and advisory service, librarians at NLB used to work alone on the reference enquiries as it is often difficult and time-consuming to find the right subject experts to help. The method of engaging assistance is also cumbersome, where they either have to send an email or call up the librarian. Finally, the onus is on the librarian who received the enquiry to track discussions and consolidate the relevant information from different parties before packaging the final response to the customer.

There were no effective and efficient means for fellow librarians to help and collaborate with each other to answer difficult enquiries. The extensive knowledge residing with the subject experts was not effectively shared or reused. It was of utmost importance to source for an effective KM tool for facilitating knowledge sharing and learning amongst the librarians.

NLB required a more mature framework for promoting its KM awareness, activism and skills in the organisation. Even though its staff were in some ways practicing KM, via their daily work, either using collaborative systems and software which are in place, or following strict project management disciplines (which ensured lessons learned are captured and reused from a KM point of view), better awareness and demonstration of 'KM in action' were required. Hence, as part of the efforts to build internal capabilities and renew the culture in knowledge sharing, NLB embarked on the Knowledge Champions Programme to address sustainable KM by building a repertoire of KM capabilities and competencies that extends beyond the central KM team and into divisions and groups. This is to ensure that the activism needed to support collaborative efforts would be further imbibed into the way things are done, proper techniques are being taught to individuals who could then demonstrate back in their workplace the techniques in action, and finally, the selection of key individuals to partake in this programme ensured that experienced and networked staff could provide a knowledge brokering role.

2.2.8. *Singapore Armed Forces (SAF)*

The Singapore Armed Forces comprises the Army, Navy, and Air Force with a current active-duty strength of approximately 55,000 and another 300,000 reservists. SAF trains in various parts of the world; at the same time its troops are assigned at international locations to support peace support operations, anti-piracy missions and humanitarian assistance and disaster relief operations. To ensure that SAF is able to deal with evolving and complex security challenges, the organisation has been constantly innovating and transforming itself. Indeed, SAF is in the process of transforming itself into a new generation SAF, dubbed as the 3rd Generation SAF, which will be a knowledge-based networked organisation.

In a global context of increasing security risks and complex conflicts, key drivers for KM at SAF included the need to deal with complex security issues, create a culture of control as well as meritocracy, accommodate the needs and skills of IT-savvy NetGeners, and learn from the fields of complex sciences. While SAF has historically been controlled through a rigid hierarchy, it has simultaneously embraced meritocracy, a social system that rewards individuals based on their achievements. Quite purposefully and with governmental support, the doctrinal changes are moving the military organisation towards integrated knowledge-based command and control, which harnesses the antecedent IT skills of computer-savvy conscripts (NetGeners) so as to develop these skills through the use of complex defence systems, all of which can be applied beyond the military system.

For example, at the 2009 Interdisciplinary Conference on Adaptation, Order and Emergence, Peter Ho, Head of the Singapore Civil Service, who is an SAF scholar as well as former Head of Naval Intelligence, remarked: "We in Singapore have begun to appreciate that complexity science has valuable insights for public sector managers. We recognise that we are a complex system, operating within an even larger and more complex environment. This simple insight has enormous implications for how we should organise and operate" (Ho, 2009).

SAF troops are trained and assigned at local and international locations, and thus another KM driver is the need to have troops with the ability to learn from diverse experiences while stationed in different locations globally, and to preserve the knowledge. In 2010, the SAF therefore created the Military Domain Experts Scheme that allows personnel with specialised skill sets to have their careers extended to 60 years of age. This is to ensure that their accumulated experience and knowledge remains available for a longer time.

2.2.9. *Singapore Police Force: Police Technology Department (SPF-PTD)*

The Police Technology Department is a department under the Singapore Police Force, located at the police headquarters. It has 250 staff, comprising uniformed police officers, national servicemen, civilian technical and administrative staff, as well as contract technical staff. The core tenets of SPF's vision are to be a sustaining force for the nation, be united with the community to ensure security, and to dissuade those inclined to crime and disorder. Within SPF, PTD's mission is to provide necessary technological solutions and services, and human expertise to enhance SPF's operational efficiency and effectiveness. Its main duty is to oversee the acquisition, development, implementation, maintenance, control and operation of all information communication technology (ICT) systems and equipment which are utilised for policing duties in Singapore.

Key drivers for KM at SPF-PTD were the need to overcome internal challenges such as risks of knowledge loss, which would lead to repeated project management mistakes. There was a need to preserve high-level tacit knowledge of experts, reduce operational mistakes during project management, and create and promote a collaborative culture. Prior to the KM journey, the organisation realised that tacit knowledge resides in the heads of technical experts and experienced project managers. As a result, there was loss of tacit knowledge when staff in the department resigned or got posted out. Project management mistakes were sometimes repeated because they were not extensively shared between project teams. There was little or no conscious effort to share knowledge within the department.

A requirement in SPF is for officers to go on job rotation, but there were challenges in ensuring that their knowledge acquired during one role would not be lost when they shifted to another role. An effective KM initiative was seen as reducing this knowledge loss while also building a culture of knowledge sharing among the rotating officers. It was also seen as important to create a habit of lifelong learning in the department. Communication about best practices as well as mistakes were seen as key to be able to learn from a diverse range of experiences; this would eventually lead to a broad spectrum of KM activities being rolled out, ranging from annual competitions and site visits to internal magazines and management retreats.

2.2.10. *Singapore Youth Olympic Games Organising Committee (SYOGOC)*

The Singapore Youth Olympic Games Organising Committee was set up in April 2008 to deliver the inaugural Youth Olympic Games in Singapore in 2010. It was a project-based organisation that was disbanded in the months following the Games, and was structured as an organisation under the Ministry of Community Development, Youth and Sports. By August 2010, it had 550 staff recruited on contract and seconded from other government agencies, as well as 20,000 volunteers recruited to assist in the games. The Singapore 2010 Youth Olympic Games (SYOG), held from 14 to 26 Aug 2010, was the first major innovation by the International Olympic Committee (IOC) in more than 80 years. After the Southeast Asian Games in 1993 and the Asian Youth Games in 2009, this was the first time that Singapore was hosting an international multi-sport event of this scale.

This Olympic-level event was a brand new world-class product for Singapore, and it had to be delivered in two and a half years. As a nation, Singapore had to maximise this one-off opportunity to learn from and retain the know-how of organising such a mega event, thus enhancing the country's ability to host future major games. This involved a wide mandate, covering venue management, parallel events, transportation, culture and media. There were clear objectives though this was a new task, and the team realised KM was a way to develop learn-as-you-go principles. SYOGOC used KM as one of the approaches to deliver on the urgency of its mission. The organising committee had little room for major mistakes or rework; there was only one attempt at presenting the Games to the rest of the world.

Having a team of supporters and volunteers consisting of diverse cultural and linguistic backgrounds meant that teamwork had to be built rapidly, which implied that simple rules and guidelines had to be established to create a sharing environment. KM was thus seen as a way of improving learning and collaboration to overcome risks and errors. Further, there was also a need to learn from external sources of knowledge (such as a domain taxonomy partly inherited from the Singapore Sports Council), develop and standardise a new set of shared acronyms and terms, and design and facilitate workshops for mapping, assessing and refining new processes. A common understanding of Games requirements and deliverables, in addition to teamwork, had to be created swiftly.

A wide range of practical and suitable knowledge assets also had to be created (e.g. venue planning toolkit, operating manuals), and there would need to be games-time reviews once the event started. Finally, knowledge transfers had to be conducted at the end of the event to both the Singapore sports organisers and the IOC. To meet all these internal and external needs of multiple stakeholders, KM was seen as an enabler to design and manage the SYOG venue and event processes.

2.2.11. *Supreme Court of Singapore (SC)*

The Judiciary is one of the three branches of government in Singapore, namely the Executive, the Legislature and the Judiciary. Judicial power in Singapore is vested in the Supreme Court. The Supreme Court of Singapore describes its vision as establishing and maintaining a world-class Judiciary, and its mission is to superintend the administration of justice. It defines its core values as integrity and independence, which leads to public trust and confidence in the Court. SC is made up of the Court of Appeal and the High Court, and hears both civil and criminal matters. The Court of Appeal is usually made up of three Judges, whilst the High Court consists of the Chief Justice and the Judges of the High Court. The Chief Justice, Judges of Appeal, Judges and Judicial Commissioners are appointed by the President on the advice of the Prime Minister.

The Supreme Court's environment and workflow are becoming increasingly information- and documentation-centric over the years, and the need to ensure that adequate justice is constantly delivered in a prompt manner leads to an increased focus on KM. At the Supreme

Court, technology is used extensively to aid productivity and to reduce errors. For instance, a wide range of services are provided by the Corporate Planning Directorate, which comprises court reporting services, interpreters and special projects sections. There are also other units for digital transcription services, library services, finance, international relations, statistics and learning, and electronic filing.

The KM efforts at the Supreme Court were preceded by several years of work on document and information management to support its work. In other words, the key drivers for KM at SC were derived internally, such as encouraging learning and innovation to maximise levels of performance; reduction of errors, coordination of a range of information and collaborative activities were also seen as KM objectives.

Weaving these threads together, the KM vision of the Supreme Court emerged to leverage on a knowledge-sharing culture and technology platforms to enable the fullest exchange of knowledge and information amongst all Supreme Court staff who are knowledge workers, thus empowering the administration of justice in Singapore, ensuring that justice delivered is timely, of high legal quality and accessible to all.

2.2.12. *Urban Redevelopment Authority (URA)*

The Urban Redevelopment Authority is Singapore's national land use planning and conservation agency. Its mission is to make Singapore a great city to live, work and play in. URA strives to create a vibrant and sustainable city of distinction by planning and facilitating Singapore's physical development in partnership with the community. It adopts a long-term and comprehensive planning approach in formulating strategic plans such as the Concept Plan and the Master Plan, to guide the physical development of Singapore in a sustainable manner. As the conservation authority, URA has an internationally recognised conservation programme, having successfully conserved not only single buildings, but entire districts. Indeed, it has successfully transformed Singapore into one of the most liveable cities in Asia through judicious land use planning and good urban design as its plans and policies focus on achieving a balance between economic growth and a quality living environment.

To turn its plans and visions into reality, URA takes on a multifaceted role. In addition to its planning function, it is also the main government land sales agent. Through the sale of state land, it attracts and channels private capital investment to develop sites to meet the island's land use needs. To create an exciting cityscape, URA actively promotes architecture and urban design excellence.

With its multiplicity of key roles, the driver for launching KM is to capture, analyse and utilise the vast amounts of information originating from multiple internal and external sources to better serve its functions. These functions include land use planning, urban design, land sales, investments, and innovative architecture. Further, to be a world-class player and to build its successes require an enormous exchange of information, ideas and knowledge externally, e.g. the type of intelligent information needed to compare Singapore with Hong Kong and Shanghai. KM is viewed as a way to harness the information, facilitate collaboration, and tap flows of tacit knowledge in these domains.

2.3. Insights from the Case Studies

As seen in the case studies, KM drivers identified by Alstete and Halpern (2008), such as overcoming repeated mistakes and reducing knowledge attrition, were a concern of SPF whilst knowledge loss due to attrition was also a challenge in AGC. Al-Hawamdeh (2002) noted that KM can help create organisation cultures that "learn from mistakes", which was seen as a KM factor in the case study of MOF. Cong and Pandya (2003) identified KM drivers such as retention of knowledge and preservation of institutional memory; this was a driver for KM in IRAS and SPF. Social media was one of the new supply-side drivers of KM in organisations such as SAF and SPF. Through KM, organisations can increase innovation, as identified by the CIO Council (2001); improving organisational innovation was identified as a KM driver for IRAS, SAF and the Supreme Court. Jain (2009) identified some challenges faced by public sector organisations, such as making informed decisions in the face of change; these concerns were some of the drivers at IPOS and AGC. The rationale for KM implementations in each case study is summarised in Table 2.2.

Overall, the rationale can be classified into two dimensions (summarised in Figure 2.2) — the scope of the drivers (internal or external) and the nature of the drivers (overcoming existing challenges or pursuing new opportunities). In brief, Figure 2.2 shows the four

Table 2.2 Summary of KM Initiatives.

Organisation	Rationale and Drivers
AGC	High workforce attrition rate, limited talent pool, duplication of work, difficulty of accessing information
DSTA	Needs leading-edge solutions, innovation, as well as knowledge retention, release and reuse
IPOS	Needs to raise IP capabilities and awareness, increase demand for knowledge acquisition and sharing, no central location for knowledge, lack of standard methods, low staff retention
IRAS	Needs knowledge to deliver performance, active discussions, limited knowledge-sharing culture, loss of institutional knowledge over time
JTC	Needs innovation capacity, enhanced resilience, sustained organisational excellence, to leverage on IT, and a work culture of knowledge sharing
MOF	Lack of information organisation, lack of specialised systems to manage large quantities of information, lack of institutional memory
NLB	Librarians isolated, difficult and time-consuming to find the right subject experts, no reuse of knowledge; need for KM awareness, activism and skills
SAF	International relationships, leadership training, IT skills, innovation and knowledge creation to meet security challenges
SPF-PTD	Knowledge loss due to resignations/transfers, repeated project management mistakes, build culture of knowledge sharing, knowledge retention and lifelong learning
SYOGOC	Short-term project, little room for mistakes, international workforce, limited technology
SC	To encourage learning and innovation for the highest levels of performance
URA	For urban design excellence via sound knowledge capture, analysis and utilisation, planning and operations

categories: internal challenges and opportunities, as well as the external challenges and opportunities. In sum, analysis of these drivers shows that KM can be seen as a source of organisational excellence and a de-risking strategy.

It appears that the bulk of the drivers for launching KM initiatives are internally focused, such as those related to human resources — employee attrition (AGC, SPF, IPOS), knowledge-sharing culture (IRAS), lack of institutional memory (MOF), and difficulty in locating

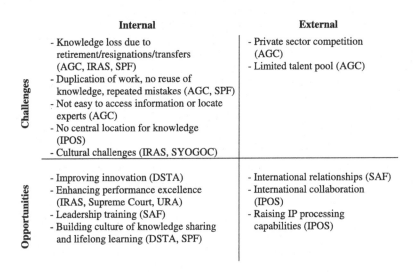

	Internal	**External**
Challenges	- Knowledge loss due to retirement/resignations/transfers (AGC, IRAS, SPF) - Duplication of work, no reuse of knowledge, repeated mistakes (AGC, SPF) - Not easy to access information or locate experts (AGC) - No central location for knowledge (IPOS) - Cultural challenges (IRAS, SYOGOC)	- Private sector competition (AGC) - Limited talent pool (AGC)
Opportunities	- Improving innovation (DSTA) - Enhancing performance excellence (IRAS, Supreme Court, URA) - Leadership training (SAF) - Building culture of knowledge sharing and lifelong learning (DSTA, SPF)	- International relationships (SAF) - International collaboration (IPOS) - Raising IP processing capabilities (IPOS)

Figure 2.2   Two-Dimensional View of KM Drivers.

expertise (AGC, IPOS). Other drivers include the perceived/internal opportunities of KM, for example, the chance to become more innovative (DSTA, Supreme Court), to promote lifelong learning (SPF), and to enhance performance (URA).

External challenges are more limited as these are government organisations and not commercial-oriented; still, challenges are perceived in the form of limited talent pool and competition for talents from the private sector (AGC), and in dealing with complex global problems like security (SAF). A few organisations also see important external opportunities via KM in the form of international collaboration and raising IP processing capabilities (IPOS), international thought leadership and alliances (e.g. SAF), and sharing the knowledge achievements with other international bodies (e.g. SYOGOC).

In brief, how an organisation defines and describes its knowledge assets as a source of organisational advantage will shape its KM journey. A number of illustrative metaphors for knowledge and KM are being used by practitioners and academics. Knowledge has been compared to oil: Its value comes across only when it lubricates, fuels, and energises an organisation. Others say knowledge is more important than oil: Oil is a dwindling resource, but knowledge always grows; there are a growing number of alternatives to oil, but there is no substitute for knowledge. Other practitioners compare knowledge to gold ('mining'), water ('wells' and 'taps') and even flowers and milk ('finite shelf life'). These metaphors for knowledge and KM tend to be long-lasting in the course of an organisation's KM initiative. How these initiatives are visualised, planned, designed and implemented will be the focus of the next chapters in the book.

A holistic set of strategies is required for putting in place a KM initiative and harnessing the knowledge advantage. According to Davenport and Prusak (1998), "the only sustainable advantage a firm has comes from what it collectively knows, how efficiently it uses what it knows, and how readily it acquires and uses new knowledge". But in contrast to individual knowledge, organisational knowledge is a more complex and murky dynamic, involving socio-political factors of knowledge buying, selling, brokering, pricing, reciprocity, altruism, reputation and trust.

In fact, O'Dell (2004) advises, "For good results, develop a vision for the KM initiative. For exceptional results, translate that vision into explicit expectations and demand tangible results." She also urges KM practitioners to develop a long-term vision with mid-term measures, and look for "teachable moments", supply magnet content, and watch how organisational culture changes as a result of knowledge sharing.

CHAPTER THREE

Plans, Phases and Frameworks

"The great end of knowledge is not knowledge but action."
— Thomas Huxley

This chapter focuses on how organisations develop a plan for their KM initiatives, and how they chart out near, medium and long-term phases in planning their KM initiatives by developing a framework.

Access to accurate and timely knowledge has been acknowledged as a critical success factor in the long-term evolution of organisations. Conway and Sligar (2002) remarked: "Knowledge has an unlimited capacity for renewal; it is expandable, self-generating, transportable, and shareable. The capacity to turn knowing into knowledge and knowledge into productivity and innovation will be the hallmark of the successful enterprise in the 21st century." For such knowledge strategies to succeed, quantifiable milestones and timelines must be identified, and KM must be aligned to and synchronised with business strategy and planning. However, as proposed by Natarajan and Shekhar (2000), knowledge strategies must also be interwoven into an organisation's mainstream activities and functions.

3.1. Planning Rationales

This section profiles KM planning literature in terms of phases and frameworks, for defining and evolving the knowledge journey. A KM roadmap typically involves knowledge needs analysis, knowledge capture (via knowledge maps), knowledge administration, refinement, and dissemination. Many KM initiatives tend to get stuck in 'pilot project' stages with an unclear focus or inadequate measures of progress, and managers tend to underestimate the complexities of technology integration and cultural changes within the workforce (Natarajan & Shekhar, 2000).

Typical steps in a KM plan include understanding the nature of knowledge in the organisation, identifying the organisation's knowledge needs, and devising steps to fulfil the needs through a combination and evolution of people, process and technology measures. Chatzkel (2003), citing Wiig (1999), identified different kinds of knowledge, for example, paradigm knowledge, methodology knowledge, decision-making/factual knowledge, routine working knowledge, and tacit knowledge. These types of knowledge manifest themselves through knowledge maps, knowledge landscapes, scripts, schemata and meta-knowledge that are factored into the different stages of the KM planning.

Planning KM should allow for the complex nature of knowledge, which can often be uncertain, difficult to capture, dynamically changing, highly context dependent, expensive to codify, and too politically sensitive to make explicit. Indeed, as pointed out by Newell *et al.* (2002), for knowledge workers who view modern firms more as "orchestras", "knowledge is simultaneously an input, medium and output for their work". Also, a more visible connection needs to be established between knowledge sharing and business strategy. For instance, the appropriate KM activities can include the transfer of best practices, expertise locator, and principal lessons learned when getting information to workers for the reusing of solutions and expertise, lowering operational costs, or improving innovations (O'Dell, 2004). Dependent upon the level of human interaction and tacit nature of the knowledge, Hansen *et al.* (1999) expounded two kinds of knowledge strategies — codification (reuse of knowledge bases), and personalisation (encouraging people-to-people networking and mentoring), although there are other emerging approaches such as social computing that promise to democratise relationships and content.

O'Dell and Hubert (2011) classify KM approaches into specific categories: self-service, lessons learned, communities of practice (CoPs) and best-practice transfer. Classification as such is seen as more than a tactical approach in organisational development. Ahmed *et al.* (2002) noted: "Managing learning and knowledge requires more than small-time tinkering within the organisation. Success demands a paradigm shift in organisational thinking." Thus, the deliberate approach to KM leads to more structured and conscious ways for organisations to manage the acquisition of knowledge as well as to manage learning.

3.1.1. *Planning Phases*

KM planning is inherently related to innovation and intellectual capital as the focus is on value creation extracted from the intellectual property (Al-Ali, 2003). In other words, KM is about increasing organisational intelligence quotient through learning, about systematising collective and creative thinking, as well as commercialising and legalising the values created in the marketplace. In successive stages, KM results in best practices and knowledge cultures, where innovation leads to product concepts, and intellectual capital leads to patents, trademarks and copyrights.

To ensure sustainable organisational capital, KM planning is important to strategise as well as to manage the organisation's intellectual capital as it requires harnessing and codifying information, and leveraging knowledge sharing for incremental or radical innovations. As part of KM planning, knowledge audits and resource maps are charted to position and enable tools for socialisation (such as expert directories), internalisation (an e-learning portal), and externalisation (databases consisting of best practices) so as to deploy the different phases of knowledge capture.

3.1.2. *KM Frameworks*

There are different frameworks or perspectives to plan for differing phases within each KM project. There is no specific order that the organisations would follow in planning their KM projects, as the mode of planning is dependent upon the context or problems that the organisations face. Thus, planning may start with identifying existing knowledge assets and mapping the gaps between the current situation and the desired objectives; or it may start with recognising different facets in the organisation and designing tasks accordingly; it may also start with re-engineering business processes to optimise organisational resources. Regardless of the choice, effective KM practices are required to align with corporate strategies and objectives.

	1. What We Know We Know	2. What We Know We Don't Know
Knowledge Awareness	Emphasis: knowledge sharing, access and inventory. Tools: benchmarking, communities of practice (CoPs).	Emphasis: knowledge seeking and creation Tools: R&D, market research, competitive intelligence.
	3. What We Don't Know We Know	4. What We Don't Know We Don't Know
	Emphasis: uncovering hidden or tacit knowledge Tools: knowledge maps, audits, training, networks	Emphasis: discovering key risks, exposures and opportunities. Tools: creative tension, audits, dilemmas, complexity science

Knowledge Content

Figure 3.1   A Knowledge Portfolio.

Source: Adapted from Drew (1999).

Drew (1999) classified four important types of knowledge that should be considered during KM planning process as follows: what we know we know; what we know we don't know; what we don't know we know; what we don't know we don't know. Through identifying and comparing the organisations' existing knowledge assets with other assets that are required to achieve the organisational vision, an organisation would thus understand the strategic gap to move forward. Adapted from Drew (1999), Figure 3.1 provides the knowledge portfolio of four types of knowledge based on knowledge awareness (whether the organisation is aware of the knowledge that exists) and knowledge content (whether the organisation possesses such knowledge). In other words, by understanding the context of the knowledge (awareness) and auditing the content of the knowledge (content), each quadrant identifies techniques and tools that will assist management to focus strategically to overcome the knowledge void in the organisation.

In another KM framework shown in Figure 3.2, Donoghue *et al.* (1999) categorised two dimensions to measure the work processes in terms of the level of interdependence (individual vs. collaborative) and complexity (routine vs. interpretive). In other words, depending on the objectives of the KM initiatives, KM planning could start with evaluating the dimensions in order to understand the various KM work process models to adopt.

3.1.3. *KM Maturity Frameworks*

Maturity frameworks have been deployed by various organisations to assess and plan initiatives ranging from quality to innovation. They

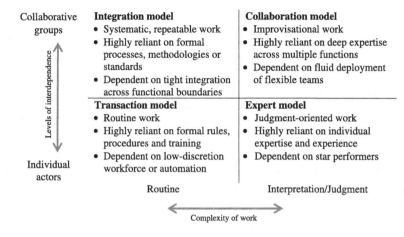

Figure 3.2   KM Work Process Model.

Source: Donoghue *et al.* (1999).

have also been used by organisations to plan their KM evolution. The American Productivity and Quality Center (APQC) defined five levels of KM maturity as follows: initiate (awareness about KM), develop (involvement through specific KM initiatives), standardise (alignment of various KM initiatives), optimise (measure outcomes of KM) and innovate (improvement of processes and quality through KM). These should be applied not just to IT and content management but culture and communication as well (APQC, 2012). Each level in turn has different outcome measures: activity, process efficiency and business performance.

Consulting firm KPMG identifies five stages in the maturity of the KM culture and its adoption in a company, depending on the processes, culture and roles in the organisation. These stages include: knowledge chaos (no structured approach), knowledge aware (basic cataloguing), and knowledge-enabled (standardised processes), knowledge-managed (integrated KM culture), and knowledge-centric (assessment and improvement of knowledge environment). Global consultancy firm McKinsey goes into further detail and examines how organisations at different levels of KM maturity deploy different kinds of IT tools and process solutions. Organisations which deploy and adapt such KM solutions fall into five kinds: conservative adopters (with basic KM functionality for cost savings), fast followers (deep KM functionality in a few critical processes), and solution buyers (who prefer all-in-one solutions), self-sufficient integrators (market leaders), and business design innovators (driven by visionary leaders).

3.1.4. Roadmaps

A number of practitioners and analysts have charted out KM roadmaps and evolutionary steps. APQC recommends a knowledge roadmap consisting of phases inclusive of assessment, strategic development, launching of KM initiatives, education/communication, expansion, and institutionalisation. Alignment with business objectives and design of effective pilot projects are important considerations. Leadership plays a key role in 'passing on the passion', devising budgets and reward/recognition schemes, and steering the core KM group.

As KM is a long-term strategy, its implementation and yields occur over a relatively long period. As Davenport and Probst (2002) puts it, "The economic value of knowledge does not lie in possessing it, but in using it. Pilot projects for KM must have clearly defined, measurable objectives that can be achieved in less than six months. However, the changeover to a knowledge-based company involves a change process that can span several years." There are therefore key issues to be resolved that include spelling out financial responsibilities, identifying internal sources, flows of knowledge, and choosing appropriate measurement frameworks. 'Hard' measures can include savings on energy, time and labour whilst 'soft' measures can include enhanced innovation, improved morale, and employee satisfaction. These measures themselves evolve with maturity of a KM initiative.

To ensure KM success, it is critical to design both corporate culture and technology to scale relative to organisational growth. At its best, KM poses challenges for managers in the organisations (Conway & Sligar, 2002). Effective leadership and long-term commitment are also seen as important success factors for KM. Davenport and Probst (2002) explained: "To successfully introduce KM into an organisation, it is important to engage an expert on KM and top managers who believe in KM. If one of the two is missing, the chance of a failure is 60 percent. Only when we have made up our minds that sharing knowledge is important, not only for efficiency's sake, but also to increase the essential humanisation of the business and social environments in which we work, will we be prepared for the tasks confronting us."

3.2. Perspectives from the Case Studies

This section describes the planning approach adopted by each of the case studies.

3.2.1. *Attorney-General's Chambers (AGC)*

AGC embarked on a KM Pilot Project under the auspices of the Singapore Government's Knowledge Management Experimentation Programme in May 2002. From the outset, it was recognised that KM is not merely an IT effort, but turns upon organisational culture. Consistent with the KM Implementation Roadmap, AGC sought to achieve greater enterprise integration and is indeed, currently on its way to the final stage of the KM Implementation Roadmap (see Figure 3.3).

Phase One of the project involved the development of an organisational blueprint with the assistance of Ernst & Young Associates and was completed in November 2002. The scope of engagement consisted of assessments in the areas of: (a) leadership and culture; (b) KM processes; (c) measurement; and (d) technology. The engagement took six months, and during that time, AGC's change readiness index was assessed, and a knowledge audit and process-mapping

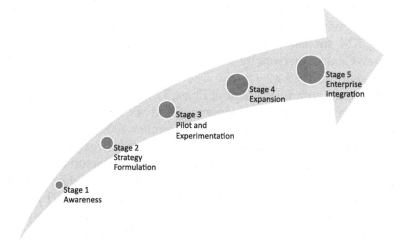

Figure 3.3   Evolution of AGC's KM Journey.
Source: Provided by AGC.

Table 3.1 AGC's KM Assessment and Plan.

Areas of Assessment	Key Recommendations
Leadership and culture	— KM vision statement — Case for change — Change management strategy
KM processes	— Content management framework — Knowledge taxonomy — Communities of practice
Measurement	— KM performance indicators — KM roles and responsibilities
Technology	— System features to support knowledge needs — Technology roadmap

Source: Provided by AGC.

exercise was also completed (see Table 3.1). A KM Visioning Workshop, involving senior management and KM representatives from the divisions, was held to develop AGC's KM vision statement — to develop their human capital and have a culture of sharing so as to provide quality legal services through the bold, effective, swift and thorough application of knowledge and experience.

During the consultancy stage, senior management actively participated by giving suggestions to improve on the KM projects and by sharing KM success stories that they came across. In addition, the Attorney-General personally championed visits to various law firms for KM sharing.

Prior to the commencement of Phase Two (implementation) in January 2003, a KM change management and six KM awareness workshops were held in November and December 2002 to bring the KM message to all staff. Messages were customised to each level of the staff so as to create a shared and common understanding of the KM vision and objectives. The benefits of KM were demonstrated and success stories were told. The KM effort was driven by a KM committee comprising divisional representatives, with support from senior management. The Solicitor-General was the project sponsor, and divisional representatives served as KM champions and domain experts to provide user input to the technology team and participated in user acceptance tests for the new portal.

Commonly used references and resources for their KM launch included the Ernst & Young KM Study Report, KM Implementation Roadmap (Civil Service College), and the KM Climate Assessment Study Report (Civil Service College).

3.2.2. Defence Science and Technology Agency (DSTA)

In 2000, DSTA put up a ten-year roadmap to chart the KM journey that comprised three phases (see Figure 3.4): exploration, foundation and growth.

Phase I — Exploration: The focus of the first three years was on engaging staff to understand their needs in information sharing, raising awareness of KM benefits, as well as shifting the mindset of the staff from a 'need-to-know' to a 'right-to-ask' mindset. Numerous workshops were conducted to engage the staff. The enterprise intranet platform for sharing information on a group basis that allowed departments to publish events, make announcements and share information was established.

Phase II — Foundation: Having understood the needs of the staff, the KM team moved on to set up an online repository, to support the

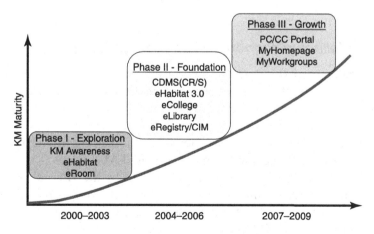

Figure 3.4 The KM Journey at DSTA.

Source: Provided by DSTA.

centralised approach of managing official documents and records. The approach included the scanning and routing of documents and records. The legacy Registry system was progressively replaced by the eRegistry initiative, which consists of features such as eFiling, eRouting, scanning and eWorkflow. The DSTA eLibrary was transformed to include eResources which were paid subscriptions to online databases of research articles such as Gartner, Jane's and IEEE. Depending on the areas and domains of interest, it was possible to forward alerts and news to the portals of the different departments. For the first time, materials of in-house courses organised by DSTA College were made available through this portal so that both participants and non-participants could access the same information.

Phase III — Growth: The last phase of the roadmap was to facilitate knowledge growth. This was performed at two levels: group and personal. At the group level, this was achieved by ensuring like-minded people came together in the sharing of knowledge. Each divisional entity was also equipped with its own portal and was given announcement channels to inform their staff of changes that affected them, updates that affected the entity and of upcoming events. In addition, the entity's portal facilitates sharing by its staff; such that CoPs were also formed in areas that were topical or domain-specific, e.g. Corporate IT Developer Network, Modelling and Simulation, and Systems Safety.

3.2.3. Intellectual Property Office of Singapore (IPOS)

IPOS first learned about KM in a variety of ways. Site visits and interviews were conducted with public agencies that had implemented KM successfully. Learnings were acquired from attending KM conferences, talks and networking sessions as well as from KM practitioners and consultants, such as in KM workshops and courses organised by Strait Knowledge and IPAM, and SharePoint related workshops.

The KM efforts of IPOS was started in 2007 by the internal research team on the feasibility and benchmarking of KM. Ernst & Young Associates was consulted at the initial assessment phase for launching its KM initiatives. Their KM audit took about four weeks which involved senior management, heads of department and content managers. The study identified the strong need for a document management system to codify knowledge, thus, its KM master plan included a predominantly codification strategy, complemented with personalisation efforts in the form of person-to-person sharing, collaboration tools and knowledge-sharing communities. Indeed, IPOS introduced KM as a journey for its officers to move towards an environment of sharing and collaboration.

As the IPOS senior management believed in and strongly supported the implementation of KM, it was not necessary to try and use IT as an angle to bring in budget support for its KM proposal, in fact the business case for KM itself was strong enough. As a first step, IPOS used technology for its officers to get into the KM initiative. The next move was to get them into the mode of sharing and this is still ongoing. The support of senior management in this aspect was a plus factor for the future development of KM.

3.2.4. Inland Revenue Authority of Singapore (IRAS)

To understand KM initiatives, IRAS invited various KM practitioners to share insights about their best practices. Based on the inputs, a timeline for its KM journey was prepared, consisting of three phases: Phase I (2003–2006), Phase II (2007–2008) and Phase III (2009–2011).

The initial phase, spanning three years, began with a knowledge audit of the organisation's knowledge strengths, weaknesses and needs. Based on the audit, the knowledge-sharing sessions were designed and launched. However, instituting a culture of sharing would not be easy, thus there were various incentives and recognition schemes built in knowledge-sharing initiatives. There was also extensive training for employees to use the supporting electronic tools and technologies for their individual as well as group work (see Figure 3.5a).

In Phase II which spanned over two years, a range of activities were introduced to further support and align the knowledge roles, in particular, providing closer integration of KM activities with existing work plans. This phase also involved increasing the number of knowledge champions, and refining the measurement metrics for monitoring and assessing knowledge-sharing behaviours (see Figure 3.5b).

The highlight of Phase III, which again span two years (2009–2011), was the iKMS Knowledge Excellence Award in 2009 (Silver Award for

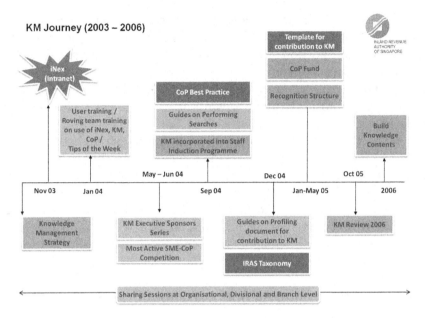

Figure 3.5a Evolution of KM at IRAS: 2003–2006.

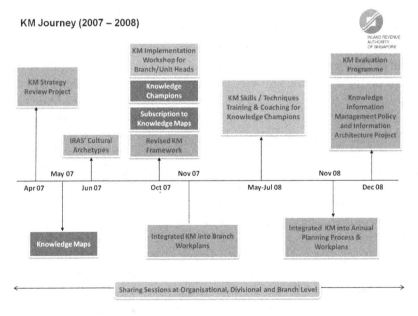

Figure 3.5b Evolution of KM at IRAS: 2007–2008.

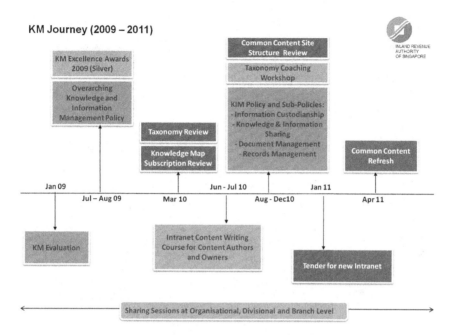

Figure 3.5c   Evolution of KM at IRAS: 2009–2011.

Source: Figures 3.5a–3.5c are all provided by IRAS.

knowledge-sharing sessions). In this phase, various technologies were included, such as a search facility and content management system. The knowledge taxonomy was also refined, and a tender for a new intranet was initiated. Writing courses were also launched for content creation on the intranet (see Figure 3.5c).

3.2.5. *Jurong Town Corporation (JTC)*

JTC recognised that to fulfil its role as a key government agency support-ing the nation's economic development, it should enhance its resilience and sustain its business and organisational excellence. A key thrust in its pursuit of organisational excellence was what lead to the pursuit of KM, which commenced a decade ago.

JTC's KM vision is to create "a knowledge-enabled organisation wherein the work culture and supporting infrastructure nurture collaboration and sharing of knowledge". Its corresponding KM mission is to formulate and drive corporate KM strategies and

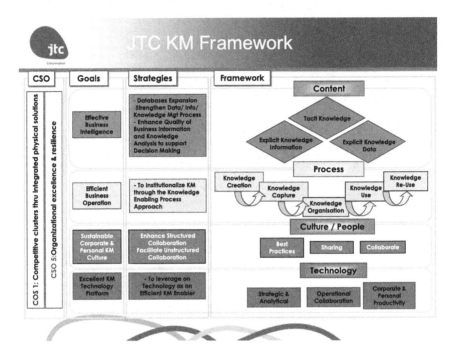

Figure 3.6   JTC's KM Framework.

Source: Provided by JTC.

implement initiatives to transform JTC into a knowledge-enabled organisation. Its KM efforts are therefore focused on ensuring that the organisation can better capture, use, reuse and leverage on information and knowledge throughout the organisation, supported effectively by IT. In fact, to guide its KM initiatives, JTC had a comprehensive framework that maps its goals and strategies accordingly to focus on the components comprising content, process, culture and technology, as shown in Figure 3.6.

JTC also strategically chartered its KM journey into three different phases focusing on three key agenda: The first was the full implementation of the electronic transactional systems; the second was the implementation of electronic platforms for the capturing and sharing of information and knowledge, and the third was the introduction of knowledge sharing and collaboration through online CoPs and workspaces. Figure 3.7 shows the various processes implemented during its KM journey.

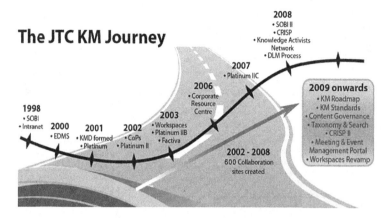

Figure 3.7   The JTC KM Journey.

Source: Provided by JTC.

3.2.6. Ministry of Finance (MOF)

KM plays an important role in the MOF. As shown in Figure 3.8, knowledge management is found under "Harness knowledge and information" in MOF's strategic plan that covers customer centricity, policy innovation and organisational learning. Indeed, its plans for improving organisational learning involved cultivating an organisational culture that recognises individual excellence and performance efficiency based on delivering excellent customer services.

For its KM plan, management systems and processes needed to be continuously improved upon to ensure that MOF could become more nimble and prepared to face new challenges in a fast-evolving environment. Indeed, its critical management capability is the implementation of KM, where an officer is able to access the required knowledge resource at the appropriate place and time. The quest for a well-constructed framework for KM forms the impetus of this KM initiative, whose individual steps are outlined in Table 3.2.

3.2.7. National Library Board (NLB)

KM planning at NLB began with an audit of internal perceived opportunities and challenges. This led to specific steps for building internal KM capabilities and strengthening the culture of knowledge sharing. Recognising that its activities are pretty diverse, its KM

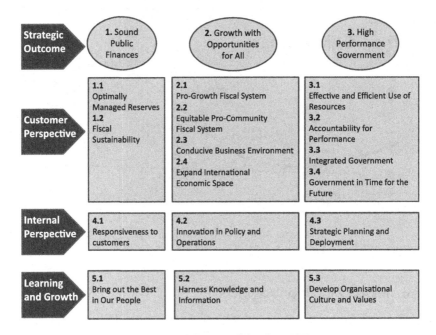

Figure 3.8   Strategy Map for MOF.

Source: Redrawn from MOF.

Table 3.2   Chronology of KM Initiatives at MOF.

2007	Appointment of Directorate Knowledge Activists (KAs)
2007	Worked with KAs to develop corporate taxonomy
2008	Endorsed corporate taxonomy
2008	Implemented the Email Repository System
2009	Won iKMS Award
2009	Adopted SharePoint platform for sharing and collaboration
2010	Roadshows to solicit feedback on requirements for new intranet portal
2010	Launched MOFi, the MOF intranet portal
2010	Migration of information from Lotus Notes to SharePoint platform

Source: Provided by MOF.

programme therefore identified knowledge champions from across the organisations, in other words, to address sustainable KM, the programmes focused on creating a repertoire of KM capabilities and competencies that extends beyond the central KM team.

In successive phases, close to 40 staff were nominated based on their experience, standing and openness to learning new techniques, and they were put through ten sessions (over ten months) covering 24 different techniques for knowledge solicitation, capture, codification, and distribution. Such techniques included Rich Pictures, Play of Life, podcasts, and storytelling. Technological innovations were leveraged to develop a collaborative platform dubbed as the Network of Specialists (NOS) for librarians and external experts to collaborate in real time, discuss and simultaneously work on one enquiry.

3.2.8. *Singapore Armed Forces (SAF)*

SAF launched its KM initiative in 2002 to support its leadership mandate to nurture first class people, strengthen professionalism, promote open learning, and create deep specialisation.

Peter Senge's Fifth Discipline played an important role in catalysing SAF's need to develop into a learning organisation. Daniel Kim and Diane Cory became core facilitators to the Army's program 'Leaders for Learning Army' which continues today. Gary Klein's work on naturalistic decision-making and his consultations with the SAF helped form the basis for much of the leadership training and education program. Dave Snowden worked with SAF on understanding complexity and storytelling. Alex Bennet and David Bennet's new theory of the firm based on complexity theory and KM, *Organisational Survival in the New World: The Intelligent Complex Adaptive System*, is a reference text for the SAF leadership team. They also serve as consultants for its KM implementation.

The consultants recommended that SAF become more involved in the international KM community to take full advantage of wider benchmarking and collaborative opportunities. Early in its KM and organisational learning journey, SAF benchmarked itself with the US Department of the Navy (DoN), which was the leading implementation of KM in the US government sector; it was also the first government MAKE (Most Admired Knowledge Enterprise) winner. The DoN effectively placed their KM program under the department-wide Chief Information Officer's (CIO) Office, and its Chief Knowledge Officer also served as the Deputy CIO for Enterprise Integration. As the KM journey continued, SAF made a conscious effort to attend selected conferences to learn how others have taken the journey and learn from their experiences. SAF continues to visit other agencies such as US Army and commercial entities like Schlumberger and Accenture.

Working with APQC, the SAF applied the KM Maturity Model to assess its progress in KM. SAF attained a maturity of Level 4 which states that its KM efforts are aligned and institutionalised across the enterprise. It is also moving into Level 5 where knowledge is embedded in key organisational processes. SAF is now actively involved in international forums such as APQC and the KNOW Network.

3.2.9. *Singapore Police Force: Police Technology Department (SPF-PTD)*

SPF-PTD's KM initiative was launched in 2005 to cushion knowledge leakage when officers go on job rotation. Its aims were to build a culture of knowledge sharing, knowledge retention and lifelong learning, as well as to align the KM initiatives with PTD's strategic objectives, and to maximise learning from mistakes and experiences. A broad spectrum of KM activities were planned in the areas of organisational learning, knowledge sharing competitions, internal communications, peer visits, and formal training. These were rolled out in successive phases, e.g. annual competitions in storytelling; internal magazines and innovation videos; management retreats and informal hobby clubs (listed in Table 3.3).

3.2.10. *Singapore Youth Olympic Games Organising Committee (SYOGOC)*

SYOGOC's KM plan was drawn up to support the overall games activity schedule. Hence, the initial timeline for the KM plan was anchored on the five major phases of its master schedule: (a) foundation planning; (b) operational planning; (c) operations readiness planning; (d) operations; and (e) dissolution.

Inputs for these phases and activities were gathered from a variety of sources. In addition to the CEO and Chief Operating Officer, it had directors for corporate planning, ceremonies, logistics, finance, venues, sports, technology, the Youth Olympic Village, sports development, protocol, sponsorships, workforce, and games services. SYOGOC also created an advisory panel consisting of the Minister for Defence and Minister for Community Development, Youth and Sports, representatives from National Trades Union Congress as well as

Table 3.3   Chronology of KM Activities at SPF-PTD.

2006	— PTD KM Day and launch of PASSION Magazine
	— Inaugural Let's Celebrate Learning (LCL)
2007	— KM Archetypes Video produced
	— Launch of PTD Training School
2008	— PTD Internal WITs[1] and SSS[2] Competition 2008
	— PTD received the KM Excellence Awards 2008 (Silver Award)
2009	— PTD Internal WITs and SSS Competition 2009
	— Capability Development Division (CDD) created
	— First issue of *Knowledge Times* published
	— KM visit to URA
2010	— PTD Internal WITs and SSS Competition 2010
	— Formation of nine hobby clubs
	— Launch of the PTD Learning Portal at the 14th LCL
	— Inaugural Director PTD Essay Competition 2010
	— First broadcast of 'Have Your Say!'
	— CDD retreat held at Civil Service College
	— Soft launch of the PTD Competency Website at the 16th LCL
	— KM visit from Supreme Court hosted
	— PTD Innovation Video produced
	— First broadcast of 'Coaching Channel'
2011	— PTD Internal WITs and SSS Competition 2010
	— PTD KM Open House
	— KM visit to Accenture
	— PTD Photo Gallery

Source: Provided by SPF-PTD.
[1] Work Improvement Teams.
[2] Staff Suggestion Schemes.

Singapore Federations for Sailing and Hockey. External advisors were members from the International Olympic Committee.

3.2.11. *Supreme Court of Singapore (SC)*

The Supreme Court has drawn on experiences from external KM practices when planning for its KM initiatives. Developed by the Knowledge Management Steering Committee (KMSC), its KM plan covers diverse aspects of activities such as establishing the collaborative space, creating the tools, and designing the processes to enable and capture the generation, retention and flow of knowledge. It also draws up precise

Table 3.4   Chronology of KM Initiatives at the Supreme Court.

2000: Electronic Filing System launched
2005: New Supreme Court building becomes functional
2005: Launch of Creanovator Room
2006: KM Portal launched
2008: Wikis created
2009: KMSC formed
2009: Addition of Legal Analyst whose portfolio includes KM
2009: Pegs and Bench Memoranda databases created
2010: Full-time Knowledge Manager recruited
2010: Supreme Court wins iKMS Knowledge Excellence Award
2011: Launch of Knowledge Retention (KRIS) Programme
2011: Site visits to other KM programmes
2012: Upgrading of intranet to SharePoint 2010

Source: Provided by the Supreme Court.

measurement metrics to ensure that its plan stays on track, and that results can demonstrated and validated.

Table 3.4 shows some of the chronological steps that Supreme Court had taken to implement its KM initiatives. It is interesting to note that its KM plan did not solely focus on creating online workspaces, it has also included integrating and aligning the online spaces with the physical space; for instance, it expanded the collaborative space to include the Creanovator room which is a physical space that involves its relocation; indeed, the plan also included the designing of new offices to provide a more conducive space for knowledge sharing. Further, various specific roles for the management of knowledge were activated, with new positions defined and filled as the initiative matured.

3.2.12. *Urban Redevelopment Authority (URA)*

In working out its framework, URA studied various planning and maturity approaches such as those of APQC. It was recognised that the KM framework for URA should be strategic in business alignment and yet pragmatic in implementation. After engaging various stakeholders, URA developed a KM framework with clear goals, deployment and desired outcomes.

One group in the governance framework focused on strategic planning and decision-making, and another addressed daily business operations for KM. The KM plan initially addressed internal issues of knowledge sharing and infrastructure, but the later mature stages focused on various benchmarking and comparison studies to gather intelligence. These strategies stemming from external knowledge were aimed at improving processes, products and services, vis-à-vis other best-in-class cities and organisations.

3.3. Insights from the Case Studies

Based on the literature review and snapshots of case studies in Section 2, the KM planning approaches are summed up in Table 3.5. The planning approaches can be described in terms of input sources or references, alignment with internal objectives, a roadmap, and steps taken towards the initiatives. These four categories are shown in Table 3.6.

Overall, many organisations used external references to implement their KM plans, for instance, input from agencies which have implemented KM (e.g. IRAS) or from external consultants (e.g. AGC). They also visited other agencies (e.g. Supreme Court) or adopted entire

Table 3.5   KM Plans and Approaches.

Organisation	KM Planning and Strategy
AGC	Pilot project, experimentation program, KM implementation roadmap, external consultant
DSTA	Three phases: exploration, foundation, growth
IPOS	Audit, consultancy, master plan
IRAS	Portfolio, system, KM roadmap, KM practitioners' insights
JTC	Three phases: electronic transactional systems, platforms for sharing knowledge, CoPs and workspaces
MOF	Corporate Strategy Map, KM Strategy Map
NLB	Audit, KM, Knowledge Champions, collaboration platform
SAF	Organisational learning, APQC KM Maturity Model
SPF-PTD	KM work plan
SYOGOC	Knowledge transfer from the IOC
SC	Site visits, workshops, full-time roles
URA	APQC KM Maturity Framework, knowledge pyramid

Table 3.6   KM Planning Procedures.

Plan Factors	Parameters
Reference points (external inputs)	— Visits to other agencies who implemented KM — Site visits to other organisations — Consultancies, IT vendors
Alignment with internal initiatives	— Corporate Strategy Map — Leadership initiatives — Learning initiatives
KM roadmap	— Internal growth phases (e.g. exploration, foundation, growth) — KM Maturity Models (e.g. APQC, KPMG)
KM steps	— Audits, master plan, pilot projects

KM frameworks from other organisations (e.g. SYOGOC from the International Olympic Committee).

Phases of the KM plan can be classified in terms of evolution (e.g. DSTA: Exploration, Foundation, Growth) or in terms of the maturity models (e.g. SAF, URA). Often, the KM roadmap is aligned with corporate strategies (MOF) or leadership and learning initiatives (SAF). Once the framework or roadmap is worked out, specific steps are then pursued, such as conducting a knowledge audit, drawing up a master plan, and launching a pilot study.

The KM plans of these organisations were developed by the top managers acting along with a team of internal experts, and often with inputs from external KM practitioners, consultants and IT vendors. Indeed, the KM plan can also change with emerging supply-side and demand-side drivers. "The knowledge-based enterprise is a sense-and-respond, intelligent organisation, and its work is conversation, characterised by building new knowledge capital with new players, new information, new perspectives, new possibilities and new responses to new consumer needs," explains Chatzkel (2003). Corporate leaders must rely on members to self-organise and design emergent strategies that move the firm forward (Lengnick-Hall and Lengnick-Hall, 2003).

Conway and Sligar (2002) also explain that various phases are needed to tackle corporate culture and technology in the KM journey, for instance, in DSTA. Long-term success will require organisations to realise that a knowledge focus is not just a component for efficiency but also a way to humanise social environments (Davenport & Probst, 2002); such thinking is reflected in some KM visions, such as in IPOS. Organisational change for successful KM can take several years (Davenport & Probst, 2002); indeed, a few of the organisations described in the case studies have been on the KM journey for more than ten years (e.g. SAF, URA).

Moving from an organisational to a national level, Singapore recognises knowledge as a key competitive force. This is reflected in the nation-state's own knowledge journey along phases characterised as labour-intensive, skills-intensive, capital-intensive, knowledge-intensive and now innovation- or experience-intensive.

CHAPTER FOUR

Leadership and Governance

"The greatest difficulty lies not in persuading people to accept new ideas, but in persuading them to abandon old ones."
— John Maynard Keynes

This chapter focuses on KM leadership and governance, addressing the 'who' of KM in the organisation. In other words, the chapter discusses the knowledge leaders of the organisation, their attributes, skills as well as the aspirations of the KM team, and the people who hold the governance roles in various KM committees.

Defining a company's conceptual umbrella, articulating knowledge aspirations, harnessing chaos, and still staying on course are key challenges faced by KM leaders and managers (Takeuchi & Nonaka, 2004). Enabling conditions for successful knowledge creation include intention, autonomy, creative chaos, redundancy and a variety of perspectives. Instilling a knowledge vision, managing conversations internally and externally, mobilising knowledge activists and creating the right contexts are important components of a knowledge advancement strategy.

Within the core KM team of an organisation, Chief Knowledge Officers (CKOs) play a crucial role in managing corporate knowledge capital and championing knowledge-centric cultures. CKOs require a blend of technical, human and financial skills (Malhotra, 2001).

4.1. KM Leaders and Managers

This section reviews literature on the human and social aspects of KM initiatives in terms of leadership, management, governance frameworks and roles. The bulk of this attention initially focuses on the CKO, but more recent research has since addressed the full gamut of knowledge workers.

4.1.1. *The Chief Knowledge Officer (CKO)*

Bennet and Neilson (2004) address the key role of the CKO, principally in public sector organisations. KM is important to public sector organisations due to its positive impacts on productivity, learning, process improvement and risk management. The role of a CKO consists of developing a KM vision with the CEO, championing KM behaviours and benefits, providing policy guidance, benchmarking internally and externally, and assessing and aligning KM practices. The competencies and skills that create a successful CKO include strategic thinking, cognitive capabilities, leadership, storytelling skills, and alignment with key stakeholders.

McKeen and Staples (2004) profiled the characteristics of CKOs, and found that they are generally hired internally because of their vast knowledge of the organisation. Their key tasks are: setting strategic knowledge priorities, establish best practices, create commitment to KM among senior executives, address customer satisfaction, and nurture a knowledge-sharing culture. Challenges they face included: lack of clarity in budget allocations (often overlapping with other functions and initiatives), change management, and measuring the impacts of KM. The authors also called for longitudinal field research to identify changes in CKO roles, perceptions, and aspirations.

Ruth *et al.* (2004) further expanded on the qualities required of successful CKOs. They must have a mix of consultant, technologist, environmentalist and entrepreneurial skills. CKOs must be able to align and integrate diverse functions, develop a culture of continuous learning, leverage organisation-wide learning, establish partnerships with senior managers, and conduct strategic planning and implementation. Thus, the three key responsibilities of CKOs include building a knowledge culture, creating a KM infrastructure, and ensuring that the KM implementations are economically viable (Davenport & Prusak, 1998). Good knowledge workers need to have a combination of 'hard' skills (structured knowledge, technical abilities, professional experience) and 'soft' skills (cultural, political and personal aspects of knowledge). The CKO also assumes the role of a leader, champion, integrator and an agent of change. "Knowledge superiority" is the key answer to dealing with the increasing complexity of this age (Chatzkel, 2002). High 'situational awareness' in all directions is called for, as well as an ability to continually make decisions based on new information. Successful KM requires a combination of 'nodes and flows', coupled with porous boundaries and requirements for continuous learning and training.

Besides the above-mentioned responsibilities and roles of CKOs, Shekawat (2002) pointed out five mistakes that CKOs should avoid in order to keep their organisations alive and thriving, and he provided solutions for each of the mistakes as follows:

- Read-Fire-Aim: KM programs should not be implemented simply for its own sake, but to tackle more specific business problems. In other words, CKOs should align KM initiatives within the context of the organisation, and then identify suitable technological solutions to address the business problems.
- Build it and they will come: The value of new KM technologies can only be actualised by employees' usage. CKOs should promote a smart adoption methodology within organisations, and execute incentive plans to boost system popularity and usage.
- People vs. documents: Though documentation can ensure longer availability and easier accessibility, it can only capture a very small portion of human knowledge, while the most valuable tacit knowledge still remains within the human mind. CKOs should assess their problems and decide whether to deploy a techno-centric or human-centric view.
- Taking a 'Big Bang!' approach: A constantly changing market, globalised competition, and high workforce attrition rate all lead to unpredicted return on investment, inclusive of KM projects. CKOs have to adopt a framework to pilot the program and utilise a staged approach for value measurements.
- Sinking in the supply-side quicksand: Supply-side approach (selection of a KM solution based on existing knowledge resources) may work well under static environments such as call centres, but it falls short in more dynamic environments such as R&D or sales, etc.

CKOs should take a demand-side approach, to meet the changing knowledge needs of employees and organisations.

4.1.2. *The KM Team*

The CKO requires the support of a diverse team, covering a range of skills and domain knowledge so as to set strategic policies for an organisation's knowledge acquisition and distribution. Davenport and Prusak (1998) identified key roles in the KM team to include knowledge project managers, coaches, trainers, counsellors, integrators, administrators, engineers, librarians, synthesizers, reporters and editors — capped by learning officers, CKOs, directors of intellectual assets, or Chief Information Officers (CIOs). Organisations should focus not just on harvesting, but also on nourishing knowledge (Edvinsson, 2004). Therefore they should not just capture the moment but also have the abilities of capturing the momentum and seizing the future. For instance, Buckman Labs has a role for 'anecdote management', which is to develop stories about successful KM in practice for capturing in the future. To practice storytelling processes, it requires support and drive from idea practitioners within the organisation, who are important players in the process of importing and implementing new ideas into businesses. They are the link between ideas and actions (Davenport & Prusak, 2003). They are not fad mongers, but are thoughtful, reflective, motivated, and moderate in temperament; they are hybrid creators and users of ideas, and multi-disciplinary boundary-spanners. They should also be aware of how each idea is positioned within and outside the organisation at any time.

Within the organisations, Wenger (2006) advocated "transversal leadership (both vertical and horizontal)" for emergent governance in a KM practice. Amidon and Macnamara (2004) further expanded on the role of knowledge leaders with their "7 Cs" framework: context (for creating the KM vision), competence, culture, communities, conversations, communication and coaching. Knowledge leadership should move beyond commanding and controlling towards creating and communicating. There is no fixed task scope for a CKO, but their job responsibilities typically involves developing a KM strategy to align with the organisation's overall objective, promoting KM initiatives within and beyond the organisation, implementing related KM infrastructure, facilitating interpersonal, inter-departmental, and inter-organisational connections and communications. O'Dell and Hubert (2011) on the other hand, identified ten characteristics of knowledge champions: progressive, investigative, all-for-one, trusted, methodical, visionary, good at implementation, observant, innovative and follower-centric. They also advocated the importance of fun during knowledge work.

4.1.3. Skills of KM Teams

Common sets of KM skills required include information searching, communication and socialising (dialogues, interviews), as well as having cognitive abilities (reflective, active learning). Socialising skills are hard to build via training, since they derive from inherent personality traits. KM practitioners should develop networking skills besides cultivating curiosity about other people's problems, and communicate to share the different perspectives.

People working in KM teams should possess hybrid thinking, integrating their visions with people across levels in various teams and departments. They should have the ability to plan and execute work plans, to manage multiple projects, to manage people, to work effectively both as a team player as well as an independent professional, and to achieve desirable end results.

Indeed, instead of just codifying best practices and enterprise portals, emphasis should be placed on unlearning ineffective best practices and the continuous refinement and pursuit of better practices. Management strategies need to shift from command and control, to sense and respond (Malhotra, 2001). KM processes should be focused on doing the right thing (effectiveness), not just doing the thing right (efficiency). KM is not merely about bottling water from rivers of data, but about giving people canoes and compasses to navigate in these rivers of data.

In terms of KM implementation, Rumizen (2002) advises companies to start with a pilot or several pilots, with clearly defined objectives and then proceed to scale up depending on the lessons learned. New roles will be created, both within a core KM group and throughout the organisation. A steering committee including senior members of diverse backgrounds — and possibly external consultants as well — is a critical success factor.

4.2. Perspectives from the Case Studies

This section explores the knowledge leadership and knowledge roles in the case studies. Based on the literature review above, each profile covers the knowledge leaders, leadership committees, governance structure and facilitating roles in the individual KM initiatives.

4.2.1. Attorney-General's Chambers (AGC)

On 2 July 2007, an Information Division (InfoDiv) was established in AGC through the merger of the Computer Information Systems Department (CISD) with the Library and the Knowledge Management Central (KM Central), for better functional synergy (Figure 4.1). The objective is to provide effective legal services through the use of Information Technology (IT) and management of knowledge assets.

The InfoDiv is headed by a Chief Information Officer, assisted by an Information Systems Director, a Knowledge Management Director and a Library Director. Assistant Directors were appointed from

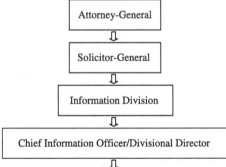

Figure 4.1   KM Governance at AGC.

Source: Redrawn from AGC.

the five legal divisions to support KM, IT and Library initiatives. The Information Communication Technology and KM steering committee (ICTSC), comprising the Solicitor-General and senior management from all the legal divisions, meets every half a year to provide leadership for directing the overall ICT and KM goals and policies, as well as endorsing strategies and plans for the programmes.

The establishment of the KM Central, in place of a KM committee, represents a further institutionalisation of AGC's KM efforts. KM Central is responsible for developing and coordinating its KM strategy, and providing guidance and support to the divisions in their individual KM projects. Senior management took part in developing the KM strategy such as the KM Vision Workshop. In AGC leadership meetings, senior management share information with cross-divisional impacts.

As of 2011, there are two full-time KM executives. The current Director of KM holds concurrent duties as a Senior State Counsel. The 13 Assistant Directors appointed from the five legal divisions also take on KM roles on a part-time basis. Their responsibilities include setting the KM goals for their respective divisions, prioritising projects and acting as a liaison between their respective divisions and the KM Central. The CIO and the KM Director hold the positions of Chairman and Secretary respective to the KM Committee since the launch of the original KM strategy and implementation design.

4.2.2. Defence Science and Technology Agency (DSTA)

To fulfil DSTA's KM vision, a KM team comprising of both the KM Programme and Portal Team was formed. In addition, the KM team also has strategic partnerships with the Centre for Information Management, Information Resource Centre, Knowledge Managers and an IT team. Figure 4.2 shows DSTA's KM organisational structure. The KM team plays a pivotal role in developing capacity and capability to learn and innovate, and to cultivate the growth of communities and workgroups. Broadly, the role of the KM team includes:

- Driving the adoption and practice of KM;
- Defining the KM landscape to ensure knowledge capturing/sharing and that work collaboration remains effective and efficient;
- Leading initiatives under the KM landscape which include rolling out KM systems; and
- Formulating holistic knowledge strategies and approaches, engaging entities for change management and growing the KM journey.

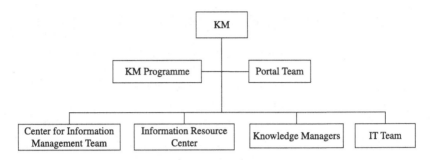

Figure 4.2   DSTA's KM Organisational Structure.
Source: Redrawn from DSTA.

As part of the organisation's transformation, a Directorate of Organisation Capability was established in 2006. The Directorate consists of eight Competency Centres (CCs) grouped in accordance to technical disciplines. Every staff member belongs to a CC which is the 'home base' for competency development and career management, and is assigned to projects that are undertaken by operating units across DSTA according to the job and competency needs. Each CC is headed by a senior executive who is responsible for the competency development, capability build-up and career progression of the staff. The CC heads also ensure that the staff have the relevant breadth and depth of their domain competencies to handle current and future demands. The CCs have since been working closely with the DSTA KM team, to tap on the enterprise's KM infrastructure and services. The CC heads have also embraced the concept of communities of practice (CoPs) as part of their CC management and staff engagement.

4.2.3. *Intellectual Property Office of Singapore (IPOS)*

IPOS introduced KM as a journey for its officers to move towards an environment of sharing and collaboration. The senior management believes and strongly supports the implementation of KM. The KM steering committee at IPOS consists of five members; the KM department consists of three members, and there are 22 KM representatives across the various departments. In the IT department, there is also a consultant to support the KM project. The KM Director's role is part-time and supported with two full-time KM officers. IPOS relies heavily on the KM steering committee and the KM working committee. The working committee members work with their officers, including their Heads of Department.

The KM Department's responsibility is to establish the KM framework and to interpret the content of the KM policy across the organisation. It ensures that IPOS maximises the value of knowledge assets, and facilitates the deployment of an information structure to enhance the knowledge creation and sharing culture. It also communicates the information sharing policy to all new staff as part of their induction programme, and reviews taxonomy annually and jointly with departments. Additional KM representatives are the intranet site owner and site administrator of KENNY (Knowledge ENterprise 'N You) .

4.2.4. Inland Revenue Authority of Singapore (IRAS)

IRAS appointed three KM officers to handle the KM portfolio and system. There is a dedicated KM team working within the Organisation Excellence Branch, with adequate linkages to the HR functions for performance management, learning and development, and clear alignment between the KM efforts and the IRAS vision and strategy. There is also a CKO as well as Branch Knowledge Champions.

IRAS Branch Heads are Directors ('branches' are known as departments in other organisations). The organisation structure of IRAS is as follows: Group Level (led by Deputy Commissioners) to Divisional Level (led by Assistant Commissioners) to Branch Level (led by Directors). The IRAS Senior Management team articulated a clear knowledge strategy and knowledge goals for IRAS; it made it a point to reiterate the importance of knowledge sharing in IRAS, through the implementation of other KM systems and tools, which sent a strong signal to all staff of its sponsorship and commitment to making knowledge sharing a norm. IRAS is currently developing a number of action plans following the completion of the KM Strategy Review Project in 2008 inclusive of the implementation of knowledge maps and a project to develop knowledge and information management policies and information architecture.

4.2.5. Jurong Town Corporation (JTC)

JTC has a staff strength of about 800 employees, making KM an imperative for its survival. In addition, due to its important role as Singapore's leading master planner and provider of industrial space solutions, it places great emphasis on customer satisfaction and holistic talent management. JTC is one of Singapore's most dynamic statutory boards, and its board comprises senior government officials and representatives from leading private sector companies.

JTC's CEO leads a panel of senior managers from different operational departments in the organisation. These units include specialised business functional teams, such as the industrial parks development, specialised parks development, customer services, and corporate planning, finance, IT, and the legal department. The KM initiative at JTC is spearheaded by its Corporate Research and KM Department, and led by a deputy director.

4.2.6. Ministry of Finance (MOF)

The Ministry of Finance (MOF) started off its KM initiative with the appointment of the Directorate Knowledge Activists in 2007. The directors from the various directorates at the Ministry were asked to nominate appropriate KM representatives from their directorates to assist in the implementation of the project. The KM representatives became the KM Working Committee which had the responsibilities of providing feedback, giving ideas, highlighting requirements and assuming the role of early adopters and change agents.

The MOF senior management team, comprising the Permanent Secretary, Deputy Secretaries and the Directors, formed the KM Steering Committee. This Committee would give the final endorsement, feedback and direction for the project. In other words, the KM initiative at MOF is guided by the Directorate Knowledge Activists, KM Representatives, and the KM Steering Committee.

4.2.7. National Library Board (NLB)

In the early 2000s, NLB started a series of KM programmes to align its strategies towards achieving customer excellence, operational excellence and innovation excellence; facilitating a seamless workflow to capture, organise, disseminate, create and exploit knowledge. The IDEAS website at NLB provides staff with information on participating in the Proof of Concept process to propose and test the feasibility of their ideas.

The staff are encouraged to take their initiatives in exploring new possibilities or ideas that leverage technology to create new and better ways of doing things. The IDEAS website also contains many examples of innovative ideas from libraries as well as from other industries. Top management provided the following objectives and desired outcomes for the initiatives:

- To enhance customer satisfaction;
- To attract and retain new customers;
- To increase public faith in the organisation;
- To strive to meet and manage customers' rising expectations; and
- To be able to justify the spending of funds allocated.

4.2.8. Singapore Armed Forces (SAF)

Helming the SAF's KM Group is the Head of the Joint Communications and Information Systems Department (JCISD), who is a Brigadier General which has oversight as both the SAF's CIO as well as the Deputy CKO. The CKO is the Chief of Staff who assists the Chief of Defence Force in development issues including that of the CIO and KM. The KM office has two full-time staff augmented by three staff on assignment from DSTA for change management support. The KM office maintains oversight of the two core teams responsible for the development of the intranet and the eSILK[1] system.

The Head of JCISD chairs fortnightly meetings to address governance issues, monitor progress and endorse project proposals. He has budget approval up till a certain value, and any amount beyond that will require approval from higher up the chain to the Ministry of Defence's CIO, and finally to the Defence Minister. Represented in the fortnightly meetings are the Heads of KM in the respective services, i.e. Army, Air Force and Navy, who are normally of the Colonel rank.

Within each of the KM offices, two or three staff would normally manage activities at the grassroots level. While they are dedicated staff, they also perform other learning-related functions. Beyond that, the respective subunits may have a variety of roles such as Knowledge Officers (usually a Captain or Major), Knowledge Systems Administrators (who are trained to manage the eSILK system at the unit level) and Community Administrators (who assist in the running of the Knowledge Communities, which are normally regarded as secondary roles).

---

[1] Enterprise System for Innovation, Learning and Knowledge.

4.2.9. *Singapore Police Force: Police Technology Department (SPF-PTD)*

SPF's Chief Knowledge Officer is also the Deputy Commissioner of Police. SPF's KM Steering Committee appoints a KM Champion, KM EXCO (a core team within PTD working on KM projects), Knowledge Managers, KM Advocates and KM PTD Training School (a training school to bridge learning and knowledge gaps). The Director of the PTD is personally involved as a KM visionary and evangelist. He plays the role of advisor to the KM EXCO with a strong management commitment to KM. The majority of PTD staff are involved in KM activities of one form or another — either as a participant or as part of the organising committee.

With regards to internal communications, the core KM team develops a KM work plan at the beginning of each fiscal year, usually during the KM EXCO retreat. The work plan, alongside target milestones, is presented to the PTD Director for approval. The KM team holds regular monthly meetings to plan for and review activities. Figure 4.3 shows a rather complex KM structure at PTD. KM-related communications are disseminated to the organisation via the KM Communications Team, a five-member team in charge of increasing KM awareness, using methods such as innovative graphics in posters via channels like email.

From 2009 to 2011, the PTD Training School's curriculum was developed and hosted in the PTD Learning portal. From an organisational perspective, the initial structure was adapted to a model, where the Capability Development Division (CDD) is the KM facilitator division that works with the subject matter experts within the other divisions. Together, they identify knowledge gaps, and craft the necessary training requirements and training format to meet the knowledge gaps. Identification of the knowledge gap is aided largely from an established competency framework. The KM EXCO retreat was adapted into an organisational format where CDD holds an annual retreat, incorporating the consolidation and assessment of KM practices in PTD. The Director of PTD remains the Chairman of KM in PTD. KM representatives from various divisions are tapped through learning coordinators or divisional webmasters.

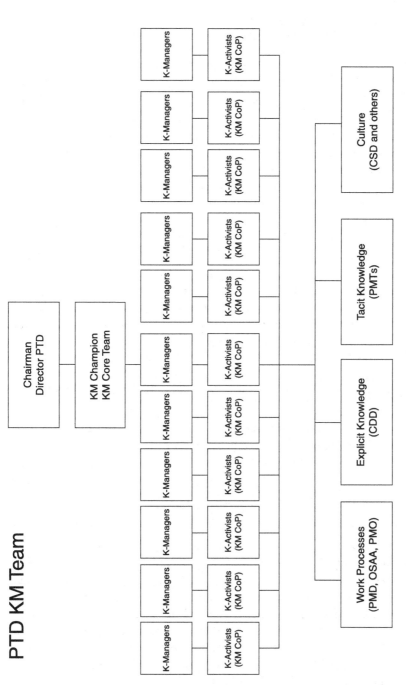

Figure 4.3   KM Team at SPF-PTD.

Source: Redrawn from SPF-PTD.

4.2.10. *Singapore Youth Olympic Games Organising Committee (SYOGOC)*

SYOGOC had more external inputs for its KM projects than any other case study. This is due to its unique positioning in a web of international event management. Some members of the senior management team were assigned by the Singapore Sports Council and Singapore National Olympic Council to support the Singapore 2010 Youth Olympic Games, starting from March 2008. The SYOGOC Chairman was formerly a sportsman and the ex-Chairman of the Singapore Sports Council, before being appointed as one of the vice presidents of the International Olympic Committee. These managers brought with them many years of sport industry experiences, and have participated in different capacities in major regional sporting events.

Other members of SYOGOC were sourced from various government agencies who were previously involved in major events, such as the National Day Parade and the APEC Singapore in 2009. Competition managers and technical officials were recruited from the local National Sport Associations. In addition, SYOGOC also recruited international talents from the organising committees of previous Games to complement the local workforce.

In order for the Games to be organised and conducted in an 'Olympic manner', the International Olympic Committee (IOC) conducted orientation seminars for the organising committee right from the start. The first orientation seminar was conducted in April 2008. The Olympic Games KM extranet containing planning documents from past summer and winter Olympic Games was made available to SYOGOC.

4.2.11. *Supreme Court of Singapore (SC)*

The Knowledge Management Steering Committee (KMSC) of the Supreme Court, led by two senior management representatives (Senior Assistant Registrar and Assistant Registrar), has been driving the KM initiatives together with the CKO, who takes a strong personal interest in KM. Whilst the KMSC drives the knowledge direction, all directorates are involved in and have ownership of KM, as KM is integral to all staff functions. Since August 2009, there has been a Legal Analyst whose portfolio includes KM — the chairperson of KMSC.

There is a network of KM activists, often holding the positions of Deputy Directors or Section Heads. The Registrar has a strong bearing on the KM initiatives, and understands the need to encourage a strong culture of connecting both 'people to people' and 'people to knowledge'. He personally champions the culture and creates the environment for others to do so.

A full-time KM officer position has been created and the organisation has recruited a Knowledge Manager with formal postgraduate KM qualifications. He reports directly to senior management (which collectively oversees the work of all the directorates in the Supreme Court). The Knowledge Manager is also chairperson of the KMSC, and has authority from senior management to implement such changes when deemed necessary, through the KM champions (all of whom sit on the KMSC).

4.2.12. Urban Redevelopment Authority (URA)

URA's KM efforts are overseen by the IT/KM Steering Committee, which is chaired by the Deputy CEO, as well as management-level members from business groups. The KM deployment group comprises the KM team, coupled with KM activists from the business groups. Knowledge roles are dispersed as per URA's view of the KM pyramid as shown in Figure 4.4.

The Knowledge Pyramid consists of four levels ranging from the most basic Infrastructure Management (level 1), to Explicit Knowledge Management (level 2), to Tacit Knowledge Management (level 3),

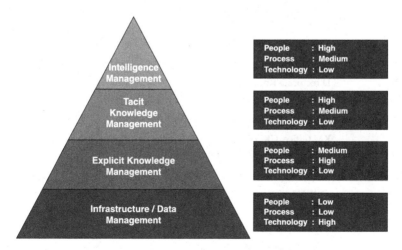

Figure 4.4   URA's Enterprise Knowledge Pyramid.

Source: Redrawn from URA.

and peaking at Intelligence Management (level 4). Level 1 focuses on the central provision of KM infrastructure, procedures and policies to ensure information quality which include the integration of 6 central information databases (over 20 systems) and information administration (Quality Check) procedures. Level 2 focuses on the extensive use of more than 20 strategic IT systems such as the Electronic Knowledge Repository Information System (eKRIS) and Integrated Planning and Land Use System (iPLAN). KM activists handle key roles at each levels, with more of an emphasis on people as one moves up the hierarchy of KM activities (especially in intelligence management and tacit KM).

4.3. Discussion and Insights

Table 4.1 summarises the KM leadership and governance of the profiled organisations. It can be seen that most organisations have a CKO,

Table 4.1   KM Leadership and Governance.

Organisation	Leadership and Governance
AGC	Divisional KM Champions, KM Director, KM Committee
DSTA	KM Team, Portal Team, Centre for Information Management, Knowledge Managers, IT Team
IPOS	KM Steering Committee, KM Department, KM Representatives, KM Director, KM Officers
IRAS	Organisational Excellence Officer for KM, KM Officers
JTC	KM Department, Senior-Level KM Council, Steering Committee
MOF	Directorate Knowledge Activists, KM Representatives, KM Working Committee
NLB	Network of Specialists, Knowledge Champions
SAF	KM Office, CKO, Deputy CKO, Knowledge Officer, Knowledge Systems Administrators, Community Administrators
SPF-PTD	CKO, KM Core Team, KM Champion, Knowledge Managers, KM Advocates, KM Communications Team
SYOGOC	KM Group, KM Coordinators
SC	Knowledge Management Steering Committee, KM Officer, KM Champions, KM Activists
URA	KM Steering Committee, KM Activists

who themselves are highly placed managers (sometimes even the CEO). They also appoint a high-level KM Committee or KM Directors. It has also been noted that most organisations establish steering committees to oversee the KM projects, such as in IPOS, URA, and the Supreme Court. In addition to hosting activities ranging from the serious to the informal, the fun element is well displayed in organisations such as SPF, where there are even essay competitions about key insights from movies. Managers need to sense and respond with regards to strategies for KM, and not just provide command and control as in URA and SAF.

There are other leaders at each divisional level, and managers for the following specific roles: knowledge sharing, portal, IT, information, organisational communication, communities, and organisational excellence. Some organisations create dedicated full-time or part-time roles called knowledge champions or knowledge activists.

Some of the KM roles are specifically dedicated to creating a culture of knowledge sharing, designing and executing knowledge processes, and leveraging existing and emerging IT tools. Perspectives in KM today thus come from a wide range of disciplines and organisational functions. Each of these throws up new kinds of roles and designations for an organisation's KM initiative. Disciplines leading into the KM body of knowledge include: organisational development, educational technology, leadership development, information policy, competency development, information design, strategic planning, systems integration, knowledge resources, cognitive studies, operational planning, and organisational excellence. Knowledge leaders are required to be proficient in a range of these disciplines, or the KM leadership team or committee will need to incorporate these diverse backgrounds and roles to ensure sustainable long-term growth and success of KM. Knowledge-based businesses need new forms of communications; this requires a continuous interplay between visionaries and pragmatists, informed by "scouts" in different domains (Chatzkel, 2003).

It is interesting to note that many of the KM champion roles in the case studies fall in the category of idea practitioners, for instance the KM office of SAF. Such idea practitioners should be aware of both the internal and external positioning of their organisations. For instance, KM practitioners, especially those in the Supreme Court and IPOS, regularly draw insights from academic institutions. In analysing the different cases, the authors identified a number of other emerging KM roles in organisations: Regional Knowledge

Manager, Principal KM Specialist, Knowledge Development Officer, Knowledge Process Analyst, Knowledge Services Analyst, Knowledge Architect, Knowledge Supervisor, and Manager of Knowledge Sharing. These have been augmented over the years by additional roles: Knowledge Principal, KM Executive, Head of Knowledge, Innovation Manager, Innovation Facilitator, Manager of Human Capital Development Centre, Project Manager for KM, Knowledge Asset Manager, Knowledge Librarian, Director of Learning and Management Development, and Knowledge Engineer.

CHAPTER FIVE

Cultivating Cultures

"If you have knowledge, let others light their candles in it."
— Margaret Fuller

This chapter focuses on the strategies for the creation and implementation of knowledge-sharing cultures. As people aspects of a KM strategy include culture, community activities and organisational attitudes, the chapter addresses the values, motivations, encouragement, and incentives to promote a collaborative culture in the organisations in order to foster more effective KM initiatives.

For KM projects to be successful, supportive cultural elements, such as interpersonal relationships (trust, value), hierarchical structure (teamwork, consensus), work nature (flexibility) and rewards, need to be incorporated in the organisations (Ahmed *et al.*, 2002). These elements are made visible through explicit cultures (e.g. artefacts) and implicit cultures (e.g. values, beliefs). Cultural traits recommended for KM include: creating a conducive environment for members to try new things with an understanding that the new projects can end in success or failure; establishing an environment whereby there can be acceptance, as well as discussion of mistakes, where there is no punishment for mistakes, and where members are open-minded in listening to and discussing new knowledge. To internalise knowledge sharing, just as it is essential to provide training to the knowledge champions, it is also important to manage both the informal and the formal learning processes, such as the building of stories, narrations, and the belief that individuals can have an impact on organisations.

Organisations must identify and overcome the impediments to knowledge sharing in order for KM initiatives to succeed. Some common obstacles include: the lack of time for employees to share their knowledge; a not-invented-here culture; compartmentalisation and dispersion of the employees; an unwillingness to share information; a lack of understanding of the importance of knowledge as an organisational asset; not aligned or poorly aligned reward systems; legal constraints; and inadequate leadership (O'Dell *et al.*, 2004).

To overcome such obstacles, human resource management policies must influence knowledge workers in three ways: incentivise them with rewards when appropriate, build a corporate culture of sharing and collaborations, and provide employees with organisational career paths. Adequate resources, appropriate breadth and depth of skills and expertise, and boundary-spanning individuals are important components of a knowledge-sharing innovative culture (Newell *et al.*, 2002).

5.1. Understanding Knowledge Cultures

This section profiles the KM movement in terms of its focus on cultural and social attributes that affect knowledge activities and behaviours. As explained by Kayworth and Leidner (2004), organisational culture is a composite of norms, practices, rituals, routines, stories, myths, symbols, power structures, assumptions, mental models, and behaviours, and these components affect or impact the manner in which KM initiatives are handled or accomplished.

Ashkenas *et al.* (2002) highlighted the need for an environment that encourages everyone who can contribute, regardless of their rank or seniority, to do so without waiting for someone to give permission. In other words, they emphasised the need for autonomy and initiative. This is important for organisations today, as technology has broken down the barriers of time and space. To achieve the flow of information and knowledge, organisations need to adopt a borderless or boundaryless behaviour, which is the free flow of information between divisions or departments in the organisation.

As boundaries are necessary to differentiate the various functions within organisations and for administrative purposes (e.g. human resource, marketing, accounting, and research & development departments), Ashkenas *et al.* (2002) suggested that they be made more permeable. This is to allow greater fluidity of information and knowledge throughout the organisation, which is necessary as the paradigm for organisations have shifted. While the outdated paradigm places emphasis on size, role clarity, specialisation, and control, the current one focuses on speed, flexibility, integration and innovation. Indeed, a boundary-less organisation provides the necessary environment allowing an organisation to thrive in the current paradigm. The permeability of boundaries enables the relationship between the management and employees to be transformed from one that is based on control, to one based on the free flow of information. In their model, they used a house as a metaphor to describe the four types of boundaries within an organisation, namely, the vertical, horizontal, external and geographic boundaries.

Firstly, a house has different levels (e.g. the basement, the ground level and the attic). These levels represent the hierarchical structure within an organisation. Just as the floors and ceilings of the house separate the different levels in the house, hierarchies in the form of titles, ranks and privileges can hinder the flow of ideas and experience within an organisation. To remove vertical hierarchies would result in chaos, but making them more permeable would make the organisation more nimble, as more people would then have access to potentially useful information towards work and decision-making.

Secondly, a house has walls, which separate the different rooms. Similarly, an organisation too has walls between different functions. The barriers created by walls can be very costly, as Xerox has learned. It failed to capitalise on the innovative breakthroughs made by its own laboratory, the Palo Alto Research Centre, which in the 1970s, invented many of the computer technologies we take for granted today (e.g. Gary Starkweather invented the laser printer, and Robert Metcalfe invented Ethernet). This was because of the cultural and physical distance between the research and development department and the marketing department at Xerox. Rigid walls between the different functions in an organisation often resulted in the development of a local agenda, which sometimes can be opposed towards the organisational mission and vision. It can also lead to the situation where 'the left hand does not know what the right hand is doing'.

The external boundary of a house is the fence that separates it from the other homes in the neighbourhood. In the context of an organisation, external boundaries are the borders between it and its suppliers, customers, partners, and even competitors. A boundary between the insiders and outsiders of an organisation is not only necessary (e.g. to provide an identity for the employees), but legally required; yet increasingly, the necessity of collaboration requires that these boundaries be made porous. In other words, a 'we-they' relationship needs to be transformed into an 'us' relationship. Similarly, win-lose situations need to be transformed into win-win situations.

Lastly, geographic boundaries exist in organisations that operate in several countries. However, such boundaries can arise from national pride, stereotyping, cultural differences and market peculiarities, and these create unnecessary barriers to the formation of good organisational relationships; Buckman Labs recognised this when they introduced their forums, TechForum and ChemForum. They realised that if the postings in the forum were solely in English, the forum would be construed as a 'US-only thing'. They therefore made the crucial decision of translating the contents of the forum to several different languages which employees use globally. More importantly, it sent the message that the forums were for everyone, not only for the employees who understood English.

5.1.1. *Attributes for Knowledge Sharing*

Organisations vary in their history, expectations, unwritten rules, social morals, beliefs and even sub-cultures or micro-cultures. Culture can be defined as a form of organisational contextual knowledge and accordingly, it should be treated as a component of KM (Holden, 2002). Just as organisations differ in culture along the parameters of involvement, consistency, adaptability, their attributes can also vary along the different knowledge processes: creation, storage, transfer, and application. For example, some organisations may be adept at creating new knowledge internally while less efficient in applying or reusing this knowledge; others, in contrast, may be more open to acquiring knowledge from the outside and rolling out new offerings.

Knowledge workers require a style of management that is more magnanimous, participatory, and which focuses more on coaching and encouraging compared to ordering and directing. Learning and unlearning behaviours are both important. A thirst for knowledge, trust, tolerance and rewards must be incorporated in community dynamics for successful KM (Figallo & Rhine, 2002). Thus, knowledge-oriented organisations should not only provide employees with opportunities to explore new ideas, they should also provide a conducive environment for them to approach their seniors.

It is important that there is a culture of cooperation and collaboration for projects to be successful (Drucker, 1999; Ives *et al.*, 2000; Kluge *et al.*, 2001). It has been demonstrated that people are more willing and comfortable to share knowledge, if they understand the benefits of the sharing activity. An effective knowledge-sharing culture is a building block of a learning organisation (Garvin, 1993), and management should avoid having silos and barriers between departments (Kayworth & Leidner, 2004). In fact, knowledge sharing can be nurtured through rewards, recognition, education and performance appraisals, for instance, rewarding employees for innovations; mentoring or assisting others; recognising team players and collaborators; and providing incentives for group achievements before individual accomplishments (O'Dell, 2004).

Like obstacles, misconceptions about KM need to be addressed, and several myths about organisational knowledge need to be debunked, such as 'people do not want to share' (they will, with appropriate cultural settings and reward systems), 'we need to codify tacit knowledge' (it can be communicated through other means like storytelling), and 'technology replaces the need for face-to-face meetings' (databases can coexist with meetings and share fairs); there must be visible support and vision from the top management in terms of providing a shared sense of direction, trust, openness, excitement, as well as a willingness to continually learn from peers. A culture of self-directed and peer-enabled learning is also pertinent for knowledge organisations at multiple levels: individual learning, team learning, organisational learning and customer learning. Knowledge-sharing facets like judgement, persuasiveness, wit and innovation should also be factored in while creating knowledge cultures.

5.1.2. *Establishing a Trusting Culture*

Trust is an important component of a knowledge-sharing culture, and it has to be maintained at the level of companions, competencies and commitments. Trust is not easy to develop, and requires prolonged interaction and common experiences to promote (Newell *et al.*, 2002). In fact, trust must be promoted at multiple levels for successful knowledge-sharing cultures to take place. According to Ford (2004), there are different types of trust: knowledge-based, cognition-based, economics-based, relationship-based, interpersonal, organisational and institutional. Trust can be strengthened through open communication, inclusion in decision-making, sharing of critical information, workgroup cohesion, social integration and mentoring.

Obstacles to knowledge sharing arising from a lack of trust include knowledge hoarding, a self-preservation mentality, a perception that KM is a fad, and organisational bureaucracy. Trust can be strengthened through knowledge-sharing proficiencies through organisational communications and facilitations (Liebowitz & Chen, 2004). To increase trust in knowledge sharing, the knowledge vision should be articulated throughout the organisation, and employees should feel empowered to use KM principles in their work environment. Approaches like storytelling work effectively (Allee, 2003). This is because knowledge-sharing communities are motivated by the strength and significance of their members' discoveries and contributions; and according to Figallo and Rhine (2002), although there is some knowledge sharing via communities, it is being regarded as too valuable to leave sharing just to chance. In fact, the risk in starting strategic knowledge-sharing networks is that the knowledge which needs to be identified by managers may not be seen as crucial to the job performance of the target employees.

Care is an important requisite for building trust to facilitate knowledge sharing. There are various modes of knowledge sharing, dependent upon whether there is low care (individuals are left to their own; employees therefore exchange explicit knowledge) or high care (individuals are supported by a strong social network; tacit knowledge is shared), and whether there is a creation of individual or organisational knowledge (Nonaka & Nishiguchi, 2001). Such humanistic models of knowledge emergence encompass 'wandering inside and outside' the organisation, and accommodate emotional facets like freedom, interest, commitment, charisma, and safety.

5.1.3. *Building Social Capital*

The human resource (HR) department plays an important role in building the social capital in the organisation; for example, in the development of employee abilities, the nurturance of structured thinking, self-reflection, meta-cognition and knowledge communication.

Through its stewardship on guiding employees without dominating, facilitating without controlling, supporting without micromanaging; employees should thus feel motivated, committed and personally incentivised (Mertins *et al.*, 2003). Further, employees must adapt in order to encourage knowledge use and if the firm is not able to alter its behaviour as a result of what it learns, then knowledge has little value (Lengnick-Hall and Lengnick-Hall, 2003).

The management should establish knowledge-sharing expectations, inclusive of the abilities to cultivate a culture of caring, promote productive cross-pollinating conversations, integrate knowledge behaviours into everyday life, and overhaul subjective appraisal and compensation practices.

To build a socially accepted culture requires a combination of persuasive business arguments, effective inducements, as well as focusing on the web of relationships as collective knowledge requires a relationship orientation that stretches across four dimensions: rapport (level of comfort, e.g. trust, empathy, respect), bonding (robustness of relationship, e.g. collaborators), breadth (scope of relationship, e.g. transactional), and affinity (level of interest and attraction). These dimensions apply to the matrix of relationships between individuals, groups and organisations, and should be prioritised appropriately such as in cross-functional team development, cellular structuring, inter-unit resource exchange and inter-firm learning. HR professionals are advised to go beyond performing as 'picnic organisers' to 'relationship brokers'. In mature KM practices, relationships extend not just towards current employees, but also towards business partners and customers, who can be considered as 'quasi-workforce members'. The most successful organisations are those in which KM is part of everyone's job. In other words, it needs the efforts of all knowledge staffers to make KM a pervasive phenomenon (Davenport & Prusak, 1998).

5.2. Perspectives from the Case Studies

This section provides the snapshots of cultural reinforcements for KM in the case studies. The organisations' cultural activities, values, messages and rewards and recognition schemes are profiled with respect to the promotion of knowledge-sharing expectations and willingness among the people.

5.2.1. Attorney-General's Chambers (AGC)

AGC nurtured a culture of knowledge sharing via a KM Change Management workshop and six KM Awareness workshops. The purpose of these workshops was to convey the KM message of creating a shared vision towards the staff, and to demonstrate the benefits of sharing through success stories. The KM effort was a top-down approach via a KM committee comprising divisional representatives with support from the senior management.

KM gradually won over the staff. They no longer feel threatened about sharing their knowledge as they understood its purpose, which is essential for KM to assist them in their work. In fact, their KM initiatives were shared at organisation-wide events such as Work Plan Day and Innovations Day. In addition, each division frequently included a KM-element within their own retreat or strategic planning cycles. The induction programme for new hires includes KM orientation and collaborative activities. The divisional heads were also involved in sharing with new officers at the Induction Programme, as well as during training sessions (when some new lawyers undergo the orientation programme at AGC). Coffee sessions were also held to encourage interactions between the senior management and officers.

Although there was some sharing, a number of cultural issues were identified. For instance, the Asian culture tends to obey strict hierarchical codes, which makes collaboration less open, also taking into account that employees are reluctant to be seen as disagreeing with their superiors. There were inhibiting factors that included work pressures and the reluctance for most people to be labelled as experts. To overcome the inhibiting factors, AGC has since been considering adopting some kind of structured rewards and recognition system; however, it has not implemented the scheme, as it was perceived to be difficult to establish the basis of the award. Even though contributions to the KM initiatives are not a formal part of performance appraisal for the employees, the senior management is aware of the officers' efforts and contributions. Thus, the staff were recognised for a job well done when they contribute their knowledge by uploading their piece of work.

5.2.2. Defence Science and Technology Agency (DSTA)

Knowledge managers act as the change agent in DSTA, to proliferate a KM culture. A comprehensive competency framework across eight competency centres is used to sustain existing capabilities and to build new expertise. To maintain diversity within the Competency Centres (CC) and to prevent specialised silos building up, all CC learning events are open to all staff.

DSTA understood that the potential of communities of practice (CoPs) can only be realised if staff, as knowledge workers, embrace good knowledge practices and develop personal KM mastery. They need to learn how to access and filter the vast amount of information and keep abreast of the progression and developments in their respective fields. For these reasons, four essential skills — connect, search, capture and share — are promoted as part of the staff's working habits.

The CCs also encourage regular seminars and knowledge-sharing sessions (e.g. the CC's Learning Day). The spirit of knowledge sharing provides staff with the opportunities to demonstrate and be recognised for their abilities. Knowledge sharing also promotes team-based learning, which is necessary in the increasingly fast-paced environment of today. To further enhance the ease of staff engagement and facilitate knowledge-sharing, a personal homepage facility called MyHomepage was launched by the DSTA Chief Executive in September 2007. Looking forward, key KM priorities for DSTA are the creation of 'vibrant' communities and the promotion of a 'wow' experience.

5.2.3. Intellectual Property Office of Singapore (IPOS)

The culture in IPOS is generally regarded as open and the leaders are approachable. However, when the new concept of KM was introduced, there was anxiety and a lot of individual approaches had to be taken to secure employees' confidence. The main hurdles IPOS faced were (a) resistance to new technology and methodologies; and (b) 'KM = Additional work!' as perceived by the staff. In an attempt to overcome these hurdles, IPOS initiated a series of in-house training sessions, combined with seminars and classes conducted by a professional training consultant. For instance, they launched some classes from December 2009 to January 2010 for all site administrators of the portal called KENNY. Throughout the duration of the course, attendees were expected to submit, as their training assignment, one automated KENNY process that was already implemented, to demonstrate their understanding and mastery of the KM system. Over this period, some 90 percent of the attendees have since been certified. The underlying principle behind this series of trainings — people are only afraid of what they do not know.

The KM Department in IPOS recognises that culture will have to be consistently nurtured over a period of at least three years (beginning from conscious implementation), before bearing any discernible fruit. Currently, it continues to encourage its colleagues via engagement exercises with the hope that as more of their staff understand KM, they will become more receptive towards accepting and seeing the benefits of KM projects.

5.2.4. Inland Revenue Authority of Singapore (IRAS)

IRAS sharing sessions were introduced as organisation-wide sessions, designed to break down functional silos, to provide a culture of learning and sharing. The sharing sessions were also intended to provide an opportunity for the organisation to capture in a central place the core aspect of IRAS' organisational memory. Understanding that cultural change is a slow and complex process, IRAS has been sustaining its efforts with consistency over several years. Its effort with twice-monthly sharing sessions is now beginning to pay off. There is greater organisation-wide awareness, movement of staff across functions, and greater development of staff. The sharing sessions are fully attended, and the sharing activity (including the mentoring of junior officers) is seen by staff as a part of their work duties. Sharing is also embedded into the performance review criteria.

These sharing sessions have enabled IRAS to improve its capabilities to resolve complex cases, detect signs of tax fraud, and improve officers' understanding of particular industries, thus enabling them to resolve cases more expeditiously. Organisational climate surveys are regularly conducted and the reviews indicate that staff are generally happy with the sharing culture, and feel that colleagues are very willing to share their knowledge.

Although in the past IRAS Legal Officers would only share cases that the organisation had won, at a recent IRAS sharing session, the Chief Legal Officer mentioned that going forward he would like to share suitable cases that they have not won. This is a significant shift in mindset in that the organisation recognises that there are great learning opportunities in 'failures' and there is now the openness in sharing not just successes but also failures. The KM team believes such a mindset will further enhance organisational capacity for innovation.

In the KM Strategy Review Project in 2007, the consultants mapped out the organisation's cultural KM archetypes based upon surveys and focus group discussions conducted among various levels of its staff. It found that there is a good knowledge-sharing culture in IRAS.

5.2.5. Jurong Town Corporation (JTC)

JTC recognises that the key to the success of its KM initiative rests upon cultural transformation. To this end, it has targeted the culture of knowledge sharing as a focal point for change. To help facilitate change, CoPs on various subject areas have been formed. Every employee is a member of a CoP, and technology is used to enable participation from different departments. With the formation of CoPs, JTC hopes to increase the level of social capital, such that "the sum of the actual and potential resources embedded within, available through, and derived from the network of relationships is possessed by an individual or social unit". It hoped the increase in the level of social capital will create behavioural changes leading to a greater intensity of knowledge sharing that, in turn, would positively influence business performance by decreasing the learning curve for new employees, responding more rapidly to customer needs, and spawning new ideas for new products and services (Lesser and Storck, 2001).

5.2.6. Ministry of Finance (MOF)

Having implemented its email management solutions, MOF's KM team looked at ways to cultivate its KM learning culture to ensure that the softer aspects of KM progress along with technology. An interesting cultural KM initiative is its 'Learning Errward', which is an award that recognises the team for trying out new ideas and in the process learns from the mistakes. MOF encourages their officers not to be afraid of making mistakes during project implementation, and to be brave to share their mistakes or leanings, so that the others can learn from the shortcomings or weaknesses.

- Senior management encourages two-way communication, discussions and learning. Flat hierarchy.
- Strong encouragement of work-life balance within the organization.
- Officers are encouraged and empowered to contribute staff suggestions and participate in open discussions.

- MOF HQ Brainstorm Sessions: Sharing of strategic thrusts and directions during Management Advance, MOF Exchange and Directorate Retreats.
- Sharing-centric meeting forums/spaces: PS 21 and Financial Staff Meetings (FSM), MOF intranet — News@MOF, informal sharing sessions (SHINE!) half time, PS lunches.
- Overseas studies, amoeba projects, cross agency projects.

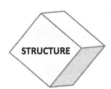

- Technology enablers, e.g. Ideabox, Ideamart, Amoeba Monitoring System, Collaborative Workspaces.
- Adoption of KEN (Knowledge Enterprise System — MOF's KM system) for a three-year trial via forum workspace (common site for all officers to access internal meeting forums and corresponding materials). The same philosophy will apply to documents, application systems and collaborative spaces — all to be housed within a single system.
- Coffee corners.

Figure 5.1 Cultural, Process and Structure Enablers for KM at MOF.

Source: Redrawn from MOF.

The KM team recognised the importance of getting both the senior management's support as well as officers' buy-in to facilitate the organisational-wide change. Two-way communication, a flattened organisational structure, and open information flows are seen as important factors for its KM implementation, as summarised in Figure 5.1.

5.2.7. National Library Board (NLB)

At NLB, management support has played a significant role in encouraging knowledge sharing and usage of KM tools. Apart from communicating with staff, they also participate actively in the KM platform by contributing inputs whenever possible. Whenever the staff have made an outstanding contribution, the management would not hesitate to highlight it in the system, giving recognition to the staff's sharing effort. The staff also share compliments received from library customers as a result of colleagues' collaborative inputs. The top three staff who contributed to these enquiries are then commended at the monthly staff communication session. The support from the management and the staff's appreciation of the sharing platform greatly help to boost usage of the system for knowledge sharing.

The Knowledge Champions programme is seen as one of the key contributors to the overall KM efforts in creating a collaborative culture in NLB. Specifically, the programme is put in place to create and raise renewed awareness in knowledge sharing, and strengthen the learning, sharing and collaboration culture in NLB.

5.2.8. Singapore Armed Forces (SAF)

SAF needed to propagate a learning culture that is receptive to new ideas and tolerant of mistakes. SAF believes that having an open culture is necessary for the KM system to thrive. However, this needed to be balanced carefully with traditional military beliefs of strict compliance with orders, regimentation and deference to authority. In 2001, the Chief of Army decided to adopt a new 'start small, scale up progressively' approach instead of the typical big-bang launch for KM. The strategy was to start small with a few committed change agents, to equip them with organisation learning ideas and implement quick wins in their workplace. Subsequently, these efforts were scaled up progressively with positive ground support to a critical mass.

To nurture a learning culture, SAF moved away from the traditional regimented culture to a new one that was receptive to new ideas and tolerant of mistakes. Numerous CoPs were set up, and knowledge capital was built up through military domain experts and professional military education. Knowledge hubs and branches facilitated cross-organisational learning. SAF is also innovating new ways of learning, for instance, its leadership competency model covers conceptual thinking, social competency, mission competency, developmental competency and self-competency.

SAF recognises and builds on new ideas as they emerge around the world, then applies those new ideas to its requirements and aspirations. With such a learning model, members of the military are encouraged to read the latest books in their areas of expertise, and leaders are continually sent abroad for advanced degrees to help build learning networks. Today, military and civilian members attend and are encouraged to present at conferences, and advanced degrees and publications are highly honoured.

SAF does not need to provide special incentives to implement KM activities since these activities are seen as something they need and are expected of their work. While knowledge contribution and learning are taken into account in all SAF awards and advancement programs, special rewards are being introduced for outstanding work. Indeed, the cultural characteristics at SAF include the learning and respect for knowledge; a young generation hungry for learning, coaching, and feedback; high collaboration and interdependence; and a positive attitude coupled with responsibility.

5.2.9. Singapore Police Force: Police Technology Department (SPF-PTD)

The KM culture at PTD is reinforced through specific activities that were put in place to ensure that its KM mission and vision are properly understood. The KM activities are highlighted on a regular basis, and exemplary KM behaviours are rewarded. These include monthly updates (chaired by the PTD Director), working meetings for each KM project, and the Quarterly KM Role Model award. Toward the end of 2009, the award was phased out and replaced with 'Pat on the Back', an award to recognise significant contributions to SPF. KM progress is monitored via the participation level and feedback from the activities.

KM Day is an annual event to celebrate knowledge activities, featuring show-and-tell competitions, quizzes, award ceremonies, in-house videos and magazines. It has been graced by its Chief Knowledge Officer (CKO), the Deputy Commissioner, for several years. Indeed, its KM Day is now integrated with Let's Celebrate Learning (LCL) which is a quarterly learning festival featuring invited speakers, training videos and workshops on topics covering project management, organisational development, and personal effectiveness to emphasise lifelong learning. Republic Polytechnic's problem-based learning methodology is utilised as a learning tool. The knowledge race (K-Race) is an event modelled after the 'Amazing Race' reality show where participants travel to different police establishments, uncovering clues to solve related puzzles. Participants expressed KM through artworks in the finale.

The 'Pat on the Back' award is bestowed periodically to staff who exhibit exemplary conduct in sharing knowledge. A portion of departmental performance bonus (averaging $50 per person) is also redistributed in the form of KM rewards for units that have contributed towards sharing knowledge. The 'Encouragement Wall' allows staff to leave messages of thanks and appreciation to their colleagues during the December festive season. In terms of formal content, PASSION magazine, chronicling PTD's KM journey and featuring essays from senior SPF management, was launched on its KM Day, 8 February 2006. That year, the KM Archetypes video was also produced (an in-house video skit featuring staff acting the role of common KM archetypes). Other creative communication techniques include introduction of email signatures with KM themes to promote the culture of 'sharing knowledge' and 'helping others learn' while sending emails. At the highest level, the Director also issues messages on KM Rules of Engagement, on the 'do's and don'ts' of creating a positive culture in sharing knowledge and avoiding negative KM practices.

5.2.10. Singapore Youth Olympic Games Organising Committee (SYOGOC)

SYOGOC is the most 'international' organisation featured in this book, in terms of number of cultures, nationalities and languages involved. The deadline of the Games served as a key driver for creating a high-performance learning culture, and concluding KM activities such as 'After-Action Reviews'. Without the luxury of large expensive IT systems, an intense 'learning on the go' culture was established; process and knowledge maps were used in disciplined ways to identify key knowledge flows, and process knowledge and learning were carefully captured.

Process knowledge was captured via workshops during which participants were oriented to the knowledge capture process via a food-related analogy. Participants were asked to imagine that they were all cooking different parts of a complex banquet. For the part that they were cooking, they had to identify the main steps and sub-steps, the cooks and assistant cooks involved, and lastly 'connect' all the interdependent parts that others were preparing to form the banquet. As food is a well-understood concept, especially in Singapore, the staff were able to learn at a faster rate.

SYOGOC had only one chance to present the Games to the rest of the world. The capture and transfer of processes and lessons learned were extremely crucial as the whole organisation had to adopt the culture of progress, learning and improvement in a rapid and integrated manner.

5.2.11. *Supreme Court of Singapore (SC)*

KM at the Supreme Court is not just about IT tools and collaboration platforms, but also about the effective designing of forums for knowledge practitioners to conveniently meet and interact. The office environment has been deliberately designed to cluster offices together so that it is easy for Assistant Registrars (ARs) to pop into each other's offices for quick consultations and sharing.

Peer-to-peer communication and sharing takes place regularly among the Justices' Law Clerks (JLCs). The Supreme Court has facilitated this by clustering the JLCs' offices (called dens) together in the same part of the Supreme Court building as opposed to having individual JLCs' offices physically located together with the offices of the individual Judges that they are assigned to. For the Supreme Court's ARs, the clustering of offices was a deliberate step taken when the new Supreme Court building was designed.

Rooms in the new Supreme Court building were also designed to facilitate informal sharing and innovation. To exemplify, the 'Creanovator' is a room with brightly-hued sofas equipped with Nintendo Wii and karaoke machines for staff to relax or to encourage informal discussions. This room provides a conducive environment and is often used by Innovation Activists for Innovation Class committee meetings to get creative discussions flowing.

5.2.12. *Urban Redevelopment Authority (URA)*

Over the years, URA has developed a very positive organisation culture based on the visibility and accessibility in relation to senior management leadership. URA's core values of Spirit, Passion, Integrity, Respect, Innovation and Teamwork (the URA SPIRIT) enables a knowledge-friendly environment throughout the organisation. Practices such as the involvement of all staff in 360-degree feedback helps to instil the URA SPIRIT as well.

It was also important for URA to create a sense of 'external' awareness in its employees, and benchmark with the crème de la crème from urban development practices around the world. Hence, environment scanning and intelligence research were accorded high priority, to assist employees with comprehending global trends and developments on a regular basis. URA also actively engaged external stakeholders (customers, service partners) to share information about their needs and concerns. Such an external orientation helped create a culture of improvement for products and services, vis-à-vis other best-in-class cities and organisations.

5.3. Discussion and Insights

As pointed out by Holden (2002), organisational culture itself should be treated as a unit of analysis of KM and in this regard, AGC showed how a culture audit was conducted to assess knowledge-sharing behaviours and attitudes that also influenced change management initiatives. The organisational facilitation to bring about better knowledge sharing is also demonstrated at SPF and IRAS. Learning and unlearning behaviours are both important, and this includes learning from mistakes, as was shown in the case of MOF.

Allee (2003) addresses 'hybrid' CoPs where online forum members also meet face-to-face, thus overcoming some challenges of purely online or purely offline forums. Many of the organisations mix online communities with face-to-face interactions and events, e.g. SPF. Interestingly, on the online front, social media is becoming a norm to facilitating online knowledge-sharing cultures, as SAF discovered, and MOF as well, has noted that some of these channels are particularly suited for greater reach in communication.

A way of building trust for knowledge sharing is via mentoring; indeed, among the case studies, SAF has a strong focus on mentoring as a way of improving trust and decision-making. However, IPOS highlighted initial barriers to their KM initiatives (e.g. KM was seen as additional work) and how they were overcome (e.g. through alignment of KM activities with workflow, and in-house training sessions about the importance of knowledge work). Trust is not easy to develop, and requires prolonged interaction and common experiences to promote knowledge sharing, which is seen in the case of SAF. However, DSTA is a good example of changing the organisational culture into a 'right to ask' mindset that requires 'low care' and 'high care' approaches to knowledge sharing in terms of the level of voluntary knowledge contributions.

Among the organisations, IRAS had a decent mix of such bottom-up and top-down approaches to learning activities across the organisation. The MOF also has particularly good examples of organisational communication to reinforce expected KM behaviours. The Learning Festivals of SPF's KM initiative is another clear example of such education and celebration of KM.

As various theories have highlighted the importance for knowledge-oriented organisations to reward group collaboration and sharing behaviours, it is therefore heartening to note that, throughout the analysis of the case studies, knowledge cultures have been created and nurtured via some kind of rewards and recognition scheme, especially in SPF. In short, most organisations put in place incentive and rewards schemes to promote collaborative behaviours, as summarised in Table 5.1. Exemplary practices included sharing of knowledge even from failures (e.g. IRAS).

Special annual events like the KM Day and Learning Festival helped periodic stocktaking and rejuvenation of KM (e.g. MOF). The Supreme Court and IRAS had specially designed workplaces where knowledge

Table 5.1   Culture Approaches.

Organisation	Culture Approaches
AGC	Culture audit, change management, people profiles
DSTA	'Right to ask' mindset, competency framework, personal pages awards
IPOS	Training sessions, overcoming fear and ignorance through engagement and education
IRAS	Top-down and bottom-up approaches, sharing both failure and success stories, learning activities, managers lead by example
JTC	Promoting awareness and trust in best practices, knowledge sharing and collaborative work; recognise staff contributions
MOF	Staff ownership, participatory branding
NLB	Management support, rewards and recognition, external/ customer orientation
SAF	Emphasise collaboration and connectedness, quick knowledge sharing ('SAF in backpack'), network and nurture
SPF-PTD	KM Day, LCL festival, KM Role Model award, 'Encouragement Wall'
SYOGOC	Culture of frequent learning, less 'micro-management'
SC	Awareness, interaction spaces, KM Quiz
URA	External awareness and benchmarking via environmental scanning

activities, brainstorming and innovation exercise can be conducted, creatively breaking away from the texture of boardroom meetings or purely online interchanges.

These analyses are in line with recommendations from KM practitioners, that knowledge cultures should be nurtured by passion and action. The change which is needed to promote and sustain knowledge advantages should be done in an assertive manner. Etienne Wenger goes further to say that knowledge workers should think of learning as 'mutual meaningfulness' and 'activism'.

CHAPTER SIX

Processes and Techniques

"Knowledge rests not upon truth alone, but upon error also."

— Carl G. Jung

This chapter focuses on KM processes such as workflows, procedures, and activities, which are connected with knowledge capture, storage, sharing, transfer and dissemination. It analyses effective processes for knowledge co-creation and codification of knowledge (e.g. via after-action reviews, repositories and taxonomies) and connecting knowledge workers.

Pentland (1995) defined KM processes as an "ongoing set of practices embedded in the social and physical structure of the organisation with knowledge as their final product". These embedded knowledge processes must also be able to blend well into the workers' routine. Thus, designing these knowledge processes require observations of how knowledge workers perform, so that tacit knowledge can be put in context. Indeed, even office space should be designed with KM synergies in mind.

Mertins *et al.* (2003) identified the following as core KM processes: identification of relevant knowledge (e.g. benchmarking), generation of new knowledge (e.g. external links), storage of knowledge (e.g. databases), distribution of knowledge (e.g. portals, newsletters, mentoring) and applications of knowledge (e.g. coaching). However, Ford (2004) distinguishes between KM processes (generation, codification, transfer) and KM practices (e.g. mentoring, storytelling, coaching).

Tacit knowledge   *To*   Explicit knowledge

	Tacit knowledge	Explicit knowledge
Tacit knowledge	**Socialisation**	**Externalisation**
Explicit knowledge	**Internalisation**	**Combination**

From (label between Tacit knowledge and Explicit knowledge rows on left)

Figure 6.1   Nonaka's SECI Model.

Source: Nonaka and Takeuchi (1995, p. 62).

6.1. KM Processes: Types and Practices

This section expands on the types of processes and practices used for implementing knowledge initiatives.

6.1.1. *Types of Knowledge Processes*

A well cited model of knowledge processes is Nonaka and Takeuchi's (1995) spiral processes, which involve four phases of knowledge conversion as shown in Figure 6.1:

- Socialisation (empathising/sharing tacit knowledge via apprenticeship, conversations, brainstorming: individual to individual);
- Externalisation (articulating tacit knowledge via concept clinics: individual to group);
- Combination (connecting or systemising explicit knowledge: group to organisation, with roots in the information processing paradigm); and
- Internalisation (learning or embodying new tacit knowledge, such as experience-based operational knowledge: organisation to individual).

Nonaka's process model provides management with a useful and systematic approach to understand the core knowledge activities within an organisation that include the following processes — acquiring knowledge from the environment, selecting knowledge within the organisation, internalising knowledge and utilising knowledge. Of course, key managerial tasks and influences in knowledge activities are coordination, control, measurement and leadership.

Before proposing KM projects, the management should conduct appropriate audits of the organisation's knowledge assets, knowledge gaps, knowledge flows, and critical processes for the evaluation of its KM gaps. Dixon (2000) demonstrates how organisations can utilise multiple ways of knowledge transfer, involving databases, response systems, monitoring, meetings, and dedicated KM staff. She identified five key categories of lesson sharing in large organisations: serial transfer, near transfer, far transfer, strategic transfer and expert transfer. They differ in terms of who the intended knowledge receiver is (same or different from the source), the nature of the task involved (frequency and routine), and the type of knowledge being transferred (tacit/explicit).

Srikantaiah *et al.* (2010) address the issue of information assets quality (via three parameters: comprehension, contextualisation, valuation) in work environments with tight budgets, pressures on time, shortening half-lives of knowledge, and rapidly changing classifications or indexes. Information in such settings must be useful, usable, dependable, sound, well-defined, unambiguous, reputable, timely, concise and contextualised.

6.1.2. *Types of Knowledge Practices*

There are three kinds of knowledge practices that are commonly used in generating, sharing and transferring knowledge: experiential, narrative and abstract/symbolic (Boisot, 1995). They reflect the following situations in the context of knowledge work: 'What do I see/hear/feel?', 'What can I say about this?', and 'What stable durable content can I extract from this?'. According to Kluge *et al.* (2001), there are six key attributes of knowledge which must be factored into KM practices so as to understand the complex nature of knowledge and the impacts of these attributes on knowledge-sharing processes. The attributes are as follows:

- Subjectivity (the context and the individual's background shape the interpretation of knowledge);
- Transferability (that knowledge can be extracted and transferred to other contexts);

- Embeddedness (that knowledge is in a buried form that makes it difficult to extract or reformulate);
- Self-reinforcement (the value of knowledge increases when shared);
- Perishability (that knowledge can become outdated); and
- Spontaneity (that knowledge can develop unpredictably in a process).

Considering the different attributes of knowledge, it requires knowledge workers to have some aspects of lateral thinking to bring knowledge into entirely new contexts, and even from entirely new industries. For instance, coping with perishability of knowledge involves continuous updating, education and training, with regards to the standards, rules, and optimisation of the domain knowledge. Thus, engaging in practices such as brainstorming and workshops can help to encourage spontaneity in knowledge articulation and exchange, but organisations must avoid lack of openness, lack of experience, and lack of focus (Kluge et al., 2001). It is not enough to simply hire people and put them to work, but rather, to create and disseminate knowledge among employees, customers and business partners. Active management of knowledge assets and continuous learning among employees (along with a focused direction) needs to be facilitated, and knowledge exchange needs to be brokered via online and offline mechanisms as well as incentive schemes.

O'Dell and Grayson (2004) distinguish between processes (identify, collect, create, organise, share, adapt, and use) and enablers (culture, technology, leadership, strategy and metrics) in the context of KM. They classify best practices into four kinds: good idea, good practice, local best practice, and industry best practice. However, the process of arriving at a consensus on what a best practice is can face barriers of entrenched mentalities, political alignments and differing priorities.

6.1.3. Communities of Practice

Communities of practice (CoPs) have emerged as one of the most common and useful knowledge practices. The processes of creating and sustaining CoPs have been identified as core KM processes. Also known as practitioner forums, they constitute combinations of three fundamental elements: domains (scope, identity), community (creates the fabric of learning via relationships and interactions), and practices (frameworks, tools, vocabulary, documents) (Wenger et al., 2002).

CoPs can be diverse; they may be unrecognised, legitimised, supported, institutionalised and even bootlegged — but if properly cultivated, they can create value in multiple complex ways. CoPs may be long-lived or short-lived, small (less than 15 members) or large (more than 150, with sub-communities), co-located or distributed, homogeneous or heterogeneous. Successful CoPs can only thrive when the goals and needs of an organisation intersect with passions and aspirations of participants. Through its practice, the community operates as a 'living curriculum'.

Allee (2003) explained that CoPs can benefit members in terms of providing self-confidence, identity, and reputation, and it also benefits their organisations by provision of quick answers to questions, strengthened quality assurance, and harnessing emerging trends. CoPs should be nurtured throughout their evolutionary phases as it can provide potential value (coaching is needed), coalescing (knowledge flows should be mapped), stewardship (career development), and transformation (storytelling, memorabilia and convening reunions).

Yet, without proper care, CoPs can turn into isolated fortresses not unlike stewards of knowledge, preserving the status quo instead of fostering innovation, and may reflect their own narrow prejudices instead of reflecting diversity. Community cultivators should be aware of the following possible risks: narcissism, factionalism, cliques, disconnectedness, mediocrity and rigidity. However, CoPs can create values at three levels: community activities (e.g. increased participation levels), knowledge assets (e.g. number of solutions submitted) and performance outcomes (e.g. number of customer problems resolved, reduction in service hours).

6.1.4. Conversation and Storytelling

Organisational storytelling is an important springboard and vehicle for effective knowledge capture and sharing. A well-structured story can stimulate people towards action, understand new realities, innovate and co-create the vision of the future (Denning, 2001). The personnel system of an organisation should include knowledge sharing and learning as part of the job, review and appraisal structure.

As pointed out by O'Dell and Grayson (2004), organisations do face a range of barriers with regards to knowledge transfer: in terms of silo thinking, valuing knowledge creation more than knowledge sharing, lack of common work perspectives, and inadequate time for reflective activities. Thus, to counterbalance these barriers, a number of frameworks for knowledge sharing via effective organisational storytelling are emerging. The key is to get people to talk meaningfully of the content as learning comes when employees are emotively engaged, especially through experiences and anecdotes ('episodic memory'). As conversations form the most natural and commonplace human activities, its importance should not be understated (Takeuchi & Nonaka, 2004). Like conversation, knowledge is a continual process, rather than in static state, it emerges in the shared communal learning space that arises between people (Allee, 2003). Cross-pollination between communities can arise via the efforts and activities of 'ambassadors of meaning' and 'theme weavers'.

6.2. Perspectives from the Case Studies

This section describes and expands the knowledge processes implemented and/or practiced by the organisations.

6.2.1. Attorney-General's Chambers (AGC)

AGC utilises a range of codification and personalisation approaches. Codification is based on an organisation-wide taxonomy, with clearly specified roles and processes for knowledge contribution and portal usage, augmented with powerful search tools. Personalisation of knowledge transfer occurs through CoPs, expertise profiles, and collaboration tools. Even though AGC's staff realise that KM is both invaluable and indispensable to the organisation, KM tasks tend to be allocated a low priority when staff are faced with the competing demands of their urgent core work. The most effective way to overcome this is to embed KM tasks into ordinary work processes. The workflow system Enterprise Legal Management System (ELMS) has streamlined the process by making the capture of electronic copies of significant documents as part of the standard workflow. In addition, comments given in the course of reviewing documents are captured to provide important insights on the changes made to documents as they are being processed and checked by reviewing officers.

Fresh graduates and junior Legal Service Officers posted to AGC are taught KM processes over six months of training. This structured learning programme exposes trainees to a wide a range of legal practices. Written guides by senior officers are made available to the rest of AGC on the KM portal, such as the Prosecutor's Handbook, the Legislative Drafting manual and guides for effective drafting.

AGC's 'buddy' and mentor system stems from the induction programme for new officers. Every new officer is assigned to a peer mentor, who provides direct guidance to the new officer in his/her work environment. This helps ensure that tacit knowledge is passed on and not haphazardly transmitted by happenstance. The new officer will thus feel less intimidated as this is not done through a superior-subordinate relationship.

6.2.2. Defence Science and Technology Agency (DSTA)

Knowledge processes at DSTA are inherently tied to the development of competencies. Much work has been done to identify and consolidate various related competencies into core domains, such as the domain of technology and safety. It constantly looks ahead for new competencies to accommodate them as they emerge. As each competency community can be fairly large, the KM team conducts basic CoP briefings and clarification of its purpose to ensure proper sponsorship and support. Furthermore, the strategy is to ensure that there is clear purpose and leadership for each CoP, such as objectives to include tech-watch, and development of new competency or standards. It is also the responsibility of the staff to develop and enhance their skill sets. The combination of top-down and bottom-up approaches has been a key feature in many CoPs. Even though some CoPs are formed for sub-domains, there are communities which bridge across the organisation. One such example is the Software Safety CoP, which is relevant to all project teams that are involved in software development.

DSTA's content repository has been configured to handle content according to their security classification. Where sharable across communities, it will be available for all staff. Otherwise, the content will be accessible within each community. There is also a provision to accept invited guests into each Competency Centre's (CC) repository. Therefore, content management and sharing are highly automated. A standard or high-level information structure is first adopted by all CCs, e.g. technical reports, events, policy and standards. Beyond that, each CC will develop their detailed competency structure.

6.2.3. Intellectual Property Office of Singapore (IPOS)

Knowledge processes at IPOS revolve around documentation and collaboration, which were started via a pilot project. The KM portal Knowledge ENterprise 'N' You (KENNY) involves three business processes from the following departments: Legal Policy and International Affairs Department, Registry of Trademark and Performance Reporting. The objective of the pilot project was to demonstrate its KM portal efficiencies through automated processes. This pilot project was first carried out for three months, followed by a three-week user requirement study to identify potential business processes that could be further enhanced from each department.

An example in KENNY is the library system used for Legal Advice and Contract, which is one of the business activities under the Legal Policy and International Affairs Department. In fact all legal documents (e.g. contract/agreements that involve IPOS and external parties) have to be reviewed or are drafted by legal counsels in IPOS. Each department is assigned a primary and an alternative legal counsel. Prior to the implementation of KENNY, correspondence between legal counsel and the staff were done via email and drafted legal documents were kept as email attachments. Duplicated copies were kept by both parties, and sometimes the same document may be kept by more than one legal counsel as each keeps his/her legal documents in the individual's local disk drives.

With the automated process on KENNY, the discussion board is used as a collaboration tool to replace the email. A discussion board was created for each department and correspondences between legal counsel and department staff are kept according to contract matters in different discussion threads. Reference documents are then kept as an attachment in the discussion board. Under the discussion board, there is a link to the latest copy of actual legal document which is kept in a contract library. Apart from this collaboration, the manual approval form for signing off the final document has also been streamlined using KENNY's out-of-the-box approval workflow. The contract library also serves as the central repository for the legal counsels of all the legal documents in IPOS. In addition, it simplifies the handover process between legal counsels as all the information is kept in KENNY. IPOS actively encourages the automation of work processes so that employees can capture and retain knowledge. The following processes have been automated in KENNY:

(a) In the Hearing and Mediation Department, KENNY is used for file management, i.e. it is used for monitoring and tracking cases;

(b) In the Enterprise Development Department, KENNY is used to track and monitor the number of small and medium enterprises engaged in IP Management Programmes; and

(c) In the Legal Policy and International Affairs Department, KENNY is used as a collaboration tool for seeking and giving legal advice to IPOS staff and also as a central repository for legal advice.

6.2.4. Inland Revenue Authority of Singapore (IRAS)

IRAS sharing sessions were introduced in 2003 as organisation-wide sessions, designed to enable knowledge sharing and capture in a central place for core aspects of IRAS' organisational memory. On a yearly basis, the Branch Heads identify interesting tax topics, technical topics on forensics, intelligence, audit and investigation or corporate development topics for sharing. Sharing sessions are then scheduled at the IRAS auditorium, and publicised to all staff. The KM team works with the Human Resource (HR) department to organise sharing sessions by staff who had attended overseas courses/workshops.

Such sharing sessions would not only cover the main contents of the course/seminar, but also the latest developments on foreign tax systems and tax administrations, learning points, as well as the staff's personal experiences during the visits. There are also ad hoc sharing sessions scheduled throughout the course of each year, e.g. when a legal case has just been decided in the court of law and it would be timely to share the findings and decision of the court with staff.

The staff are encouraged to attend courses to further their knowledge. They are also expected to share their learnings upon returning from the courses. This is a two-fold benefit of reinforcing what officers pick up from the course while enriching their fellow colleagues.

6.2.5. Jurong Town Corporation (JTC)

JTC places emphasis on two learning processes, namely 'Learning during Execution', and 'Learning after Execution'. It also rolled out information technology systems containing KM tools which assist their employees in codifying lessons as they carry out their day-to-day work. As an example, their 'Knowledge Discovery Points' system encourages employees to reflect on their work, and to suggest improvements. These improvements are then captured by the system, and used as a basis for future modifications to the work process. Employees are exhorted to practice experiential learning by documenting key learning points throughout the lifespan of a project, and put the principles of double-loop learning into use.

JTC's 'Learning after Execution' system encourages employees to critically review and compare what was achieved, with the goals which were set at the beginning. This practice avoids repetition of mistakes and improves work performance over time.

6.2.6. *Ministry of Finance (MOF)*

Codification and taxonomy alignment of documents and emails were key knowledge processes for MOF. Its enterprise taxonomy was built via a bottom-up approach, by working closely with KM representatives who were officers working on the ground and were known to be familiar with the breadth and depth of their work. Furthermore, it was important for the staff to have a feeling of ownership of their own taxonomy. To create the taxonomy, the KM team brainstormed with broad subject classifications of the various types of work that MOF does. These eventually helped form the 16 subject classifications as part of the Level 1 taxonomy. Once these were endorsed, the team proceeded to Level 2 and Level 3 classifications. The process was relatively long and tedious, due to a lot of toggling back and forth in the discussion of where certain subject areas should belong within the subject-based structure.

The KM team placed a considerable amount of emphasis on communications and organisational outreach. As learned from previous initiatives, keeping officers aware, informed and engaged is central to facilitate and manage change. Thus, while in the midst of the testing stage of the KM tools and taxonomy, the KM team routed weekly emails and posters to align with the various milestones of the project as a means to maintain the interest and momentum prior to the actual rollout. The vendor provided hands-on training sessions to the users. Each training session began with an introduction to the system, explaining the rationale behind its usage and some broad guidelines for filing and usage. Officers were guided through installation and navigation of the system. A copy of the corporate taxonomy was also disseminated, so that officers could familiarise themselves with it.

Other KM processes implemented at MOF include Free Sharing@ MOF, ExCO Meeting, KM Roadshows, Amoeba Project Presentations, after-action reviews (AARs), and Staff Engagement Sessions. The ExCO meeting is chaired by the Permanent Secretary and involves all the directors in the headquarters as well as the heads of departments. In the Free Sharing@MOF sessions, anyone who has an item to table can send it to the secretariat who would then consolidate the items for discussions.

6.2.7. National Library Board (NLB)

NLB's Network of Specialists (NOS) approach for KM comprises various subject and special interest online communities, such as the Arts Subject Community, Business Subject Community and the Singapore/ Southeast Asia Subject Community. A librarian receiving a difficult enquiry can send an email to the relevant subject community to seek assistance, and it will then be broadcasted to all the community members simultaneously. Members of the community can review and add to the contributions in a common web-based e-space. This means that anyone in the community who has an internet-enabled device can access the collaborative platform any time anywhere.

Through the sharing process, learning takes place as the initiating librarian continues to take ownership of the reply to the enquiry whilst getting inputs contributed by others in the community. This improves the staff's capability in handling the more challenging reference enquiries. The interactions between staff and subject experts are also captured and archived to form part of the library's KM data as shown in Table 6.1.

6.2.8. Singapore Armed Forces (SAF)

In the course of its KM journey over the past decade, numerous CoPs were established within SAF as core knowledge processes, augmented by regular training, leadership development and expertise hubs. Parallel to these, the leadership formed the Leadership Dialogue where open discussion and debate on important and complex topics were

Table 6.1   A Community of Specialists Contributing to an Enquiry on NOS.

Response by 1 Librarian	Response from Community of Specialists

Sample Enquiry: What are the addresses of Buddhist temples or monasteries belonging to the Mahayana tradition in Singapore?

Recommended Solution:	*Recommended Solution:*
The Singapore Buddhist Federation is the umbrella body for Mahayana Buddhism in Singapore. This is their homepage: http://www.buddhist. org.sg/ Most information on the homepage is in Chinese. Examples of three major Buddhist temples for Mahayana Buddhism are: • Phor Kark See Temple • Kwan Im Thong Hood Cho Temple • Shuang Lin Cheng Huang Temple (Formerly known as Siong Lim Temple)	The Buddhist community in Singapore does not have a complete list of Mahayana Buddhist organisations. Nevertheless, a list of almost all the 136 Buddhist organisations in Singapore can be found on this website. This website is used frequently by the local Buddhist community for events and courses: Source: For You http://www.4ui.com/activity/activity.htm Click on the individual temple listing to view their addresses. Most of the organisations in the list with Chinese names are Mahayana Buddhist organisations. We have also gotten in touch with the Buddhist Library in Singapore and the librarian will be sending us a book containing the print version of the list similar to the website listed above. We will get in touch with you again when we receive the book. The Buddhist Library has also advised us that if you would like to visit a Chinese-speaking Mahayana temple, then any Chinese Buddhist temple is Mahayana. This includes Bright Hill Temple (at Sin Min Road), Shuang Lim Temple (at Toa Payoh) and the Venerable Ming Yi's temple in Paya Lebar. If you would like to visit an English-speaking Mahayanist temple, then perhaps a trip to the Tibetan temple in Pasir Ris would be helpful.

Source: Provided by NLB.

conducted. SAF wanted its people to make sense of the evolving operational environment and system. As much of the tacit knowledge will continue to reside in people, SAF has focused on continual education for the regulars, leadership development as well as the staple Professional Military Education and Training.

SAF profiled its people and created a new Military Domain Expert Scheme to build up deep knowledge. The learning opportunities in SAF have groomed many leaders that later on became key players contributing to Singapore at large. For example, in 2003, at the height of the Severe Acute Respiratory Syndrome (SARS) epidemic, the current Civil Defence Force played a pivotal role in establishing the national contact and tracing system.

SAF also created Knowledge Hubs where various Task Forces could draw upon each other's expertise and knowledge to achieve integration in relation to war-fighting techniques. These Joint Task Force headquarters comprises experts from various knowledge hubs and networked back to their respective knowledge hubs, thereby creating a pervasive matrix in a knowledge-based organisation. For example, the Navy established the Changi Command and Control (C2) Centre for synergistic inter-agency and multi-lateral cooperation. The information fusion centre within Changi C2 Centre facilitates the consolidation and distribution of operational knowledge from partner navies and maritime agencies. The Army has since restructured its functional departments into five interlinked knowledge hubs. The Air Force has also reorganised its airbase-centric structure and networked the new warfighting commands to achieve greater effectiveness. At the SAF level, the MINDEF SAF Operations Centre networks the Navy, Army and Air Force operations centres into an integrated structure to support knowledge-based operations.

Another KM initiative is called Innovating New Processes, to move from being technology and concept 'adopters' to becoming 'innovators'. For example, with the eSILK[1] repository system, SAF was able to transform the workflow of its registries to be more efficient and environmentally friendly, with users doing their own filing and downloading e-documents meetings. Further, it transformed its processes in training such that core learning processes such as coaching, facilitation, reflection and journaling, are incorporated into existing processes. New

---

[1] Enterprise System for Innovation, Learning and Knowledge.

processes such as the Action Learning Process which reviews SAF operations before, during and after execution are also incorporated.

6.2.9. Singapore Police Force: Police Technology Department (SPF-PTD)

A number of offline and online forums were conducted to promote
knowledge sharing and strengthen collaborative relationships. These
ranged from the formal to the informal. For instance, the PTD Coffee
Corner is a set of informal monthly meetings among departmental
heads, intended to bridge knowledge gaps and create better inter-unit
cooperation. KM Sharing @ Staff Meeting is a slot for all units to give
short presentations on any topic of interest during the monthly meeting. We Hear You (WHY) is a structured interaction process developed
based on the feedback of the organisational health survey. The staff
are given opportunity to meet a senior staff of their choice to provide
feedback or seek clarification on any work-related issue.

The Software Design Competition is a way to encourage innovation, where the staff could submit proposals for target problems, such
as a software to build a secure, efficient and intelligent lift system.
More informal competitions included essays on movies, which feature include high technology and action. For example, in one such
essay competition, the staff watched the movie 'The Bourne Ultima-
tum' and named the technologies and equipment which are mentioned
in the movie. This was a fun activity which encouraged curiosity and
reflection on the possible uses of technology. Other knowledge-sharing
forums extended outside PTD and SPF. For instance, KM101 consists of
sharing of KM experiences with other divisions in SPF such as the Police
Psychologists' Services Division (PPSD) and the Home Team Academy
(HTA). PTD shared their learning and understanding of KM concepts
and practices with these external departments. PTD further augments
its KM competence by peer visits to other organisations to learn about
their KM practices.

PTD also produced a KM Archetypes Video. It was an in-house
video skit featuring staff actors playing the role of common KM
archetypes. The same year also witnessed the launch of the PTD Training School (PTS) by the then Chief of Police, Khoo Boon Hui. From 2008
onwards, annual competitions were launched for Work Improvement
Teams (WITs) projects and Staff Suggestion Schemes (SSS). In 2009,

an internal publication called 'Knowledge Times' was published, to increase internal awareness about KM practices and trends.

The Coaching Channel was then launched with the aim of raising awareness of supervisors in PTD on what coaching is about, and to highlight coaching best practices. Another knowledge initiative was the production of the PTD Innovation Video; this video was PTD's submission for the SPF Innovation Video Competition organised by the Service Development and Inspectorate (SD&I) Department.

6.2.10. *Singapore Youth Olympic Games Organising Committee (SYOGOC)*

Process mapping and AARs were the key KM techniques used by SYO-GOC. Systematic learning processes based on AARs were applied to the Games, whereby knowledge managers captured lessons learned from venues and events on a daily basis. These lessons learned were then shared the same evening, so that they could be applied to the following day's events. There were two main types of knowledge transfer: one for Singapore's own sports community to enhance its ability to deliver major Games in the future, and the other to the IOC and Nanjing, the host city for the 2014 Summer Youth Olympic Games.

Observers and Visitors Programmes provided knowledge transfer opportunities for other Games organisers. The SYOGOC team comprehensively and carefully planned these knowledge transfer tasks. Since the organisation would be disbanded after the Games, there was the risk of dispersal of the hard-gained know-how. Figure 6.2 demonstrates the phases of knowledge capture and transfer processes, during and after the Games.

The KM Group team consisted of three KM staff and two registry staff. The KM staff planned and rolled out the KM initiatives with two objectives: capturing knowledge and transferring knowledge during and after the Games in a systematic manner. The registry staff worked closely with the KM staff in terms of creating and synchronising the taxonomy, managing the records, and planning the logistics support. As the team was small, SYOGOC leveraged on 28 divisional KM coordinators during the implementation of the KM initiatives. Figure 6.3 shows the organisational chart of SYOGOC.

An important aspect of the planning is the knowledge 'synthesis' which came in the form of standard templates for the process maps, standard shapes to use to represent different types of activities and

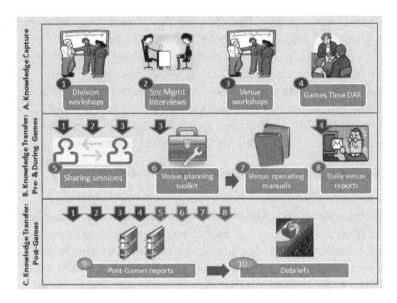

Figure 6.2   Phases of Knowledge Capture and Transfer.
Source: Provided by SYOGOC.

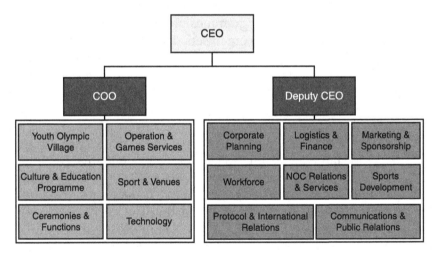

Figure 6.3   Organisational Alignment at SYOGOC.
Source: Redrawn from SYOGOC.

steps, and standard names to use for each group of people or actors in the process map. As the processes were derived from the main milestone map, they were already sequenced in a logical manner. SYOGOC also put in place a process to allow 'extensions' of process maps. For instance, if the process or activity cut across two planning phases, the workshop participants had to quote the process reference number of the first map. The process reference number clearly identified which division the process belongs to.

The flow from the phases of knowledge capture to final reporting and sharing was continuous and dynamic. In the post-Games reports, the process maps would be arranged according to the divisions. SYOGOC-wide sharing sessions were scheduled after the completion of each series of division or venue workshops and senior management interviews; typically it took about seven to eight months. Other KM Group (KMG) activities include facilitated sharing sessions, pre-venue planning briefings, overseas trip sharing sessions, the post-Asian Youth Games sharing sessions, and overall AAR sharing.

As SYOGOC moved nearer to the inauguration date of the Games, the sharing sessions became more focused on operations and executions. Lessons learned were immediately used to tweak and improve operations. Functional groups tended to rely less on the KMG team to facilitate these sharing sessions. Due to the tight timeline, not all staff had the luxury to go through all four AAR questions in a sequential manner. What was most important to them was to identify the issues and impact, the lessons learned and the follow-up needed. They quite often missed out the 'What was planned' and 'Explain the difference between planned and actual' questions, simply because these did not enhance their work in an immediate manner.

SYOGOC was also concerned that the context of some situations may not have been fully captured, but it was also very aware of the realistic concerns of staff. Hence, they did not 'over-police' what was being captured in the AARs, as long as the output helped staff in their work. Furthermore, it was impossible for the KM team to monitor and facilitate all AARs as they only had three members.

6.2.11. Supreme Court of Singapore (SC)

The Supreme Court's KM processes are designed around knowledge stocks and flows, supported by active roles such as KM Champions and

KM Activists. Information updates are systematically recorded and captured. For instance, the Registrars' homepage is updated by the Assistant Registrars (ARs) after the monthly Judicial Officers' (JO) Meetings. In the case of the Justices' Law Clerks (JLCs), updates to the database called Pegs take place whenever new points of research turn up, which occur throughout the year. All ARs and JLCs have been designated as KM Activists.

Peer-level sharing takes place regularly between the ARs. ARs' judicial decisions are thus not derived from a top-down process. Rather, the decision-making process is flat, which makes peer-level sharing all the more important, so that the AR making a particular decision is cognisant of all relevant factors to be taken into account.

In the case of the Legal Directorate, the process by which 'core material' is generated is a dynamic one, which is dependent upon a multitude of factors, such as developments arising in the course of Registry operations. As such, identification and uploading of material to the Legal Directorate homepage takes place throughout the year, as and when the need to do so arises. The content on the individual homepages are constantly monitored by its owner, the webmaster.

The Legal Directorate KM Champion is its Director while the KM Activists are the Directorate's Assistant Directors and Section Heads. The role of the KM Champion, supported by the Activists, is to identify crucial information, knowledge and work processes in the Legal Directorate that should be documented. This is done with the objective of retaining and transferring knowledge and allowing easy access to knowledge. The Activists identify the sources of such information and where this information should thus reside. The Activists would then upload, maintain and update information on the KM portal which the Legal Directorate KM Champion has identified as worth institutionalising.

Each knowledge process has a specific owner. The Assistant Director (Civil) is the KM Activist in charge of all information/materials relating to civil proceedings. The Assistant Director (Enforcement & Support Services) is the KM Activist that oversees the uploading of all information/materials related to criminal proceedings. The Assistant Director (SLU) is the KM Activist who ensures that the monthly management reports are uploaded to the KM portal on a timely basis.

The Pegs database and the Bench Memoranda database are evidence of the 'collaboration', 'capturing', and 'reuse' sub-components of the 'process' aspect of KM. Both the Pegs and the Bench Memoranda databases capture current legal knowledge, allowing the JLCs to reuse each other's research so that they do not waste time covering the same ground from scratch.

6.2.12. *Urban Redevelopment Authority (URA)*

URA has devised a number of processes for learning, sharing and collaboration among its officers and teams within the organisation. There are formal CoPs such as an active online Planners' Club for planners, architects and management in URA. This online discussion forum allows staff to share information and knowledge freely on an informal basis.

Organised Learning Forums such as the 'Learning Day' are also convened. Learning Day is a session where officers get together to learn and share on various subject areas. It is conducted at a group level on a bi-monthly or quarterly basis. The presentation materials shared in Learning Day are stored in the corporate intranets for future reference.

Higher-level KM processes include environment scanning, intelligence research, and benchmarking/comparison studies. URA conducts regular scanning of external and internal environments to understand global trends and developments. It also actively engages stakeholders (customers, service partners) to gather information about their changing needs and concerns. It further conducts benchmarking studies to gather intelligence to improve processes, products and services, vis-à-vis other best-in-class cities and organisations. These studies are shared with the management and officers before they are filed in the electronic Knowledge Repository Information System (eKRIS), and the resource centre portal for future reference.

6.3. Discussion and Insights

Overall, most organisations in the cases do actively promote KM processes and practices to suit their environments. Some of the key success factors range from getting management support to the building of structured information, and from reviewing external environments to establishing internal sharing participatory platforms. For instance, in terms of leadership development and mentoring, AGC, SAF, and the Supreme Court are seen to be active and deliberate in getting top management involvement; in terms of building structure information, it was necessary for MOF and AGC to have a proper taxonomy process to spearhead the knowledge process. However, to implement KM processes for enabling knowledge to be transferable within and between the organisations more effectively, establishing CoPs — both diverse and heterogeneous — were essential; thus, we see DSTA, IRAS, IPOS, NLB, SAF and URA creating such environments for knowledge-sharing practices. Many of these organisations also conduct site visits and benchmarking to share their KM expertise; and workshops are a regular part of KM activities in organisations such as URA, SPF, and MOF. Table 6.2 provides a summary of KM processes identified in each case.

Workshops and site visits are common ways of increasing knowledge abilities (e.g. in IPOS), as well as training sessions. KM tools are well-aligned with workflow (e.g. IPOS, Supreme Court). Qualitative methods to knowledge sharing via storytelling, Anecdote Circles and

Table 6.2   KM Processes in Singaporean Organisations.

Organisation	Processes
AGC	Cross-divisional sharing, codification, mentoring, search, taxonomy, workshops, Innovation Day
DSTA	Competency Centres, CoPs, peer sharing, workshops, e-workflow
IPOS	Site visits, workshops, CoPs, online workflow, taxonomy, knowledge audit, storytelling, knowledge cafes, KM bulletin
IRAS	Strong HR linkages for performance management, learning and development, organisation-wide sharing sessions, structured process for sharing sessions
JTC	Workflow features for AAR submission, processes for reminders and document expiration, categorisation
MOF	Corporate taxonomy, filing policies, KM briefings, KM roadshows, AAR, Free Sharing@MOF
NLB	CoPs, training sessions, Rich Pictures, Play of Life, podcasts, storytelling
SAF	Continual education, leadership development; reflection, journaling, coaching, action learning, CoPs, taxonomy
SPF-PTD	Training school, capability development, annual competitions, suggestion schemes, We Hear You (WHY) structured interaction, Software Design Competition
SYOGOC	Value network analysis, process mapping, AAR, organisation-wide sharing sessions, Anecdote Circles
SC	Peer-level sharing, legal taxonomy, case management workflow
URA	Quality checks, CoPs, Learning Day, review meetings

Knowledge Cafes are also prevalent (e.g. IPOS, SYOGOC). Strong HR linkages for performance management, learning and development have also been established (e.g. IRAS). KM activities have been raised to the level of value networking mapping (e.g. SYOGOC) and organisational leadership development in some cases (e.g. SAF). Tight external deadlines can help create a sense of urgency and foster tighter cooperation and more rapid knowledge-sharing behaviours, while also diminishing the need for expensive enterprise IT tools (e.g. SYOGOC).

Classic KM approaches such as CoPs have now reached a higher plane benefiting from new interaction methods, social media and inter-organisational initiatives. These KM sharing techniques include world café and fishbowl (experts in inner circle, observers in outer circle, novices in between). CoPs need to balance online and offline interactions; face-to-face connections help build trust, respect and comfort, and online interactions leave a useful knowledge trail. In fact, if CoPs' processes are seamlessly intertwined with organisational work procedures, it should also help to have a certain amount of time for introspection and refining past knowledge assets, and this is where knowledge retreats and events are useful.

CHAPTER SEVEN

Tools and Technologies

"The new source of power is not money in the hands of a few but information in the hands of many."

— John Naisbitt

This chapter focuses on the technological applications along with considerations of usability for effective knowledge systems. It also addresses the types of collaboration features and functions such as connectivity interfaces, devices, and tools that knowledge workers deploy for digital content management, search, visualisation, authoring, expertise directories, and social networking.

Although organisation-wide access to technological architecture, web-based applications, groupware, data mining tools, mobile devices, high performance and monitoring systems have emerged as key components of the supporting KM infrastructure, it is important to note that technology is not the panacea for a KM practice, though an easy-to-use knowledge sharing infrastructure is an important enabler. According to Koulopoulos and Frappaolo (1999), "If the smart manager knows one thing, it is that knowledge management is not just about technology. But, if the smart manager knows two things, the second is that in today's age of technology-driven communication and information-production, the role technology can play to facilitate knowledge management should be examined."

It is true that advanced information communication technologies can play an important role in KM; however, proactive exploration of new information technologies (IT) gives companies a leading advantage by having better insights of the market, and how it triggers broader market changes (Carr, 2003). However, the technological advantage has since become difficult to sustain, due to its rapidly decreasing cost and increased accessibility. Carr even suggested that companies delay IT investments, to cut cost and reduce the risk of being saddled with rapidly changing technologies. The priority of companies thus shifted from aggressive advantage seeking towards effective cost saving and efficient risk managing. Carr's advice for IT management is to spend less, follow rather than lead, and focus on vulnerabilities instead of opportunities.

According to Dewett and Jones (2001), information technologies could impact an organisation through its characteristics such as structure, size, learning and culture; the inter-organisational relationships are shown in Figure 7.1.

7.1. KM Tools: Overview

Marwick (2001) discussed KM technologies under the framework of Nonaka's SECI model, classifying different categories of technologies by reference to the notions of tacit and explicit knowledge. Due to the nature and characteristics of such knowledge, Marwick (ibid) argues that this could help people better understand the limitations of technology, and guide future developments. Figure 7.2 provides a snapshot

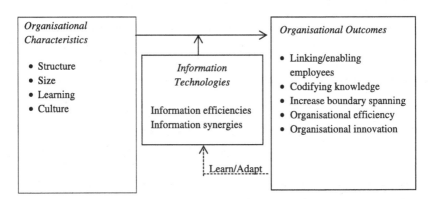

Figure 7.1   IT's Impact on the Organisation.

Source: Adapted from Dewett and Jones (2001).

Tacit knowledge   *To*   Explicit knowledge

	Socialisation	Externalisation
Tacit knowledge	• Groupware • Expertise locator	• Online discussion • Newsgroups
From		
Explicit knowledge	**Internalisation** • Visualisation • Online education • Distance learning	**Combination** • Search • Classification • Summarisation

Figure 7.2   Nonaka's SECI Model.

Source: Adapted from Nonaka and Takeuchi (1995, p. 62).

of the types of technologies that are appropriate for eliciting tacit and explicit knowledge.

Reflecting the evolution of KM technologies and techniques, this section profiles the following key sets of KM tools: content management, taxonomies, portals, and social media. Tools that currently fall under the KM umbrella have evolved in various phases since the 1980s, starting with IT tools for computation and databases, followed by publishing and communication tools, and then sophisticated platforms for collaboration, wireless delivery, search and network modelling. From automated agents to wikis, KM technologies span almost the entire alphabetical spectrum.

KM Tools: The Alphabet Soup

Abstraction, agents, authoring systems, best practice repository, blogging, business intelligence, case-based reasoning, categorisation, clustering, competitive intelligence, content management, collaboration, collaborative filtering, creativity tools, data mining, document management, e-learning, expert systems, expertise directories, expertise locators, groupware, heuristic software, idea management, intellectual property inventory, knowledge blogs,

(Continued)

(*Continued*)

knowledge dashboard, knowledge discovery, knowledge mapping, knowledge mobilisation, knowledge portals, knowledge visualisation, meta-data, micro-blogging, neural networks, online communities of practice (CoPs), personal KM, profiling, P2P knowledge networking, search, semantic nets, Skandia navigator, skill inventories, smart enterprise suites, social media, social network analysis, story templates, taxonomy, text mining, topic maps, validation, wiki, workflow...

Source: Adapted from Rao (2005).

Tiwana (2002) outlines a 'Knowledge Management Toolkit' that focuses on a practical ten-step roadmap to KM implementation. However, he cautions that KM should not be reduced to a 'fix-it-all' technology, a smarter intranet, a seductive silver-bullet solution, a canned approach, or a one-time investment. The ten steps of KM roadmap can be grouped into four phases: infrastructure evaluation, system development, system deployment and system evaluation. He identifies technology enablers for a range of knowledge activities such as knowledge finding (e.g. search, yellow pages), creation (collaboration tools), packaging (digital publishing), applying (classification), and validation (CoPs) and reuse (project record databases).

7.1.1. *Collaboration Tools*

Anumba *et al.* (2001) developed a space-time communication matrix to classify collaboration technologies. Shown in Figure 7.3, the

	Same Time	Different Times
Same Place	Face-to-Face Collaboration	Asynchronous Collaboration
Different Places	Distributed Synchronous Collaboration	Distributed Asynchronous Collaboration

Figure 7.3   Space-Time Communication Matrix.
Source: Anumba *et al.* (2001).

collaboration modes are based on either the same or different space-time matrix, and hence different technologies are being deployed. The scenarios are described as follows:

- Face-to-face collaboration: This mode of communication within the 'same' space-time scenario would involve meeting at a common venue such as a meeting room, and participants would engage in face-to-face discussions, e.g. a meeting between an architect and a client for a project briefing session.
- Asynchronous collaboration: This mode of communication happens in the 'same' place but at a 'different' time, it can be conducted using media, e.g. notice/bulletin boards within an organisation.
- Distributed synchronous collaboration: This mode of communication occurs in a 'different' place but at the 'same' time; it would involve real-time communication using technologies, e.g. telephony, video conferencing, and electronic group discussion or application sharing.
- Distributed asynchronous collaboration: This mode of communication describes the situation of a 'different' place and time; it would involve communications via the post (e.g. periodic letters/news bulletins), fax machines, telephone messages/voicemail, pagers, electronic mail transmissions, etc.

7.1.2. *Content Management*

Organisational content typically includes a range of textual and multimedia information assets: documents, presentations, research materials, workflow manuals, project reports, memos, minutes, white papers, guidelines, instructional materials, employee profiles, structured records and unstructured emails. A content management system is a set of tools to systematically control how the organisational content is created, structured, classified, validated, archived, accessed, browsed, retrieved and searched. An effective content management system makes it easy for knowledge workers to create, locate, access, and share relevant content with fellow workers in an efficient manner. Features of such content management systems include version control, secure access, compliance guidelines, automated search, and analysis of access patterns.

A growing number of organisations have therefore currently instituted content management systems to effectively utilise their accumulated information resources towards best practices, lessons learned, product development knowledge, customer knowledge, and human resource (HR) management knowledge. Content-centric KM approaches like codification focus on efficiency and effectiveness of information flow in value chains, while collaborative strategies focus on people-centric group activities in organisational value chains.

Advanced content management systems include features for seamless exploration, authoring templates, maintaining integrity of webpages and links, periodical review, meta-data, rule-setting, indexing, audits, authorised access, administration alerts, and flexible repurposing for multiple platforms and formats. Rumizen (2002) claims that an organisation's ability to create, share, capture and leverage knowledge is dependent upon the quality of connectivity and the simplicity of the intranet's interface and application.

Until recently, KM took a back seat to other management efforts, such as quality or performance management. However, Conway and Sligar (2002) have noticed an increased interest in KM, as the management turns its attention to the value created by knowledge workers with improvements in the connectivity; indeed, the economic leverage of knowledge is much valued. In brief, as much of the codification approaches focuses on content management repositories, for which validation, layering and version control are important features, enterprise content management has emerged as a set of tools and methods used to capture, manage, store, preserve, and deliver content across an enterprise. It is more than simply technology; it is an activity that involves a concerted investment in policy development, training, change management, risk assessments, and other issues of process and technology (Blair, 2004).

7.1.3. Taxonomies

Successful codification of organisational knowledge is implemented via taxonomy, a systematic and dynamic classification scheme of knowledge types and attributes in alignment with business views, goals and operations. This can include unstructured external knowledge (e.g. competitive intelligence) or structured internal knowledge (e.g. research reports). The Association of Information and Image Management professionals (www.aiim.org) defines taxonomy as a mechanism to provide a formal structure for information, based on the individual needs of an organisation. Categorisation tools automate the placement of content for future retrieval based on the taxonomy, while users can also manually categorise documents. Within these organisations, taxonomy thus presents an employee's view of organisational assets, activities, expertise and priorities.

The vast volume of information stored by the organisations, especially online information resources has made it necessary for organisations to adopt systems, processes, and technologies to organise it. Within organisations, knowledge taxonomy focuses on efficient retrieval and sharing of knowledge for employees by building the taxonomy around workflows and knowledge needs in an intuitive structure (Lambe, 2007). Organisations expand their KM initiatives by creating processes that identify, collect, categorise and refresh content using a common taxonomy across the organisation. The content templates and taxonomy must be customer-driven and domain-driven (Hasanali & Leavitt, 2003). Hence the content architecture for KM must be devised by a cross-disciplinary team.

Indeed, data management vocabulary, descriptive taxonomies and navigational taxonomies of an interactive and evolving nature are crucial components of knowledge taxonomy. Yet, maintaining taxonomy is an often overlooked requirement and underestimated cost (Conway & Sligar, 2002). Types of taxonomy can range from industry to clustering to search engine query logs and subject experts. Meta-data features like classification, tagging and validation are crucial in converting information to intelligent content. Indeed, they help ensure compliance, relevance and consistency.

7.1.4. Corporate Portals

A portal is a website, usually with little content of its own, created for providing links to various other sites and services that can be accessed directly by clicking on a designated part of a browser screen. Portals can provide links to all the enterprise-relevant sites (internal content providers) as well as to some external information; the information is found through extended search facilities or by following an enterprise-defined taxonomy, which is usually created by subject matter experts or competency communities, and organised by professional librarians (Tyndale, 2002).

The enterprise portal is an IT-enabled platform to implement a range of activities for information access and communication. It is a secure gateway interface towards content archives, corporate newsletters, employee profiles, search tools, and work applications. The portal helps provide consistent views of the organisation to all employees and is available via personalised access for employees and cross-media communication (Collins, 2003).

Corporate portals offer powerful capabilities for companies to embark on significant business model transformations and leverage collective intelligence (Terra & Gordon, 2003). KM is a step beyond information management with respect to dimensions like context, validation and human referencing. It involves components that are strategic (e.g. intellectual capital management, organisational core competencies) and tactical (e.g. knowledge creation and transfer mechanisms, KM roles, incentive measures). Terra and Gordon (ibid) classify portal implementation into six categories of intent: communications (internal and external), pushing information to employees (e.g. frontliners), knowledge reuse (e.g. expertise maps), collaboration (CoPs), human capital management (improve retention, get new employees up to speed quickly), and external relationships (reduce customer service costs).

7.1.5. Social Media

Emerging digital environments such as social media are changing the communication landscape in societies as well as within organisations. The internet, intranet and wireless media are transforming the way knowledge is being transformed and experienced; the earlier wave of emails, portals, groupware and desktop-based tools (Applehans *et al.*, 1999; Collins, 2003) has now been augmented by social media and mobile workflow tools.

As compared to broadcast media, social media enables people-to-people communication through interpersonal or group collaboration, narrative forms, and multi-media content sharing and rating. Social media on the internet and organisational intranet are real time in flow, and allow for powerful search and analysis features so that larger patterns can be unearthed, such as overall popularity of content, influence of a content creator, and trends in a debate. Social media have also emerged in the form of blogs, micro-blogs, wikis, podcasts, personal diaries, affinity clubs, event forums and social bookmarks. Many of these are now emerging in varying forms on the organisational intranet as well.

According to Norris *et al.* (2003), digital tools have triggered off a cascading cycle of reinvention of organisational education (e.g. just-in-time learning) and organisational collaboration (e.g. tradecraft knowledge mobilisation via handheld devices). Within enterprises, the original concept of KM has evolved into broader notions of knowledge ecology, knowledge experiences, knowledge habitats and knowledge marketplaces. For instance, visualisation tools, knowledge blogs ('klogs'), P2P collaboration tools, and semantic searches are interesting developments on this front. Indeed, Norris *et al.* (ibid) predict that over time, the strategic importance of fusing e-learning and KM will become abundantly clear to policy-makers and practitioners alike.

Thanks to the rapidly falling costs of communication, the web has been instrumental in catalysing opportunities for knowledge sharing via connection and collection strategies (Ahmed *et al.*, 2002). Knowledge managers should not only try to imitate what works in consumer social media, but also observe what really happens in the enterprise. The key is to mix communication and education without sidetracking into frivolity, and find a balance between security and flexibility (O'Dell & Hubert, 2011).

7.1.6. Mobile Tools and Applications

Another fast-growing trend has been the use of handheld wireless devices, especially smartphones and more recently tablets, in consumer life and organisational workflows. They help mobilise knowledge and provide 'anytime, anywhere, any device' access to intellectual assets and human expertise. Even in the early years, Keen and Mackintosh (2001) observed that the knowledge mobilisation opportunity using wireless technologies is so huge that no company can afford not to grab it fast and hard. This is because mobile technologies enhance communication, information and collaboration, the three cornerstones of knowledge building and usage.

Mobile computing has the potential to become an important part of the KM process not only because of its ability to access information anytime and anywhere, but also because of its ability to capture and transmit information in the original context (Shen, 2003). Contextual cues about the physical environment and the knowledge worker's immediate social setting can be captured via multi-media applications on mobile devices, thus assisting the tacit as well as explicit framing of the learning context in real time, e.g. case studies about repairing a machine, or handling a customer complaint.

Research on the use of mobile tools by knowledge workers will help design next generation KM systems, which utilise a range of mobile tools and applications ('apps') to create new kinds of information flows, collaboration opportunities and work processes. Mobile tools and workflows also open up interesting possibilities in the design of situation-aware information processing in the field of ambient intelligence environments (Balfanz *et al.*, 2005). The integration of KM and mobile technologies can make KM ubiquitous (knowledge access away from the office) and also make mobile computing useful (through new user-focused processes and services). Mobiles can help fulfil the "just-in-time" need for actionable information and knowledge (O'Sullivan, 2011).

7.2. Perspectives from the Case Studies

This section describes the KM architecture and tools in the case studies. Based on the broad category of tools described in Section 7.1 and illustrative screenshots, if examines how these tools are accessed and used.

7.2.1. Attorney-General's Chambers (AGC)

The AGC Portal, SA-GE, was soft launched in September 2003. It replaced its intranet, enabling easier web-content management and personalisation of Portal pages; one-stop access to its multiple repositories and frequently used transactions systems, enhanced search functions and a platform to facilitate collaboration. Federated search allows users to search across platforms. Figure 7.4 shows its KM architecture.

To generate interest and awareness of KM prior to the soft launch of its portal, contests such as the 'Name Our KM Portal', 'Design a KM Logo' and 'Banner Contest' were held. The winning entry 'SA-GE' was chosen via electronic voting that was opened to its entire staff. The name denotes 'knowledge acquired from a wealth of experiences'. The 'A-G' in SA-GE is the acronym for 'Attorney-General'.

Over the years, enhancements have been made to SA-GE, with more links for research materials added under the Legal Matters pull-down menu. Divisional and committee pages allow members of individual divisions or committees to share documents, make announcements and

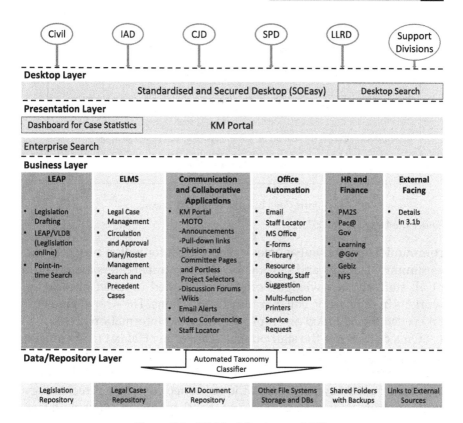

Figure 7.4   KM Architecture at AGC.

Source: Redrawn from AGC.

to hold discussion on forums online. Training sessions and self-help animated training guides are also provided for users. In 2007, a new Information Division (InfoDiv) was established through the merger of the Computer Information Systems Department, the Library and the Knowledge Management Central for better synergy in their various functions. Its mission is to help AGC provide effective legal services through the use of IT and the management of knowledge assets.

7.2.2. *Defence Science and Technology Agency (DSTA)*

DSTA's KM initiative was meant to promote peer sharing and a more efficient workflow. Its corporate intranet, eHabitat, is a one-stop staff-centric information platform for organisation-wide staff

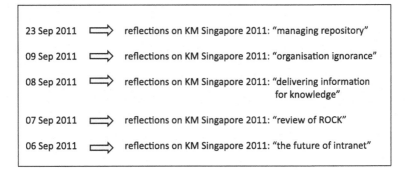

Figure 7.5   Blogposts on KM Portal.

Source: Redrawn from DSTA.

communication and engagement, corporate information services, and community learning and sharing. While the intranet caters to the needs of all staff, the Knowledge Portal is positioned to assist knowledge workers in their work, collaborations and actions. The Knowledge Portal is customised based on employee roles and information needs.

On a daily basis, the staff publish content in eHabitat to share with colleagues. In some channels, an editor is included to review the content before it is being published. In fact on a regular basis, Knowledge Managers and content owners review the published content (e.g. technology write-up from open source) to ensure that they remain relevant. In fact, content such as announcements which is more than a specific number of days old (e.g. three days) will be archived. Interestingly, some of the more recent forms of social media content include blogging, with topics ranging from the informal (e.g. ride information) to the more formal (e.g. knowledge retention in exit interviews). Members regularly attend KM conferences, and share some of their learnings with other colleagues via blogposts (see Figure 7.5).

Each community owns a CC portal which becomes the default browser homepage based on one's community (see the Chief Information Officer's (CIO) Office Portal in Figure 7.6). Each community also has a Knowledge Hub, which is set up and organised based on the required information structure and needs. Search and ASK are also integral parts of the CC portal where the staff receive updates on news and changes in their communities, as well as access policy, standard and information resources related to their area of work via navigation and search.

Figure 7.6   CIO Office Portal.

Source: Provided by DSTA.

The KM portal was largely designed in-house. Requirements were taken from various stakeholders through discussions and meetings. The eHabitat leverages commercial off-the-shelf products, and through working within a wireless infrastructure environment, this new modus operandi has allowed staff to work efficiently and effectively as each staff is equipped with a laptop.

All staff are strongly encouraged to contribute and share their learnings and technical reports through the Knowledge Hub. The personalised MyHomepage provides a template for every staff to share their career aspirations, working experience and other personal interests. Although participation is voluntary, with the CC Heads and senior management leading by example, MyHomepage achieved a participation rate of 70 percent, six months after it was launched.

7.2.3. Intellectual Property Office of Singapore (IPOS)

A top-down approach was used to understand the core departmental business needs at IPOS so as to design appropriate tools for content and collaboration. Each departmental head was consulted on its taxonomy and work processes with their representatives working with the KM team in the design and implementation stages.

IPOS selected the IT vendor by open tender based on their proposal which met its requirement and budget. The technical competency of the project team was one of the key factors in the evaluation, and the team was able to deliver the system according to the specification and timeline. It is important for the KM manager to understand both the KM tools and the internal work processes of the organisation as this will help to deliver a KM portal that benefits its users.

Knowledge Enterprise (KEN) was launched by the Singapore government in 2007 to foster the collaboration among government agencies. However, KEN was launched in IPOS in July 2008 as a pilot for the KM portal. The two portals — KM and corporate — are separate. To select the name of the portal, IPOS held a naming contest. All staff was invited to submit a portal name and 15 percent of the staff participated. The staff were then asked to vote from the names submitted, of which there was 95 percent participation in the voting. The name with the highest votes was chosen: KENNY (**K**nowledge **EN**terprise '**N**' **Y**ou). Interestingly, through the naming exercise, IPOS did not have to do a major marketing exercise to promote its KM initiative.

The implementation of its KM portal started with the pilot project to demonstrate the KM portal efficiencies through automated business processes, with three business processes from the following departments: the Legal Policy and International Affairs Department (LPIAD), Registry of TradeMark and Performance Reporting. IPOS automated the work processes for the capture of information directly into its portal. However, to provide a more efficient document capture, it developed the taxonomy according to the various departmental needs, as well as designed the KEN search interface to integrate with its taxonomy. KEN's search facility was then further customised for its site navigation features which were developed according to its divisional/departmental sites. In order to allow the flexibility and to encourage contribution, IPOS introduced sub-site administrators for those departments with various activities. These site administrators are given SharePoint training and autonomy to manage their own site, such as creating their own subject matters within the document library.

KEN was used as a key collaboration system to enhance operation-wide efficiency. The system provides a platform for users to work on the same piece of information to produce an outcome. Email can alternatively be a collaboration platform, but it did not serve the purpose of a central repository, as information is kept in the individual's mailbox and it may create duplicate information; whereas KENNY serves the purpose of both being a central document repository and a collaboration platform. Besides collaboration, the contract library also serves as the central repository for the legal counsels to have an overview of all the legal documents. In addition, it simplifies the handover process between legal counsels, for example, between primary and alternate legal counsels to follow up on the issues, as all the information is stored in KENNY.

An illustrative example is the collaboration between the Ministry of Law and IPOS on IP International Policy. One of the business activities of LPIAD is to review the IP International Policy and it requires the interaction between the legal counsels from Ministry of Law and IPOS to give comments on policies that are captured in Word documents. Prior to the implementation of KENNY, the consultation between the two parties was done using email and Word documents as attachments. A secretary was assigned to compile all the comments after the legal counsels have given their comments. This process has since been automated on KENNY using the wiki library.

7.2.4. Inland Revenue Authority of Singapore (IRAS)

As the sharing sessions play an important role in its KM strategy, IRAS has implemented not only the e-learning tools for building the staff's knowledge capacity and skills but also incorporated in its intranet a structured knowledge repository that is stored centrally for its staff to access the content, outcomes and artefacts of the knowledge sharing sessions. There are also clear roles for the KM officers from the Organisation Excellence Branch to upload the schedules and materials of the sharing sessions in a timely manner and the staff are informed of its availability via announcements in the Intranet.

To support the sharing, IRAS launched its information architecture in 2008, made major improvements to the search engine, culminating with the launch of a new search engine in 2010. In addition, various supporting infrastructure, such as iNex and the employee intranet portal, was implemented to further enhance their e-learning tools. There are also ongoing efforts to include integration of social media tools on the existing intranet.

7.2.5. Jurong Town Corporation (JTC)

The System of Business Information (SOBI) was one of the early initiatives that was developed using Lotus Notes in 1998 (Version 1) with the purpose of creating a centralised system for the reviewing of policies and processes, as well as to provide a single access to data through categorisation and search. Its web-based Domino Lotus Notes Version 2 was launched in 2005 and its latest revamp was developed using Microsoft SharePoint Server. Besides a better interface and look, this migration also enabled KM to be embedded in major work processes. For example, officers involved in reviewing policies are prompted by the system to review the policies and route the revised policies to the approving officer before dissemination.

Prior to this, such documents were stored separately as hardcopy or softcopy files in various groups and departments, and not easily retrieved and shared among them. This caused knowledge (both explicit and tacit) to be lost when the staff leave the group or department due to resignation or upon job rotation. The revamped solution includes a collaboration platform, structured review workflow, policies and process documentation initiation workflow, feedback and approval workflow, and other workflow features for after-action review (AAR) submission, reminders and document expiration.

With its new version called SOBI 2, employees now use SharePoint search to look for relevant documents, such as industry knowledge of key customers. The same IT platform has also transformed its intranet into a state-of-the-art employee portal ('Platinum'), to facilitate sharing and to provide a one-stop platform for selected business applications, HR, and other administrative systems. Indeed, JTC's use of IT infrastructure for KM has provided many useful lessons, and the organisation has been able to discuss these experiences in sharing sessions with other agencies.

JTC's Corporate Reporting Information Services Portal (CRISP) was designed for better reporting processes as shown in Figure 7.7. Prior to CRISP, aggregation of performance data was manually compiled. Performance reporting draws from a range of sources: balanced scorecard, business performance reports, macroeconomic indicators and articles, real estate reports, business statistics and ad hoc queries. However, manual and non-standardised compilation methods meant that due to multiple sources of information, there were inconsistencies in terms of definitions, data values and inclusion or exclusion of cases. The basis of computation and exceptions were not properly documented and knowledge was lost over time. Information was scattered and disjointed, e.g. in spreadsheets and individual hard disks; there was thus a strong need to provide a more systematic governance of the data and information-capturing process.

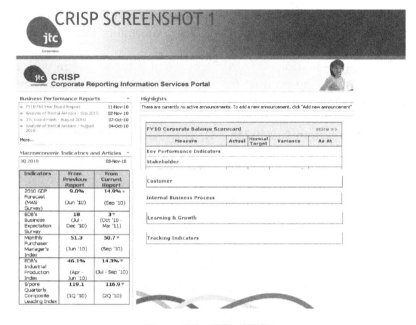

Figure 7.7   JTC's CRISP.

Source: Provided by JTC.

With the new tool, the data is reliable as there is now a single source with minimised inconsistencies, verified and reconciled. Users are also able to use the information more meaningfully, supported by a range of tools that enables trend analysis. There is a shorter learning curve, and knowledge is not lost. CRISP has also set the starting point for JTC's business intelligence journey.

7.2.6. Ministry of Finance (MOF)

The choice of KM tool at MOF reflects existing communication patterns and desired knowledge goals. MOF officers carefully sift through and select from a wide and diverse range of information for planning, day-to-day management and improvement. For a start, its KM team looked around the market for a tailored solution, which could help to address the issue of capturing knowledge through emails, the dominant communication channel at the time of launch of the KM initiative. The team eventually commissioned Third Sight, a local small and medium enterprise whose product Insight was designed for email mining and management that allowed for easy filing, retrieving and tracking of emails.

The implementation of Third Sight email solution began with the customisation of the product for MOF, to be introduced as its email repository. While firming up policies prior to its implementation, it was decided by MOF Steering Committee that all emails would have to be filed into the system (see Table 7.1). This being the case, each officer

Table 7.1   Third Sight Email Tool Features.

Email Filing Policy	Configure your email filing policy to *Optional-Silent, Optional-Prompt* or *Mandatory* (rule-based soon).
Email Capture	We *auto-capture* entire email conversations *into the future* for completeness and efficiency.
Email Browsing	We offer a power-mode *relational browsing* to show relationships, not just content.
Email Search	We contextualise search results on the fly to allow search results to be *browsed in context*.
Email Context	We apply email mining to *extract additional tacit relations* (e.g. *social networks*) beyond content.
Email Attachments	We apply *implied versioning* and *de-duplication* to all attachments to allow *attachment management*.
Email Collaboration	We mark emails to allow permitted recipients direct access to *secured collaborative workspaces*.
Email Workflows	We embed *mini-workflows* into emails for auto-tracking (even with external users).
Email Storage	We *fully optimise storage* at three levels: email, attachment and transmission.
Email Analytics	We offer *in-depth, on-demand analytics* into email activities — by projects, teams, users etc.
Email Extensibility	We *'bridge data silo's'* to interface emails with Enterprise Content Management, Microsoft Project etc.
Future-Proof Email	We offer *freedom from email format lock-in*! Store in open-standard and revive on demand into email.

Source: Provided by MOF.

would be given a personal folder accessible to only himself/herself for the purposes of storing personal or non-corporate emails.

Some of the highlights of the system include the ability to save and capture email threads as a whole, coupled with the availability of a contextual analysis function. It is also possible to derive names of all officers involved in a certain discussion topic and to further narrow down to the various attachments and documents that each officer disseminated. Tracking was not merely available — it was effective, detailed and useful, allowing for the saved emails to function as adequate reference materials.

A feature of its KM was the deployment of the multi-level taxonomy, which had varying levels of access and features based on employees' seniority and project experiences. A pilot was used to implement the system by the KM representatives. Working on a rather tight timeline, the KM representatives were engaged to test the product, with minor configurations at first, in conjunction with their everyday work over one month.

Response from the pilot stage was positive and enabled the KM team to move on to the next phase of testing. Allocated with only two weeks, the KM representatives used the same product, with more significant customisations that included the addition of a function which allowed officers to retrieve emails from the central repository for reuse.

7.2.7. National Library Board (NLB)

NLB's solution was to leverage on technological innovations to develop a collaborative platform called the Network of Specialists (NOS) for librarians and external experts to collaborate in real time, discuss and simultaneously work on one enquiry. With the collaborative platform in place, the next step was to plan for its rollout and get buy-in from staff. The staff's inputs were sought at the conceptualising stage, as the intention was to involve them right from the beginning to ensure a greater sense of ownership. When the first prototype of the product was completed, the staff was given demonstrations of the system, followed by hands-on training sessions.

They were also provided with user manuals and standard operating procedures to guide them along in the usage. To encourage usage, the management took opportunities to stress the importance of collaboration and knowledge sharing using the system. Figures 7.8 and 7.9

Figure 7.8   Email Broadcast Feature by Subject Community.

Source: Provided by NLB.

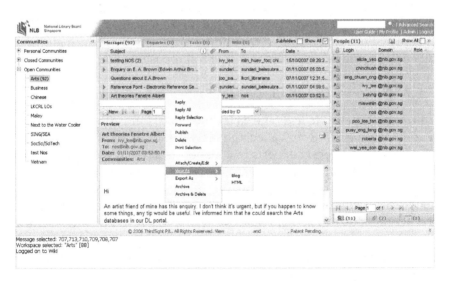

Figure 7.9   NOS Display of Subject Expert Inputs in Threaded Format.

Source: Provided by NLB.

illustrate the NOS portal and features like threaded discussions and email broadcast.

7.2.8. Singapore Armed Forces (SAF)

Using the evocative metaphor of a tree for its KM initiative, SAF wanted a single and strong 'trunk' for its diverse and rich KM initiative. Hence, it implemented a unified IT system: disparate IT systems were consolidated to become an enterprise KM and learning system known as the 'Enterprise System for Innovation, Learning and Knowledge,' or eSILK. It consists of a common repository for official documents and enabled explicit knowledge to be searchable. Lessons learned from military exercises are made accessible on demand. It also provides collaborative tools to support various communities in creating and sharing knowledge across the Navy, Army and Air Force and their organisational boundaries. To reach out towards the wider National Service populace, eSILK also supports self-directed learning on the internet.

SAF has also embarked on Integrated Knowledge-Based Command and Control to harness the power of the networks to create a knowledge-based environment for commanders to see first, understand better, decide faster and act decisively. Each 'knowledge branch' in the KM tree is the champion for a selected field, and freely shares knowledge with the other branches. In fact, SAF created its Knowledge Hubs where various task forces could draw upon each other's expertise and knowledge to achieve integrated war-fighting.

In terms of IT tools, social media are a natural attraction for the young NetGeners who make up the largest populace within the SAF. Many knowledge communities have been formed, leveraging on the knowledge system tools such as blogs, e-forum, and wikis for collaboration, and the creation and sharing of unstructured knowledge. These tools are used for interactive knowledge collaboration and dynamic discussions, supporting over 200 active communities, and over 450 blogs and wikis. The blog is essentially a learning and journaling tool; it allows individuals to reflect on recent learning experiences — this supports leadership development in which coaching, journaling and reflection are some of the key pedagogies. The approach allows users to publish their journals to everyone within their community or across communities. The e-forum is a tool made available to communities to support threaded discussion based on suggested topics. SAF also deploys newsfeeds using RSS for updates on what is happening globally as well as within the organisation. However, the necessity for security measures especially in a military organisation therefore requires it to balance open communications, knowledge sharing and transparency with security needs. SAF takes very serious views on the need to know and the need to hold as part of the overarching security governance to ensure access control to sensitive materials.

For day-to-day applications, SAF takes a more conscious approach in adopting commercial mobile technologies, and these are deployed only where security is of lower concern. For example, SMS alerts are used for mobilisation exercises, tablet PCs are deployed to entry-level training schools like Basic Military Training Schools and Officer Cadet Schools. Tablet PCs are part of the LearNet solution to leverage the internet and rich media such as YouTube in order to transform learning pedagogies and keep pace with the learning styles of the net generation.

With the eSILK repository system in place, the process of managing and retrieving e-documents is reduced to simple steps. As SAF transformed the workflow of its registries, it is also starting to see users doing their own filing and downloading e-documents to attend meetings. The re-engineering of the eRegistry and e-Meeting workflows made SAF more efficient and environmentally friendly. One of the most important feature that eSILK provides is the ability to connect the user with the right information, and thereafter connect the user to the party who owns the information. In the Athena system, all information is categorised by domain, subject, owner, author, and the like. The taxonomy interoperates closely with a meta-tagging system to support a faceted taxonomy.

With the successful implementation of eSILK, SAF has now ingested a substantial number of documents across the various platforms such as ECM, wikis, and blogs. The challenge now is to be able to allow knowledge users to swiftly locate contextually relevant information. The use of a traditional search engine such as Verity was deemed insufficient, so a sense-making tool was added by incorporating KARTOO, an information-mapping tool.

7.2.9. *Singapore Police Force: Police Technology Department (SPF-PTD)*

SPF-PTD's KM goals were to improve project management, increase domain expertise and promote knowledge sharing. Prior to the KM approach, technologies and applications used primarily were Lotus Notes (sharing via email), and basic 101-level information on the PTD intranet. Tools subsequently adopted included Lotus Notes Email, SharePoint (PTD intranet), Project Management Blog (freeware), Lectora (for e-learning content development), and FrontPage (for SPOTTIN — personal home pages). Figure 7.10 shows a snapshot of the PTD portal.

The core infrastructure consists of the intranet, which anchors shared folders, staff homepages, and orientation information. The most common themes of content relevant to PTD are information and communications (ICT) security, IT projects, IT equipment, and project management. Conversations about such topics are supported through

Figure 7.10   PTD Portal.

Source: Provided by SPF-PTD.

Table 7.2   KM Tools and Services at PTD.

Tool	Services
SPF intranet	SPF's intranet serves as a repository of knowledge, containing standard operating procedures, relevant media articles, department webpages, contact lists, announcements, links, and an events calendar.
Shared folders	The use of a document repository to provide common access to softcopy documents.
Simple Personnel Online Territory in the Net (SPOTTIN)	The staff create their own personal homepage or 'SPOT' to introduce themselves and their interests. Enables everyone to know each other better, fostering better working relationships.
Websites — Newcomers' Portal	An intranet portal specially designed to cater to PTD newcomers, where they can obtain all the necessary information about PTD, allowing them to better orientate themselves into a new environment.
SPF Discussion Forum	The Discussion Forum allows all staff to participate in active discussions and to exchange ideas.
Project Management Blog	The Project Management Blog pools together PTD's collective wisdom and encourage the discussion and spread of best practices.
Innovation Portal	A portal with various articles and entries that promote innovation in the workplace.
Lectora	Lectora is a software to create and construct e-learning courseware.
e-Learning packages	The following e-learning packages have been completed: Project Management, Access Control Technology, IT Security, SPF ICT Security 101, RFID Technology 101, 3G Manpack, CCTV 101, Introduction to Electro-Optics, EPRS Self-Help User Guide, iDEN Self-Help User Guide, Introduction to IP Telephony, Smart Card 101, WTMD Calibration Self-Help User Guide, eServices 101.

Source: Provided by SPF-PTD.

blogs (e.g. on core topics such as project management) and a discussion forum for idea exchange and validation. Table 7.2 provides an overview of the KM tools and IT-enabled services (such as folders, blogs and e-learning).

Learning and innovation are key activities at PTD, and a specific Innovation Portal provides useful resources on innovation techniques and emerging technologies. The scope of the e-learning courses ranges

Figure 7.11   Learning Blogs.

Source: Provided by SPF-PTD.

from access control technology and IT security to requirement writing and CCTV operation. The Learning Portal is open to all staff of SPF except for core PTD courses residing in the Learning Management System (LMS) (PM 101 and ICT Security — to track the staff's progress). The Learning Portal has a feedback channel and the Learning Blog as avenues to highlight matters regarding training and development (see Figure 7.11).

The KM portal (also known as PTD Learning Portal) was created in-house using a Microsoft-based search engine to crawl the websites for relevant files. It also develop meta-tagging to enable a SharePoint-based photo gallery search.

7.2.10. *Singapore Youth Olympic Games Organising Committee (SYOGOC)*

The core KM approaches at SYOGOC were process mapping, after-action reviews and frequent organisation-wide sharing sessions. Unlike many corporate-wide KM projects, the SYOGOC did not invest in any KM IT system. They leveraged on the Singapore Sports Council's IT system to store the legacy documents after the Games. In the meantime, SYOGOC maximised the usage of the network drives by ensuring a standard file organisation and structure for easy retrieval of documents.

Without the procurement of an IT system, the operating costs remained very low, with more than half of the costs attributed to postage. In this sense, the cost-benefit ratio for the KM initiatives remained relatively low. This relatively unsophisticated IT platform was complemented heavily by 'human processes'.

The network drive was structured to follow the corporate taxonomy, and mirrored the Registry's filing lists. The storage space was divided into major chunks according to the phase and nature of work. The corporate vocabulary dictionary was maintained by the KM team to ensure that the same 'language' was used across different functional areas. The KM team also helped to create many of the organisation-wide templates — this facilitated standardisation of information collected, thus making it more easily sharable. This was complemented by the regular sharing sessions within divisions, and across SYOGOC.

7.2.11. *Supreme Court of Singapore (SC)*

Under the leadership of the Supreme Court's Chief Knowledge Officer, who is also the Registrar/CEO, KM tools and approaches have been integrated into all work processes such that KM becomes second nature to all staff in all areas of work. This thrust is in line with the Supreme Court's overall KM vision, in that the organisation leverages on existing technology platforms to enable ease of use in codifying and sharing information, and to remove barriers that impede knowledge sharing.

In addition to the KM portal, the Knowledge Management Steering Committee (KMSC) has driven the e-Practice Directions and e-Rules of Court programmes which, in line with the paperless filing system that has been put in place through the Electronic Filing System, will provide the Supreme Court's immediate customers, i.e. lawyers and court users, with instantaneous online access to the latest versions of these two bread-and-butter tools of the trade. The KMSC has also been looking into a revamp of the Supreme Court's internet website with the aim of utilising Web 2.0 technologies to better engage the public and stakeholders. These are examples of the Supreme Court's KM efforts in using KM processes like 'creation', 'capturing' and 'reuse' in order to innovate and reach out to external parties.

The Pegs and the Bench Memoranda databases are evidence of the 'collaboration', 'capturing' and 'reuse' sub-components of the 'process' aspect. Both databases capture current legal knowledge, allowing the Justices' Law Clerks to reuse each other's research to avoid wasting time covering the same ground from scratch, and the wiki-style format allows for collaborative work where one person builds upon the work of another. Organised around the legal taxonomy utilised by LawNet, the leading local legal website run by the Singapore Academy of Law, the Pegs database, in combination with the Bench Memoranda database, is one of the first ports of call for Justices' Law Clerks when conducting research for Judges. Plans are currently underway to expand the entries in the Pegs database to include more references to supplement the points of law that currently exists.

The KM portal provides a convenient one-stop resource that captures the results of discussions between the Assistant Registrars in the form of decisions, taken on by matters of civil procedure and administration. These decisions are captured as updates to the material on the Registrars' homepage, such as the Registrars' Duty Manual and the Guidelines and Standard Minute Sheets, ensuring that they are conveniently located when required for use. The decision as to what content makes its way onto to the portal for sharing is determined by the KM Champion of the relevant Directorate or functional group, acting in accordance with a set of guidelines which describe the broad categories of how information should be preserved. Public documents are those that are accessible to all Supreme Court users whereas private documents are those accessible only to particular users or groups of users. The decision as to whether documents are to be treated as public or private is taken by the KM Champion of the relevant directorate or functional group. The KM portal is meant to be the first source of information for the staff from other directorates who want to understand more about the work of a given directorate or who require working-level information from another directorate. Since each directorate's homepage is based upon a template, the staff can easily understand the information architecture of each homepage and swiftly locate the required information.

7.2.12. Urban Redevelopment Authority (URA)

To achieve its goals towards the capturing of sound knowledge and utilisation at varying levels of detail, URA developed a Knowledge Pyramid to categorise various KM efforts within its organisation. The Knowledge Pyramid has four levels: Infrastructure Management (level 1), Explicit Knowledge Management (level 2), Tacit Knowledge Management (level 3), and Intelligence Management (level 4). URA developed an Integrated Information System Architecture Plan to ensure integration and interoperability of various KM systems. Under the plan, the central information database consisting of 6 databases were derived from the integration of over 20 systems. The corporate intranet, appropriately named URANIUM, is a one-stop gateway to a vast repository of information and services for staff. It facilitates communication between the management and staff, information sharing and learning among teams, business KM across groups, and quick access to various e-services.

There are also more than 20 strategic IT systems to facilitate usage and analysis of information. For instance, the electronic Knowledge Repository System (eKRIS) is an enterprise-wide electronic document management system that centrally captures the organisation's unstructured knowledge, automates the registry and facilitates staff to search and retrieve documents online. This knowledge system is also integrated seamlessly with other business application systems to centrally manage unstructured information (e.g document, emails). One of the key eKRIS modules received The Enterprise Challenge's funding and award in Singapore.

The Integrated Planning and Land Use System (iPLAN) is an integrated enterprise Geographic Information System (GIS) utilised by more than 40 percent of the staff to perform various physical planning and urban design functions. The system was conferred the Distinguished Systems Award from the Urban and Regional Information Systems Association in 2007 for exceptional achievements in the application of IT that had improved the delivery and quality of government services.

7.3. Discussion and Insights

Technology is inescapably a part of all but a small number of KM success stories. Successive waves of technology are transforming the way knowledge is experienced and transformed (Norris *et al.*, 2003). Koulopoulos and Frappaolo (1999) predicted that technology will play an important role mainly in managing explicit knowledge, rather than tacit knowledge, which still relies on interpersonal transfer. IT can also increase productivity by releasing people from routine tasks, and instead focus on tasks that require profound human understanding and insights.

Amongst the range of KM tools, content management tools have been extensively used in many organisations, such as AGC, DSTA, MOF and the Supreme Court. In terms of more specific types of KM tools by process and knowledge type such as e-learning and mining tools, various other organisations such as SPF and MOF have implemented them (for knowledge externalisation and extraction). Keen and Mackintosh (2001) explore the use of handheld wireless devices in workflows to "mobilise" existing knowledge and connect experts to remote knowledge workers. Organisations such as SAF are adapting their KM tools to the mobile phone usage habits and preferences of its workforce.

Terra and Gordon (2003) describe the wide range of KM contributions made by powerful enterprise portals. Indeed, the portals constitute the backbone of a range of information and communication tools (see Table 7.3); in the analyses of profiled organisations, KM portals have been effectively implemented by organisations such as AGC, DSTA, IPOS, SAF and SPF. The names chosen for these KM tools reflect internal considerations of branding, e.g. AGC's portal is termed SA-GE, DSTA calls its portal eHabitat, and SAF's intranet is named eSILK. URA's corporate portal is known as URANIUM. Microsoft SharePoint seems to be the most common portal platform across these cases.

In addition to legacy enterprise tools, some organisations have added social media or Web 2.0 components such as blogs (e.g. DSTA,

Table 7.3   KM Tools and Platforms Used in the Singaporean Organisations.

Organisation	KM Tools and Technologies
AGC	Portal (SA-GE), LEAP, ELNMS, repositories, wiki
DSTA	WorkGroups, eHabitat Portal, ASK query system, MyActions, Blogging, eRegistry
IPOS	SharePoint portal, search engine, repositories, wiki
IRAS	KM repository, e-learning
JTC	Corporate Reporting Information Services Portal (CRISP), single access, proper categorisation and search
MOF	MOF Email Repository, Third Sight email mining and management, MOFi intranet Portal, search
NLB	Balanced scorecard, self-service enquiry database, collaboration platforms, blog site
SAF	Intranet, eSILK system, eForum, social media (wikis, blogs)
SPF-PTD	Lotus Notes Email, SharePoint, Project Management Blog, Lectora, Frontpage, Learning Portal, e-learning courses, KM Archetypes Video, internal publication '*Knowledge Times*'
SYOGOC	Planning toolkits, basic network drives, simple templates
SC	Electronic Filing System, KM Portal, wikis, legal databases, secured access
URA	Electronic Knowledge Repository System (eKRIS), corporate intranet (URANIUM), GIS, benchmarking

SAF and SPF) and wikis (e.g. IPOS, AGC, Supreme Court). e-Learning tools for capacity and skills building have also been implemented in a range of organisations, e.g. IRAS, SPF and AGC. Search and query systems for quick knowledge retrieval have been implemented in DSTA (ASK query system) as well as MOF's email management and mining solutions. Many of the collaborative tools focus on project management activities, e.g. SPF's Project Management Blog. On the other hand, SYOGOC stands out in its very simple technology approach: basic network drives and simple templates for information sharing. This is due to the temporary nature of the Olympics as a specific project activity, and should be distinguished from long-term organisational IT infrastructure.

Tools for online CoPs have helped break past traditional departmental barriers. Expertise locator tools have also found use; tools have emerged for dynamic expertise profiling (e.g. email mining) in addition to static approaches. On the narrative tool, KM blogging is being increasingly adopted; for instance, SPF uses blogging tools to share project management experience and lessons. In fact, a number of tools for personal KM are also being used and gaining acceptance, such as social media and social networks.

In summary, even a simple move to a basic digital platform for content storage has helped some organisations realise significant efficiency increases and better knowledge sharing as compared to prior paper-based workflows. KM approaches like collaboration, content management, expertise locators, and integrated learning systems will become increasingly institutionalised into business processes (O'Dell & Grayson, 1998). KM tools have been successfully used in project management, content management, networking, brainstorming and collaborative activities, e.g. enterprise portals have contributed to the creation of knowledge repositories. More sophisticated collaborative tools have helped extend teamwork from internal employees to external partners and customers as well.

CHAPTER EIGHT

Measures and Impacts

"An investment in knowledge pays the best interest."
— Ben Franklin

This chapter focuses on the outputs and outcomes of the KM initiatives in the case studies. It also covers the metrics, in addition to explaining the effectiveness of these measures, and how they guide future actions and policies of KM.

Successful outcomes of KM initiatives include practice and process improvement, increased innovation, enhanced employee capabilities, improved organisational learning, increased business growth and customer satisfaction. These measures can be classified into operational excellence, product/service leadership and customer intimacy (O'Dell *et al.*, 2004). At the end of the day, measures for evaluating KM programmes will be applied; however, the issues surrounding such intangible assets are not easily resolved. For instance, assessing intellectual capital covers not just financial returns but should also include customer satisfaction, employee capability profiles, effective business processes, and charting performance trends (Gamble & Blackwell, 2001).

KM efforts typically focus on organisational objectives such as improved performance, competitive advantage, innovation, the sharing of lessons learned, and continuous improvement of the organisation. These help share valuable organisational insights, reduce redundant work, avoid reinventing the wheel per se, reduce training time for new employees, retain intellectual capital and adapt to changing environments and markets (McAdam & McCreedy, 2000; Thompson & Walsham, 2004).

8.1. KM Impacts: Metrics and Measures

This section reviews the diverse literature on the KM impacts and the pros and cons of KM metrics. According to Allee (2003), KM has helped us move beyond a training perspective to a learning perspective. KM has also helped create a sense of 'oneness' in the organisation, even for new employees who have just joined.

8.1.1. KM Impacts

Holsapple and Singh (2004) analysed a range of KM case studies and classified KM outcomes into four categories: productivity, agility, innovation and reputation (PAIR). These arise as a result of the primary activities in the knowledge chain: knowledge acquisition, selection, generation, internalisation and externalisation. Boland and Yoo (2004) identified the contributions that KM can make to organisational sense-making: It can provide powerful ways to encourage reflective activities.

KM provides two major benefits to an organisation: improving performance (through increased productivity, effectiveness, quality, innovation) and increasing the financial value of the organisation (Hanley & Malafsky, 2004). Key issues to address in KM measurement include: the focus of the measurement instrument, the method of gathering indicators, choosing the right framework and tools, and assessing and aligning the measures to the objectives. Hanley and Malafsky (ibid) also distinguished between KM outcomes and KM outputs; outputs can include reduced time to solve problems, or number of problems solved, or number of apprentices mentored; whereas the outcomes would include reduced operating costs, quality improvement, and customer satisfaction.

KM can also help develop better client-centred knowledge, improve processes, cultivate expertise in areas like project management, and develop knowledge products (Smith & McKeen, 2004). Strategic, tactical and operational KM benefits include improved efficiency, enhanced sustainability and continuity of the organisation, as well as having better synergy between knowledge workers (Ahmed *et al.*, 2002).

Common benchmarks of KM success include innovativeness, coordination, adaptability and responsiveness to changes (Gold *et al.*, 2001).

Cortada *et al.* (1999) noted that some companies (e.g. 3M) clearly understand the potential of KM. For instance, 3M prides itself not only for its ability to 'learn from mistakes' but also to turn them into profitable products, such as the oft-cited 'Post-it Notes' product as an epitome of achieving success through errors.

KM has also been credited for its role in preserving corporate memory, which can help ensure organisational effectiveness by combating the effects of staff turnover (Davenport & Prusak, 1998). Downsizing can create 'knowledge scarcity' with layoffs of personnel with the needed corporate knowledge; KM can help retain this critical knowledge.

8.1.2. *Categories of KM Metrics and Measurement Tools*

Rao (2005) classified KM metrics into five types, depending on their focus: activity (based on tool usage), business process, knowledge (stocks and flows), people (cultural attitudes and performance) and business (economic impacts). Table 8.1 summarises the KM metrics with sample measures in each category.

Far too often, metrics analysis stop short at only one or a few of these five categories. All categories of measures are needed to ensure that KM practices and tools steer the organisation towards the right direction and are delivering value to the organisations. For instance, mere increase in social media communication (an activity metric) after the KM tool deployment need not imply that users are communicating and collaborating more; this may just be an initial novelty effect.

Many early business process re-engineering rollouts improved process efficiency (a process metric), but they sacrificed knowledge exchange opportunities (a knowledge metric). Online communities of practice (CoPs) may increase knowledge contributions (a knowledge metric), but may also promote conforming behaviours and create cliques among employees (a people metric). Many organisations have extensive knowledge repositories (a knowledge metric) and high levels of motivation and retention among employees (a people metric), but are unable to convert this to market leadership and profitability (a business metric). True organisational success, therefore, lies in maximising performance along all the five dimensions of KM metrics listed in Table 8.1.

Table 8.1   Scope of Metrics.

Scope	Sample Parameters
Activity metrics	Number of CoPs, number of emails, usage of online forums, number of database queries, website traffic, duration of portal sessions, number of search queries, number of blogs, number of alerts, number of members on social media
Process metrics	Faster response times to queries, meeting international certification standards, more real-time interactions with clients, tighter collaboration with partners, more direct channels to citizens, more accurate content taxonomies, more secure communications
Knowledge metrics	Number of employee ideas submitted, number of knowledge asset queries, number of knowledge assets reused, best practices created, rate of innovation, active CoPs, knowledge retention, quicker access to knowledge assets, fewer steps to distribute/repackage knowledge ('flow' and 'stock' measures)
People metrics	Degree of bonding with colleagues, improved performance in CoPs, peer validation, feeling of empowerment, growth in trust, satisfaction with reward/recognition, retention in company, more accountability, responsible risk-taking, increased motivation
Organisational metrics	Reduced costs, less travel costs, greater market share, increased citizen satisfaction, customer loyalty, profitable partnerships, conversion of knowledge assets into patents/licenses, improved productivity, risk reduction, crisis management

Source: Summarised from Rao (2005).

It is important to choose the process and business metrics with care. For instance, for more effective metrics, it is better to measure the rate or frequency of employees' contributions than to simply use the amount of contributions in a database or discussion forum; in some cases, quantitative measures can be overlaid on qualitative assessments (e.g. likes and dislikes) or semi-quantitative measures such as employee satisfaction with a KM initiative. Also, actual customer satisfaction is a better success measure than mere reduction in the number of customer calls to a contact centre. Anecdotes or testimonials from employees and customers can sometimes be more convincing as a measure than mere numbers of call centre traffic. Another way of analysing these metrics is by their nature: quantitative, qualitative or semi-quantitative, as summarised in Table 8.2.

Table 8.2 Quantitative and Qualitative KM Metrics.

Nature of Metrics	Sample Parameters
Quantitative	— Reduced clerical work, less duplication of documents, reduced admin costs, less paper flow, reduced telecommunications costs, lower travel costs, lower customer service costs
Semi-Quantitative	— Productivity (e.g. reduced training time, speedier information access) — Satisfaction (e.g. improved morale, job satisfaction) — Knowledge assets (e.g. usage of portal, reuse of best practices)
Qualitative	— Better innovation, reduced knowledge hoarding, empowered frontline, stories/anecdotes

Source: Summarised from Rao (2005).

There are also numerous organisational measurement tools, such as the balanced scorecard (financial results, customers, internal business processes, and learning), benchmarks tools by APQC, Celemi, Skandia Navigator, and the Intellectual Capital Index. Further, new kinds of 'knowledge toolboxes' are called for to effectively measure human capital and organisational culture elements like trust; stakeholder knowledge values; employee (self-actualisation), customer (product adoption capability), and the top management (cohesiveness, motivation).

8.1.3. Challenges in KM Measurement

There are frequent debates on how well KM impacts can be measured, how often they should be measured, and whether practitioners are paying adequate or excessive attention to impact measurement. The 'Achilles heel' of KM is the measurement of performance beyond mere anecdotes (Rumizen, 2002). Quantitative and qualitative metrics for actionable understanding should target return on investment, barriers to the sharing of knowledge, employee attitude and aptitude, level of knowledge standardisation, maturity levels of KM systems, and assessment of intellectual capital and knowledge assets.

A number of discussions continue to focus on the value and limits of KM metrics and return on investment. For instance, some practitioners argue that excessive measurement can be 'overkill', yet others justify it from a chief financial officer's (CFO) point of view of accountability. The challenge in KM metrics, however, is proving causality rather than just correlation. Some practitioners observed that measures of KM success should also include the engaging of associates, knowledge enablement, continuous improvement, operational effectiveness, productivity improvement, accelerated innovation cycle, and higher employee motivation.

8.2. Perspectives from the Case Studies

This section describes the KM outcomes and outputs of KM implementation in the case studies covering the qualitative and quantitative impacts of the KM initiatives that include measures such as productivity, quality, learning, satisfaction and innovation.

8.2.1. *Attorney-General's Chambers (AGC)*

With the implementation of KM, AGC has been able to handle the increasing workload both in quantity and complexity without a proportional increase in manpower. For instance, it has been able to comply with various ministries' request for shorter turnaround times for legal advice despite the stringent approval processes, which require evaluation of previous queries and responses, and ensuring the accuracy of the advice given. As the legal advisor of the government and the guardian of the public interest, it is important for AGC to maintain a clear and consistent legal stand. KM is essential for ensuring that its officers render legal advice based on the best available knowledge. It also helps to ensure that where departures from the past are required, it must be because there has been a considered decision, informed by a re-assessment of previous advice, and not because of any lack of awareness of past legal advice.

Its KM portal brings together both internal and external legal knowledge resources. Access to the organisation's authoritative policies and past advice is of utmost importance to ensure "quality legal services through the bold, effective, swift and thorough application of knowledge and experience". KM allows easier and faster location of relevant information. In the past, finding the relevant paper file would often depend on the memory of individual officers and even then, it was necessary to pore through multiple volumes of files to locate the material. With electronic search, the process which previously could take days or weeks could be achieved more thoroughly in a matter of minutes or hours.

KM also enhances team collaboration and coordination with the use of the committee and division webpages, duty rosters, group calendars and discussion forums. This is especially important for AGC as it currently has more than 300 staff and is still expanding.

KM in Action at AGC: Quotes/Testimonials

(a) Jefry Bin Mohamad
(Chief Registry Officer, Legislation and Law Reform Division)

"With the emergence of the KM portal in AGC, officers and staff (including myself) have benefited from the enormous capability of this technology as information on the KM portal is readily searchable across different platforms/databases, hence, improving operational efficiency and performance standards."

(b) David Chew
(Deputy Public Prosecutor / Senior State Counsel, Economic Crimes and Governance Division)

"We recognised from early on that if we hoard information, we will not get far as an organisation; yet we need to find a balance between public-sensitive information (where a need-to-know policy is applicable) and the need to share the latest developments both on the legal as well as policy front. This used to be shared through informal networks when AGC was a small organisation but as we got larger and our job disciplines got more varied, we specialised into special directorates, and it became necessary to concretise KM into something that we can pass on. KM has existed to fit a clear felt need that keeps it relevant. We have evolved from hardcopy directives and submissions into softcopy html webpages (in the 1990s) to a sophisticated KM portal. KM will always be a 'work in progress'. KM has to evolve with our needs; it has already evolved with our growth in size and complexity."

As a result of AGC's success in implementing its KM, it has received numerous requests for sharing and demonstrations of its KM and information technology (IT) systems from other government agencies, both local and foreign. Indeed, its KM effort also resulted in improved transfer for learning and shorter learning curves for new officers. With easy access to the collective wisdom of the organisation, and the best thinking and experience of their senior colleagues, junior officers have been shown to progress more quickly to perform higher-level work.

8.2.2. Defence Science and Technology Agency (DSTA)

In terms of KM impacts at DSTA, the overhauled approach to managing web content helped to ensure timely updates and the sharing of information on the intranet. It has also changed the learning culture in the organisation. DSTA has learned that to encourage sharing, the information update process must not be restricted to only a few staff. Instead, the approach should be catered to the masses and the steps to do so should be few and simple. Consequently, the staff are now more interested to share information.

The new Centre for Information Management harnesses existing resources to better organise the knowledge repository, and to create synergy between document filing and knowledge sharing. It helped to reduce the duplication of effort and resources as well as the potential risk of loss of records. Inconsistencies in practices and workflow among the various registry teams were removed. The streamlined Information Resource Management framework has led to archiving accountability, productivity, and effectiveness in daily operations. Capacity has been increased for more advanced KM practices such as coalition and collaboration among various communities.

DSTA is now widely regarded as being a public agency right at the forefront of KM. To date, more than 25 statutory boards and government organisations have requested briefings or arranged KM learning visits to DSTA to understand its successful KM program. The organisations include the Civil Aviation Authority of Singapore, Civil Service College, Corrupt Practices Investigation Bureau, Defence Science Organsation, National Laboratories, Economic Development Board, Government of Singapore Investment Corporation, Housing Development Board, Health Promotion Board, Infocomm Development Authority of Singapore, Intellectual Property Office of Singapore, Jurong Town Corporation, Land Transport Authority, Ministry of Home Affairs, Ministry of Information, Communication and The Arts,

Ministry of National Development, Ministry of Finance, Ministry Of Manpower, National Archives of Singapore, National Library, National Environment Authority, Singapore Sports Council and the Supreme Court. Overseas institutions such as the National Science and Technology Development Agency of Thailand and the Bank of Thailand have also visited DSTA to learn about its KM journey.

8.2.3. Intellectual Property Office of Singapore (IPOS)

IPOS uses the following proposed calculation to determine efficiency: the percentage difference in time spent on a manual process as compared to one automated via KENNY (Knowledge ENterprise 'N You). IPOS estimates the actual usage of the portal to be about 75 percent and thus will continue to urge its KM Committee members to encourage more active participations. It also monitors the effectiveness of KENNY by the number of contributions and number of processes automated (see Table 8.3). IPOS finds this method effective as it approaches and deals with individual problems.

Quotes and testimonials from users of the IPOS KM portal

"KENNY has streamlined many work processes and allowed quick access to department information from a single webpage."
"KENNY is a useful platform for keeping the department's work in good order."
"KENNY is an excellent platform for intra-departmental sharing and collaborations as well as to function as a knowledge repository."
"In the beginning, I needed to adapt myself to KENNY as it was a totally new platform for me. With much practice, I have come to realise that KENNY is user-friendly."
"It is a resource where institutional knowledge can be retained/captured and where the rationale of our policies and decisions can be tracked. KM also aids in helping new staff to be more efficient and effective in their work."

8.2.4. Inland Revenue Authority of Singapore (IRAS)

IRAS sharing sessions have made a number of notable contributions towards the organisation's KM success. It assisted the development

Table 8.3   KM Benefits at IPOS.

Business Benefit	Illustration
1. Efficiency/ Cost savings	An online library service, built from scratch and customised using SharePoint's out-of-box features, meant that we have been able to discontinue an external electronic library system which was costing IPOS *S$9,000 every year.*
2. Service improvement 3. Customer satisfaction 4. Employee satisfaction	Among some of the automated business processes IPOS KM Representatives have put together are: ○ Legal advice to IPOS departments: a series of discussion boards per department, assigned to specific legal advisors. New queries along with uploaded contracts are posted for advice from assigned legal counsels. This board utilises the Alert Me function ○ Vendor contract renewals: a custom list outlining said function (so that contracts are renewed on time and service disruption minimised) ○ A CRM-type customer history log documenting service, data and exchange of information between customers and service personnel ○ Online library management system enabling staff to browse books, journals, magazines, newsletters etc. and borrow them online All of the above illustrate a significant improvement of service and a degree of meeting both internal and external customer satisfaction.
5. Greater innovation capacity	In our last KENNY Training for Site Administrator where 90 percent of attendees were SharePoint Administrator certified, attendees were expected to submit assignments of an automated process they have implemented within their departments. At the end of this training, 14 submissions for automated process customised utilising KEN's out-of-box features across 14 departments were recognized. This translates to 73.6 percent automation.
6. Improved learning processes	With almost all key information and departmental processes already available in the KM portal, new staff need only log in, access and orientate. The handover process has reportedly increased 50 percent in efficiency.

Source: Provided by IPOS.

of employees' competence and commitment. Staff at various levels recognised the importance of knowledge sharing and felt significant progress had been made. Indeed, the sharing sessions improved the staff's presentation skills, built teamwork and enhanced the pride and passion in working together as part of the IRAS family. The mindset of learning from successes as well as failures further enhances the organisational capacity for innovation.

In a recent Organisational Climate Survey (OCS), the staff were asked to identify two to three areas where they felt IRAS has done well. For both of the surveys done in 2007 and 2009, one third of the OCS participants identified the Learning and Sharing category as one of the areas in which IRAS has excelled. In 2009, the Learning and Sharing category was again most frequently mentioned by the staff as an outstanding area in IRAS.

KM Testimonials at IRAS

"Knowledge is shared and easily available online in iNex [IRAS' intranet]. The management fully encourages learning and sharing."

"There are many opportunities to learn, by attending sharing sessions organised by other branches, attending workshops, and courses. IRAS actively encourages staff to seek more knowledge and share knowledge with peers."

There is an improvement in percentage of OCS participants who scored the Learning and Sharing category favourably as shown in the OCS results for 2004 (67 percent), 2007 (69 percent) and 2009 (76 percent). Results for this category demonstrated that IRAS' overall score is better than Singapore's national norm by 1 percent for OCS 2007 and by 4 percent for OCS 2009. A KM evaluation done in 2009 revealed that Branch Heads appreciate the improvement in knowledge through the sharing sessions. In the KM Strategy Review Project in 2007, IRAS' consultants then mapped out the organisation's cultural KM archetypes based on surveys and focus groups conducted among various levels of IRAS staff, and found that there was a good knowledge-sharing culture in IRAS.

In 2009, according to the Information Architecture Review, the consultants shared that the culture of learning and sharing within IRAS is strong and pervasive, with systems in place to support learning and encourage sharing on different levels. The number of IRAS sharing sessions averaged 24 per year for the last two financial years, and on average, more than 80 percent of the auditorium was filled for each sharing session.

8.2.5. *Jurong Town Corporation (JTC)*

Impacts of the System of Business Information (SOBI) solution include clear ownership and responsibility, improved awareness of the policies and procedures across the organisation, increased collaboration between the subject matter experts, more confidence and trust, quick and easy access to a large pool of knowledge resource, consolidated feedback from after-action reviews (AARs) auto triggers, scalability and quick setup, and extension beyond Policies and Processes clusters.

Its key KM initiatives were conceptualised and implemented based on the KM vision and premised upon the four key pillars of content, process, technology, and culture/people. Such an approach was crucial to ensure integration with the overall KM framework as well as to ensure the success of these projects in contributing to the organisational excellence. These clear and strongly positive outcomes are evident in the following key KM initiatives: SOBI, Knowledge@Work, Corporate Reporting Information Services Portal (CRISP) and the KM Activist Network. Figure 8.1 shows the workspace of JTC.

Workspace impacts have increased staff familiarity with regards to creation and usage of collaboration tools, better capture and organisation of relevant information and knowledge, and knowledge reuse, especially those benefiting new entrants or existing staff who are new to an area of work, i.e. the workspace facilitates a shorter learning curve. The list of workspaces are centralised at the Knowledge@Work website and the staff can quickly look for information in a particular area of work.

8.2.6. *Ministry of Finance (MOF)*

MOF's staff have adapted smoothly to the KM solution (based on email management, taxonomy and repository), and have grown to rely on the central database as a means of referring to and referencing various emails. Compared to various attempts in the past to

Knowledge@Work Portal

Figure 8.1   JTC's Workspace.

Source: Provided by JTC.

Table 8.4   Results of a Survey on the Email Repository System.

- 144 out of 200 staff (72 percent) participated in the survey.
- 100 percent are aware of the MOF email repository system (MOF ERS).
- 78.5 percent are agreeable or strongly agreeable that MOF ERS allows them to retrieve information easily.
- 75 percent are agreeable or strongly agreeable that MOF ERS does not interfere in the way they usually work.
- 87.5 percent are generally positive about using MOF ERS.

Source: Provided by MOF.

implement a form of KM within the organisation, the implementation of the MOF Email Repository is one of the few that has proven to be successful (see Table 8.4).

With a total of 279,057 emails posted in a recent six month period (for more details of its usage, see Tables 8.5 and 8.6), the MOF Email Repository has effectively served to institutionalise and retain corporate correspondences and transactions. The average number of content shared per user is 1,274 emails. The system has helped create the foundation for corporate institutional memory as well as facilitate knowledge sharing throughout the organisation. In the initial stage, almost 75 percent of emails posted were put into personal folders. Currently,

Table 8.5   Number of Posts in Oct 09–Mar 10 and Apr 10–Oct 10.

	Oct 09–Mar 10	Apr 10–Sep 10
Number of users	247	229
Number of posts made	10,4251	10,3614
Average number of posts made monthly	17,375.2	17,269
Average number of posts per staff per month	70.3	75.4
Average number of posts per staff per day	3.2	3.42

Source: Provided by MOF.

Table 8.6   Number of Reads in Oct 09–Mar 10 and Apr 10–Oct 10.

	Oct 09–Mar 10	Apr 10–Sep 10
Number of users	247	229
Number of reads	10,006	11,037
Average number of reads made monthly	1,667.7	1,839.5
Average number of reads per staff per month	6.8	8
Average number of reads per staff per day	0.31	0.37

Source: Provided by MOF.

60 percent of emails are filed into corporate folders while 40 percent are classified into personal folders.

News of the successful implementation of the MOF Email Repository spread across a number of agencies within the Singapore Public Service. With many requests to visit MOF for sharing its implementation, the MOF KM team conducted a mass sharing session, attended by 36 government ministries and statutory boards on March 5, 2009. Having heard how the MOF KM team shared their journey of implementation, it is interesting to note that various agencies are hence contemplating the same product and some are even in the stage of procuring the system.

8.2.7. National Library Board (NLB)

NLB's Knowledge Champions programme is deemed as one of the key contributors to the overall KM efforts in creating a collaborative culture in the organisation. Of the 24 techniques taught, 60 percent of the techniques practiced during the course were described by the

Knowledge Champions to have helped them in recognising a tangible value (better, faster, and cheaper), whilst 30 percent of the techniques practiced resulted in an indirect value (building knowledge culture). Indeed, NLB has realised a number of benefits from its Network of Specialists (NOS) system as follows:

- *Service quality* — By enabling collaboration and sharing of knowledge in an efficient and effective manner, the system has made a significant impact on the service quality of the NLB's Enquiry Service, on top of bringing with it many other benefits.
- *Efficiency improvement* — The staff no longer need to spend hours relentlessly searching for answers to challenging enquiries as the system efficiently allows them to tap onto their mutual expertise and capabilities and that of external experts. This increases the staff's productivity and saves them valuable time. On average, the time taken for a reference librarian to answer a challenging reference enquiry is 5 man-days. By escalating the enquiry to the NOS platform, the staff are able to respond to the customer within 3 man-days. An average of 8–10 reference enquiries are sent to the NOS platform monthly and hence there is a total saving of 20 man-days per month or 240 man-days per year.
- *Quality improvement* — The system facilitates the depth and breadth of knowledge sharing and improves the quality of answers to library customers. Answers are enriched by a whole community of specialists contributing to an enquiry on NOS instead of just one respondent.
- *Customer satisfaction* — The numerous compliments from library customers are strong evidence of their satisfaction with the substantial list of recommended resources sent to them.
- *Employee satisfaction* — This improves learning curves for new employees, and staff are happy as they enjoy the benefits of sharing and collaborating and they are able to bring about a better level of service to customers. New staff or staff who are not knowledgeable in the subject areas can also learn and enhance their reference capabilities by viewing the discussion threads and contributions made in the subject communities. All these have led to an exponential growth in knowledge within the division.
- *Greater innovation capacity* — The collaborative platform has led the project team to further innovate in the areas of KM. A new project looks into the packaging of the reference enquiries and answers into

a self-service enquiry database for librarians and library customers to access and reuse.

- *Better reference and advisory services* — The provision of reference and advisory service is an important and core function of NLB. The system has helped librarians to discover knowledge experts, to share and to collaborate. The end result is a higher and better level of reference and advisory service for all library customers.

Citizen Testimonials: Effective Responses from NLB

(i) "Well done! A comprehensive response to my enquiry. Appreciate the provision of various website addresses. The directory posted on the 'For You Magazine' website is especially useful."

(ii) "I'm so happy! Just read the attachment after replying to your email a few seconds ago. The short write-up of Mr. Yong Nyuk Lin is good enough for my NE display board. FYI, I have been searching for Mr. Yong's info for quite some time. Finally it is done!"

8.2.8. *Singapore Armed Forces (SAF)*

The SAF KM initiative has had a number of positive impacts, and yielded useful learnings as well as recommendations for other KM practitioners. The key outcomes are described as follows:

Accelerating the creation and sharing of expert knowledge

By creating knowledge nodes and a networked-enabled SAF, a whole range of divisions, formations, and combat units can now provide rapid, integrated mission support. Anecdotal evidence shows how a dental assistant on a mission in Afghanistan was able to use expert knowledge and lessons learned resulting in rapid, integrated mission support.

Providing SAF with multiple, deep knowledge resources

KM has provided knowledge resources in training, operations, systems development, and administration. The creation of knowledge communities in the training and operations area has increased their effectiveness, by providing SAF with a strong and large enterprise-level operational experience for planning, doctrine development and decision-making. Through sharing knowledge in systems development, the complexities in systems integration have been mitigated, resulting in a key transformation enabler in the build-up of the 3rd Generation SAF. For example, a significant indicator of this improvement is the reduction in the rate of safety violations. Determinants of success are in the anecdotes collected from CoP members, the new ideas emerging out of the communities, and repeated engagement and participation.

The Enterprise Content Management (ECM) tool in the eRegistry system allowed for a significant reduction of administrative support staff workload, enabling relocation of five personnel, which translated into a 10 percent reduction of support costs (and a subsequent 10 percent increase in personnel available for other priorities).

Throughout 2008 and 2009 there was an average increase of 23 blogs and 25 wikis each month, to a current total of 867 active blogs and 841 active wikis. Further, in 2008, there was an average of 20 forums created per month, and by 2009 there was an average of 26 per month. One of the more successful communities is the Joint Capability Development Hub, where planners across the three services identify staff officers from their respective Plans departments to be co-located at the Joint Staff level; of which on a daily basis they sustain each service abreast of what the other services are doing and collaboration is supported at this level via eSILK.

A more effective networked structure

There is now a more effective networked structure across the MINDEF/SAF, and better online training that can be engaged as and when required. For example, an Army KM office with a CKO currently provides governance, support, facilitation of process changes, and the design of education and training activities that directly and continuously support SAF's 'Learning Army, Thinking Soldier' vision. Increased networking reduces time for making decisions and improves the quality of those decisions, leading to faster response and improved effectiveness of mission implementation. This was evident during on-the-ground relief efforts in Bandar Aceh and Medan. It only took a couple of days for logistics support to move into an intelligent systems approach, becoming a comprehensive, tight and responsive system that could deliver the right aid to the right people at the right time.

Testimonial by MWO[1] Toh Chen Seng, OC CCIS[2], Signal Institute

"The Enterprise System for Innovation, Learning, and Knowledge (eSILK) has not only moved the SAF into 3rd Generation information handling, but also been integral in accelerating and improving the manner in which I am able to conduct my work.

For instance, the information organised on eSILK enables me to quickly and comprehensively search for resources across the SAF and extract them using the 'search' and 'wiki' functions. This is especially critical when time is of essence.

Following a Signal Institute Commander Conference, I would use eSILK to extract relevant documents to aid my crafting of a particular proposal or paper. I have noticed that the time taken to complete my work has decreased as a result. Furthermore, any redundancies can be counter-checked against by simply keying in the key phrases used in my document.

Gaining a broader insight into the work of my colleagues in the SAF has also been easier through interfacing with eSILK. Being able to read up prior to supporting any joint activities places me in a better position to address the various operational requirements of external units.

The Command and Control Information Systems Training Company in Signal Institute prides itself in contributing to training and shaping the network administration landscape in the SAF. In this context, the eSILK is a truly an asset in an information organisation. I see obvious benefits from the continued use and development of eSILK."

8.2.9. *Singapore Police Force: Police Technology Department (SPF-PTD)*

SPF-PTD has analysed specific aspects of its KM infrastructure and their impacts, as well as overall cumulative impacts of its KM initiative. For example, the Newcomers' Portal helped new employees integrate swiftly, and the Project Management Blog helped younger managers learn from the experience of their seniors. Other high-level metrics tracked productivity, employee satisfaction, and external impacts.

---

[1] Master Warrant Officer.
[2] Officer Commanding, Command Control and Information Systems.

Impacts of the portal and blog

The Newcomers' Portal provided a friendly environment that made newcomers feel more welcomed than was previously the case. The portal directed newcomers towards key information they required for their first week of work, which also aided them to feel comfortable in a new environment. This included the director's welcome message, organisation structure of PTD, nearest eating places, FAQ, and a list of useful websites.

The younger project managers found the Project Management Blog to be a useful platform for them to learn from their seniors. It provided firsthand narratives on important issues like how to secure export licenses for sensitive equipment, best practices in managing vendors, and so on. The Personal Home Page (SPOTTIN) has enabled PTD officers to know one another better. There was almost full participation; officers who may not know each other well were now able to visit their colleagues' home pages to learn more about their hobbies, vacations, likes and dislikes.

High-level metrics

PTD has also tracked higher-level impacts at the level of productivity, employee satisfaction, innovation and overall performance. To elaborate:

- *Productivity metrics* — reported significant efficiency improvements (e.g. cost savings) and quality improvement (e.g. better project management through sharing, less repeated mistakes).
- *Employee metrics* — witnessed better employee satisfaction from the staff, particularly in the area of development. More officers also embrace lifelong learning. There is an improved learning curve for new employees, e.g. through the Newcomers' Portal, e-learning packages (e.g. Smart Card 101 e-learning) and induction programmes. There is also better responsiveness to change; people have become aware of the need for lifelong learning and developing agility to change.
- *External stakeholder metrics* — reported significant improvements in the annual customer satisfaction survey and improved responsiveness to customer requests and feedback. Customer care has improved due to the new processes, a new reward system (CARROT), and

a weekly email broadcast on Tips for Customer Care. There was also better partner and stakeholder satisfaction, e.g. better customer engagement through regular meet-the-customer sessions with the Operations Department, Criminal Investigation Department, Traffic Police, Commercial Affairs Department, and Security Industry Regulatory Department.

- *Innovation metrics* — has greater innovation capacity through the Innovation website, as stories are shared from outside the Singapore Police Force, thus increasing bandwidth and timeliness in awareness of relevant technology innovations in the security industry.
- *Business metrics* — credits its business success with avoidance of business risk; for instance, its project management risk is reduced through PMP Certification and narrative features such as the Project Management Blog. Customer service has improved, and AARs have improved future operations. The alignment of the KM strategy to PTD's business strategy has been a crucial success factor.

8.2.10. *Singapore Youth Olympic Games Organising Committee (SYOGOC)*

The activity and action review processes in SYOGOC helped formalise the learning culture, shorten learning curves, and leave behind a valuable legacy both for Singapore and for international sporting organisations.

Formalising a learning culture

Having gone through three rounds of the division knowledge workshops, and various rounds of venue workshops, staff became familiarised with the conduct of AARs. In fact such reviews became so common that divisions no longer needed the KM team to help facilitate sessions. Often, the AARs were planned during debrief sessions for upcoming test events without any prompting needed by the KM team. It was such an accepted phenomenon that variants of it started appearing: for instance, the plus/delta exercise initiated by the Workforce Division that was done at the end of selected Executive Group meetings. In addition, sharing sessions that followed each series of AARs became expected occurrences within the organisation. This was further reinforced by other types of sharing sessions facilitated by the KM team, for instance, the overseas trip sharing sessions and the post Asian Youth Games sharing session.

Shortening the learning curves of venue planning teams

The venue planning toolkit that the KM team helped to develop proved to be very useful to the venue planning teams. It guided the venue planning teams on specific activities that needed to be completed and corresponding deliverables that needed to be submitted. Initially, many venue planning teams had little knowledge of what venue planning was all about. This was made worse by the lack of reference resources on the subject matter. The toolkit, developed by the first venue planning team, reassured them that what they set out to do was indeed achievable.

In addition, the toolkit helped to standardise the venue planning process across all the venue planning teams. This was extremely important because quite often the same functional area staff had to attend different venue planning sessions. With a standard process, it was easier for functional area staff to understand what was required and to contribute effectively, as the planning process used in one venue is the same as that for another venue. Using the venue planning toolkit as a guide, more than 30 venue planning teams were able to get their plans approved and 25 venue operating manuals were completed by January 2010.

Leaving a legacy for Singapore and international sporting organisations

The outputs of the KM activities were consolidated and incorporated into post-Games reports. These reports serve as useful references for other Games organisers who are planning for events of a similar scale. The contents of the reports can thus be shared via debrief sessions to key stakeholders like the IOC and future organising committees of the Youth Olympics Games.

8.2.11. Supreme Court of Singapore (SC)

KM at the Supreme Court has paid off in its key performance indicators (KPI) despite overall increases in case filings. For instance, since 2005 the Supreme Court has met or exceeded its target of disposing of 85 percent of all writ actions within 18 months of being filed in court (see

Table 8.7　Monitoring the Supreme Court's KPI.

Year	Period Filed	No. of Writs Filed	No. of Writs Disposed of Within 18 Months	Percentage of Writs Disposed of Within 18 Months to Writs Filed (KPI)
2006	July 04–June 05	1216	1055	87
2007	July 05–June 06	1071	906	85
2008	July 06–June 07	1040	914	88
2009	July 07–June 08	1080	961	89

Source: Provided by the Supreme Court.

Table 8.7). Indeed, it is recognised internationally for its efficiency and effectiveness. Employee interviews by third party assessors (e.g. from iKMS) reveal steady improvements in its willingness to share, and in the usefulness of the KM resources. New officers acknowledged that they were enabled to raise their competency levels swiftly. There is also an active culture of proactive learning and sharing, with supporting processes including horizon scanning.

Workflow Impacts

The most observable change within work processes is the evolution of the Justice KM Portal as the main operating platform for all work processes done by all Supreme Court staff. There has also been an increase in sharing of working as well as technical knowledge, including sharing of experiences and learning points after completion of major projects such as The Living Courthouse and iBE certification. This is done not only at the director level, but also amongst staff committees. Examples would include the institutionalisation of the activities and action reviews, which previously was not used often, and an increase in the regular staff lecture series conducted. The core material identified by the KM Champions and Activists forms the current nucleus of knowledge and information for sharing on the KM Portal. This has enabled the KM Portal to become the first port of call for anyone seeking information from a particular directorate. Judicial Officers' meetings are specific to the Assistant Registrars and are held regularly on a monthly basis. It is only with consistency that litigants and lawyers will know what to expect when filing a particular application and this translates directly into cost savings for parties, and the saving of judicial time in dealing with applications.

Performance impacts

In successfully executing its core organisational strategy, the Supreme Court has maintained a high level of performance, in terms of meeting and exceeding various targets in its portfolio of operational results.

- *Clearance rates and waiting times* — These goals are supported primarily by core organisational strategies, in particular the innovative IT solutions to improve service delivery, where Supreme Court utilised an electronic filing system to digitise court documents, so as to facilitate time-savings in case management. Without these, court processes would be paper-based and more time-consuming. Tried-and-tested case management strategies were another important KM contribution, where the Statistics and Learning Unit was formed and the Application and Case E-management System was developed to monitor case management processes. These two key KM initiatives enabled the Supreme Court to monitor case progress, for the betterment of efficient case management. Indeed, the Supreme Court's clearance rate (percentage of cases disposed of over those filed) for all civil and criminal actions has been very healthy (above 95 percent). And for its waiting periods of court processes, it endeavours to achieve 90 percent compliance of all targets set for waiting periods in various court processes, and these have been consistently achieved.
- *Customer satisfaction* — This achievement is aided by the Supreme Court's KM initiatives including morning briefing sessions by the Legal Directorate (where staff have the opportunity to share customer service practices and to provide feedback to management for process improvements) and the drive to create a knowledge-sharing culture allowing improvements to be made (demonstrated by a high customer satisfaction rate). The Supreme Court targets to get 90 percent of the respondents in its Annual Customer Satisfaction Survey to rate themselves as 'Usually' and 'Always' satisfied with its services. This target has been consistently achieved and maintained.
- *International standing in judicial systems rankings* — In order for the public to have confidence in Singapore's Judiciary, it was imperative that Judicial Officers and Legal Directorate staff be well-informed of case management procedures and updates in law when performing

their duties. The KM initiatives that enabled swift updating of the Registrars' Duty Manuals, Counter Manuals and the like, as well as the sharing of judicial policies during regular Judicial Officers' meetings, ensured that the Supreme Court is well-ahead of the curve in the areas of law. Supreme Court plays its role in ensuring top rankings in international survey results such as IMD and PERC, which reflected not only the public's confidence in the Judiciary, but also the world's confidence in Singapore's Judiciary.

8.2.12. Urban Redevelopment Authority (URA)

The KM framework has aided URA in formulating a clearer roadmap to identify, consolidate and formalise all its KM-related projects. It has also helped to provide a better mutual understanding of KM and to ensure alignment of KM efforts with corporate business objectives.

More specifically, CoPs, learning forums and review meetings have collectively fostered sharing, learning and collaboration in the organisation. The Integrated Planning and Land Use System was bestowed the Distinguished Systems Award from the Urban and Regional Information Systems Association in August 2007 for their outstanding application of IT that improved the delivery and quality of government services. In addition, one of the key eKRIS (electronic Knowledge Repository Information System) modules received an award and funding from The Enterprise Challenge.

8.3. Discussion and Insights

Holsapple and Singh (2004) organised KM outcomes into four categories: productivity, agility, innovation, and reputation. Among these, innovation impacts have been realised in cases such as IRAS whilst productivity improvements were found in a wider range of organisations, such as AGC, DSTA, SAF and SPF. Boland and Yoo (2004) maintained that KM can aid organisational sense-making and reflective activities; and such contributions were witnessed in DSTA, IPOS and IRAS. KM benefits include better synergies between knowledge workers as shown in SPF; a well-designed KM initiative could also help an organisation learn from both mistakes and successes, as seen in MOF. KM had also been credited for its role in preserving corporate memory in the face of staff turnover as shown in MOF.

Rao (2005) explains that qualitative metrics of KM should also be addressed in assessments, and these can include anecdotes, stories and testimonials. Employee testimonials have been provided in the KM journeys of Singapore's AGC, IPOS, IRAS and SAF. Specific quantitative assessments for the return of investment have been derived from organisations such as IPOS, IRAS, MOF and the Supreme Court. In brief, based on the literature review and case study snapshots, the KM impacts for the profiled organisations can be classified into the following four categories: process, knowledge, people, and organisation. These four categories, analysed in Table 8.8 and clustered in Table 8.9, cover efficiency, quality, knowledge resources, learning times, risk management and innovation.

Query and search times were reduced within a number of organisations (e.g. AGC), thus resulting in an improved quality of service. Workflow processes were streamlined (e.g. IPOS) and collaboration and intra-departmental sharing were improved in several cases (e.g. AGC, IPOS). KM also improved employees' willingness to share knowledge (e.g. SC).

Also, employees were better able to locate experts (e.g. DSTA), and community engagement improved (e.g. DSTA). At the level of risk management, KM aided detection of tax fraud (e.g. IRAS), reduced safety violations (e.g. SAF) and reduced overall risk (e.g. SPF). On the learning front, KM accelerated the training of new hires (e.g. IPOS), improved mentoring (e.g. SAF) and proactive learning (e.g. SC). As for knowledge stocks, KM helped the retention of critical knowledge (e.g. IPOS) and created a foundation for corporate institutional memory (e.g. MOF).

In terms of the people matrix, people evolved in terms of competency and commitment (e.g. IRAS). Employee satisfaction improved in a number of organisations (e.g. SPF). In terms of capacity, KM improved capabilities to resolve complex cases (e.g. IRAS). At higher levels, KM led to informed decision-making and industry thought leadership (e.g. DSTA) as well as greater innovation (e.g. IRAS, SPF), more effective networked structure (e.g. SAF), and clarity of long-term roadmaps (e.g. URA). Externally, customer satisfaction was also positively impacted (e.g. SPF, SC) and lessons were transferred to other international bodies (e.g. SYOGOC).

An intriguing set of questions arises on valuing the organisational KM practice. At what level do these measures apply? How is anecdotal information assessed? How urgent is it to come up with value measures

Table 8.8 KM Impacts in Singaporean Organisations.

Organisation	KM Impacts
AGC	Ability to handle increasing workload, shorter turnaround times for advice, quality legal services, search time in minutes rather than weeks, enhanced collaboration
DSTA	Better location of expertise, extended space for learning, better community engagement, quicker connections, informed decision-making, thought leadership
IPOS	Improved efficiency, streamlined work processes, one-stop access, better intra-departmental sharing, retention of critical knowledge, faster training of new hires
IRAS	Greater organisation-wide awareness, improved capabilities to resolve complex cases and detect signs of tax fraud, resolving cases more expeditiously, more competent and committed people, greater innovation capacity
JTC	Increased collaboration between SMEs, more confidence and trust, consolidated feedback, scalability and quick setup, knowledge reuse by new entrants
MOF	Retention of important corporate correspondences, foundation for the corporate institutional memory
NLB	Better enquiry service, less search time, shorter learning curves, employee satisfaction, greater innovation capacity
SAF	Accelerating the creation and sharing of expert knowledge, reduction of safety violations, reduction of administrative support staff workload, more effective networked structure, better online training, better mentoring
SPF-PTD	Quicker and more insightful learning for new hires, more familiarity between employees, cost savings, better employee satisfaction, better customer satisfaction, greater innovation capacity, reduced risk
SYOGOC	Effective execution of Games, useful insights for next Games
SC	Improvements in willingness to share, more usefulness of KM resources, writs disposed faster, quicker clearance of cases, speedy attainment of competence for new officers, proactive learning, customer satisfaction
URA	Clearer roadmap, increased learning and collaboration in the organisation, improved delivery and quality of government services

Table 8.9   KM Impacts by Category.

Category	Impacts
Process metrics	Ability to handle increasing workload, shorter turnaround times for advice, quality legal services, search time in minutes rather than weeks, enhanced collaboration, better community engagement, quicker connections, improved efficiency, streamlined work processes, one-stop access, better enquiry service, less search time, reduction of administrative support staff workload
Knowledge metrics	Better intra-departmental sharing, extended space for learning, better location of expertise, retention of critical knowledge, faster training of new hires, greater organisation-wide awareness, retention of important corporate correspondences, foundation for corporate institutional memory, accelerating the creation and sharing of expert knowledge, quicker and more insightful learning for new hires, speedy attainment of competence for new officers, proactive learning, better mentoring, knowledge reuse by new entrants, shorter learning curves
People metrics	More competent and committed people, more confidence and trust, employee satisfaction, better familiarity amongst employees, better employee satisfaction, improvements in willingness to share
Organisational metrics	Informed decision-making, thought leadership, improved capabilities to resolve complex cases, detect signs of tax fraud, resolving cases more expeditiously, greater innovation capacity, scalability and quick setup, reduction of safety violations, more effective networked structure, cost savings, reduced risk, writs disposed faster, quicker clearance of cases, clearer roadmap, better mutual understanding, better customer satisfaction, useful insights for next activities

of KM? What additional skills and competencies are required to measure KM effectively? What is the timeframe for these measures? Benefit areas can be in tactical or strategic dimensions, or in job and enterprise effectiveness. Accordingly, KM effectively moves from sharing and collaboration to innovation.

CHAPTER NINE

Learnings and Recommendations

"Knowledge gives choice."

— Peter Drucker

This chapter provides some reflections from the practitioners on their respective KM journeys, and shares some of their learnings and recommendations such as challenges encountered and recommendations from the experience.

Various KM practitioners have offered a wealth of advice for implementing KM programs. For instance, O'Dell and Hubert (2011) advised that any implementation of KM programs would demand enormous organisational resources, in terms of time and expertise for planning as the management needs steadfast conviction, stamina and persistence to communicate KM benefits and most importantly the courage to institute changes in the organisations. Kluge *et al.* (2001) suggested that to leverage the push as well as the pull factors to grow holistically and share knowledge, management needs to create the right cultural context that nurtures reciprocal trust, openness and cooperation. Employees must be enthused with a desire for world-class performance and 'lust for knowledge', from within and outside the company. It is important to avoid micro-management and encourage self-steering mechanisms. However, many KM initiatives tend to get stuck in the 'pilot project' stage with an unclear focus or inadequate measures of progress; and managers tend to underestimate the complexities of technology integration and workforce cultural changes involved (Natarajan & Shekhar, 2000). Hence, for KM projects to succeed, it must be interwoven into an organisation's mainstream activities and functions, and quantifiable milestones and timelines must be identified. In other words, KM must be linked to and synchronised with business strategy and planning, and should not stand on its own in a silo manner.

9.1. Learning from the KM Journeys

Extensive assessments of KM initiatives in organisations around the world have been published, with a wealth of learnings and recommendations for success. The assessments cover issues on obstacles, problems, and challenges to success factors in the KM journeys.

9.1.1. *Obstacles in the KM Journeys*

Similar to other projects that organisations need to implement, Akhavan *et al.* (2005) identified the top management's lack of familiarity with dimensions of KM and its requirements, thus they end up selecting an unsophisticated and inexperienced person to lead the KM team. Worse, there is no concerted effort to ensure that proper and adequate criteria are used to select appropriate members for the knowledge team to lead the change.

Fontain and Lesser (2002) notice that KM initiatives tend to have little alignment with the organisation's strategic objectives and planning. In more specific cases, there is a failure to understand the context of the problem, hence leading to the creation of repositories without addressing the need to manage content; there is also a failure to understand and connect KM activities into the individuals' daily workflow. For instance, Beerli *et al.* (2003) cited that when organisations do not formulate the correct codification strategy, the problem of information overflow and the increasing difficulty of structuring the vast collections of documents may be exacerbated. Yet, on the other hand, those adopting only the personalisation strategy cannot cope with the challenge of speed in the new economy (Malhotra, 2001). Equally daunting towards complicating KM efforts is an overemphasis on formal learning as a mechanism for sharing knowledge, hence leading to the focusing of KM efforts solely within organisational boundaries. In fact, dealing with complexity, equivocality, uncertainty, and ambiguity in today's environment can lead to information overload and a collapse of sense-making in a company.

Table 9.1   Inhibitors in KM initiatives.

Category	Inhibitors
Culture	Lack of assurance against negative responses
	Lack of time
	Lack of recognition and tangible rewards
	Lack of directive from the reporting officer
	Lack of assurance against belittling by colleagues
Process	Lack of integration of the process with day-to-day work
	Lack of feedback
	Lack of mandatory organisational policy on contributions
	Lack of protection of intellectual property
	Lack of contributions from colleagues
Knowledge	Lack of awareness of knowledge requirements
	Lack of awareness on the significance of the contribution
	Lack of awareness of the process of contributing
	Lack of awareness of the utility of the contributions
Capacity	Lack of expertise in organising the available knowledge
	Lack of assistance in the domain contribution
Technology	Lack of user-friendly technology infrastructure
	Lack of quality assurance in the organisational knowledge repository
	Lack of weightage for contribution in performance appraisal

Source: Kuriakose *et al.* (2011).

In brief, Kuriakose *et al.* (2011) identified and clustered a range of obstacles or inhibitors unearthed in organisational KM journeys into the following categories: organisational culture, processes, knowledge, skills and capacity of employees, and technology infrastructure, as summarised in Table 9.1.

9.1.2. Success Factors for KM

Chong and Choi (2005) posited that successful implementation of KM program depends on 11 critical enablers which include: employee training, employee involvement, teamwork, employee empowerment, top management leadership and commitment, understanding organisational constraints, deploying information system infrastructure, performance measurement, cultivating an egalitarian culture, providing benchmarking and knowledge structure.

Davenport and Probst (2002) provided an in-depth analysis of KM success factors at the Siemens group of companies on leadership contributions, as well as organisational support in the planning, including training boot camps and provision of interesting structures with regards to motivational systems (via 'shares' for contributions which can be exchanged for equipment or conference fees). Of course, cultivating the organisational culture that is conducive to sharing knowledge is important, such that promoting messages like 'Unlike in school, copying is not only allowed — it is required' forms a core component of its success. Finally, in any management activity, the impacts need to be quantified, such as through cost savings, alignments with customer needs, and the ability to sustain its competition by spotting the dynamic trend of business.

According to Boisot (1998), KM tools can effectively empower employees and improve work in two ways — the 'Diffusion Effect' that brings about a wider reach for knowledge created, and the 'Bandwidth Effect' where media richness brings the communities closer. In other words, at an individual level, social network tools can serve as external scaffolding for the mind, allowing for extended and collective minds.

9.1.3. Recommendations for KM Practitioners

In addition to identifying barriers and success factors, a number of researchers and practitioners offer actionable advice to KM professionals. Care must be taken to roll out a KM system with a specific purpose in mind, otherwise there is a danger of information overload, increased bureaucracy, and excessive stockpiling of purposeless knowledge, as Newell et al. (2002) have warned. Indeed, Ahmed et al. (2002) observed that knowledge programmes succeed not so much because they have some brilliant and complex magical potion, but because they harmoniously blend and combine knowledge activities and processes. Knowledge sharing should not be reduced to appendices of everyday practice, but must become intertwined with practice; for instance, case writing about each sharing is a useful learning tool and knowledge recap mechanism due to its ability to tease out details and provoke or inspire further action (Davenport and Probst, 2002).

In all purposes, it is pertinent to guard against both 'not invented here' and 'knowledge is power' syndromes as they can lead to the shunning of external knowledge or the hoarding of personal knowledge

(Kluge *et al.*, 2001). Alfs (2003) recommends that KM structures should give more room for inspiration and creativity; however, lack of alignment between KM components and knowledge behaviours can be problematic. Therefore, it is important to align individual motivation with corporate goals, in other words, helping workers perform different roles: as a knowledge source, a knowledge seeker, a knowledge advocate, and a knowledge coordinator. Increased group contact, cross-hierarchical teams, cross-functional teams, and job rotation can improve cooperative behaviour.

Honeycutt (2000) offered several recommendations such as building KM tools incrementally on existing technology or selecting a pilot group carefully for speed, momentum and strategic relevance, perhaps by using early prototypes. This KM system must also include good administration tools for measuring usage of the KM base, supporting community activities, and managing meta-data. In other words, KM practices should be rolled out via smaller pilot projects if necessary, with swift solutions to ignite interest in the system. Although the information technology (IT) infrastructure is important, it is necessary not to confuse information management with KM.

9.1.4. *KM as an Organisational Priority*

KM will continue to be important and it has succeeded where it is seen as an organisational priority. It has formed part of the largest global transformation where connectivity, collaboration, and common standards have enabled people to communicate and share knowledge and information in a fast-paced knowledge economy.

Indeed, the great challenge of organisational life is how to build stability while retaining adequate flexibility to adapt and change with regards to the dynamic environment. Thus, organisations need to learn how to self-organise to live on the creative edge of chaos.

9.2. Perspectives from the Case Studies

This section expands on the learnings and recommendations from each of the KM case studies. It covers a wide range of issues: management support, technology design, personalisation, change management, needs and matrix assessments, organisational communication, training strategies, rewards, and feedback mechanisms.

9.2.1. Attorney-General's Chambers (AGC)

AGC's success factors are manifold; however, the most significant factor is the rigorous support from the senior management who literally championed the KM projects from the very beginning. Thus, there was widespread buy-in from members on the importance and benefits of KM. Unsurprisingly, with good leadership, both the knowledge strategies and processes have been closely aligned with the organisation's business direction and objectives.

KM systems promote the sharing of information on the one hand, but on the other, they require security mechanisms to prevent unauthorised access and misuse. Security is a major issue for AGC as it is privy to classified government information. Because of this constraint, AGC adopted the 80:20 rule for highly classified information. In other words, instead of holding back on having a KM system because it was infeasible to deal with the security controls for highly classified content, it was decided that the bulk of content (approximately 80 percent) should be shared through the portal, since the relative proportion of such highly classified material makes up only about 20 percent. To allow access, the Enterprise Legal Management System (ELMS) enables searches to locate all relevant information, although access to the documents is still subject to access rights control and approval.

Even though the staff realise that KM is both invaluable and indispensable, KM tasks tend to be given a low priority when the staff are faced with competing demands of their core work. To overcome this problem, the KM tasks are designed as part of the daily work processes. Previously, key legal advice was uploaded to AGC's Civil Opinions Database (on a Lotus Notes database) as an additional step after the advice had been approved in hard copy. ELMS has now streamlined this process by making the capture of electronic copies of significant documents part of the standard workflow. Additionally, comments provided in the document review process are also recorded to provide insights on the drafting of the document.

At AGC, the sharing of tacit or intangible knowledge was a challenge, as the skills and the know-how reside within the individuals, and in order to capture the collective wisdom of the individuals, a 'buddy system' was introduced whereby new officers are paired with more experienced officers to ensure that tacit knowledge is transmitted to newer officers, thus providing a sharing and collaborative culture.

Similarly, experts from each division were appointed to provide assistance to their colleagues. Indeed, AGC learned that human factors are as important as (or even more important than) technology solutions. To this end, close working relationships were established between IT and KM departments as well as users — with proper understanding of the mechanics and work processes, problems can be appropriately solved.

Despite the collaborative approach that was introduced, there were other cultural issues that AGC had to overcome, such as motivating employees to take on leadership roles to champion projects as well as getting them to voice their contributions without fear of reprisals.

According to AGC, there was also a problem with IT vendors as they do not have sufficient knowledge of how highly specialised legal services are deployed. Therefore, KM professionals must be heavily engaged in specifying their needs in order for the right product to be implemented. In fact, there is little assurance that the vendor will actually deliver the promised product even with a comprehensive evaluation process. This is because the high staff turnover in the IT vendors' organisations may create a significant risk in the KM project.

AGC's Six Key KM Recommendations

(a) Before undertaking a KM initiative, it is important to gain a thorough understanding of the organisation's strategy, culture and capabilities, and its implications for KM.
(b) The senior management's support is critical for success.
(c) For knowledge to have value, it must have an impact on the way core functions of the organisation are performed.
(d) Technology is just an enabler. There is no single KM technology solution as all available products have their limitations.
(e) Appropriate steps are required to protect security.
(f) For KM initiatives to succeed, users must experience the benefits.

9.2.2. Defence Science and Technology Agency (DSTA)

A critical success factor at DSTA was that the respective heads of each Competency Centre (CC) owns and leads the implementation of various KM initiatives. The overall implementation was phased to provide all staff the time and opportunities to familiarise themselves with the new online community environment and culture. However, the most challenging task was to encourage the staff to share information or knowledge on a voluntary basis, especially if one belongs to a relatively large community. The KM team has to work closely with the CC Heads to gather feedback, review the progress and continually devise the engagement approach, which includes the use of various incentive and promotion schemes. An important lesson learned was that it is not a one-time launch of the CC Portal that brought about successful sharing, but rather a continuous process of leadership by example and staff engagement.

Another key strategy is to use IT as a KM enabler. With Web 2.0, DSTA successfully deployed the CC Portal without the need for webmasters. The KM applications are largely intuitive by nature and easy to use. As such, all staff are able to participate and share information as content owners. In fact, as the staff learn and share, many more can now learn and connect quickly from each sharing.

9.2.3. Intellectual Property Office of Singapore (IPOS)

IPOS has learned three key lessons from its KM journey as follows:

- A highly personalised approach (in tangent with an introverted corporate culture) has proven more effective. It managed to attain 50 percent user acceptance.
- It is important to gain buy-in and support from middle-to-higher management as they are critical in the driving and encouragement of the initiatives from within their own departments.
- Its KM team recognises that change resistance is not necessarily derived from old habits, it can stem from a lack of understanding, such as the fear of the unknown and/or a series of intrapersonal and professional needs that have not been met.

Overall, IPOS provides three key recommendations for organisations trying to implement their own KM initiatives:

- Understand the current processes and culture of the organisation as these will affect the design of taxonomy and the execution style of the key initiatives.
- Understand core departmental business needs as this will help the organisation design and customise the portal.

- Conduct customised in-house training for tools such as SharePoint so that the core users (e.g. KM representatives) can trickle this knowledge down to team members.

9.2.4. Inland Revenue Authority of Singapore (IRAS)

IRAS provided a range of useful learnings in its KM journey. Interestingly, it did not set any target for each division to conduct sharing sessions, due to the concern that doing so might not get people on board the learning and sharing culture willingly. However, the only target set was for the staff who had attended a course/seminar overseas to share upon returning from their overseas trip. The branches were gently encouraged to identify suitable cases to be presented at the IRAS sharing session. Some of the senior management staff also encouraged their branch heads to contribute cases for sharing. With such an approach, the number of sharing sessions has been successfully increased from one per month to an average of two per month.

Multiple approaches were used in capturing, storing and sharing the materials presented at the IRAS sharing sessions. In the past, when the turnout was overwhelming for some of the sessions, a second run had to be organised so as to cater to staff who missed the first run. Sharing sessions were also video-recorded for staff who might want to view the presentations again. In fact some of the sharing sessions were telecasted live, so that any staff who is unable to be present at the auditorium can still view the presentation via their desktop PC. However, there are concerns about the increase in its staff choosing the more passive way of participating in IRAS sharing sessions; it is still preferred that the staff be present at the auditorium to be able to take part in discussions. Indeed, such development requires continuous monitoring, assessment and interpretation.

Management support is a key success factor. They help identify topics and cases for sharing and encourage the staff to attend the IRAS sharing sessions. Critically, it is important that the senior management team articulated a clear knowledge strategy and knowledge goals; it also made a point to reiterate the importance of knowledge sharing in the organisation, and through the implementation of other KM systems and tools, a strong signal was sent to all staff of its sponsorship and commitment to making knowledge sharing a way of life in IRAS.

Various motivational structures were introduced to encourage knowledge-sharing behaviours. For example, incentives such as recognition were given to staff who conducted sharing sessions after their attendance in courses/seminar overseas. For example, some maintenance points were awarded to its Accredited Tax Specialists when they conduct sharing sessions. The Accredited Tax Specialist Scheme is an in-house scheme to recognise the staff who have achieved the required standards to be accredited as Tax Specialists — they have to remain involved in learning and sharing activities in order to maintain their status as a Tax Specialist.

9.2.5. *Jurong Town Corporation (JTC)*

A number of key recommendations which emerged from JTC's decade-long KM journey are as follows:

- Strong senior management support is critical to driving KM efforts in the long term and its culture should be institutionalised with the support of a formal KM department.
- KM tools and workspaces should be managed in a dedicated and consistent manner throughout their life cycles.
- IT infrastructure needs to be continually updated and integrated to offer diverse but consistent process support, given the rapid pace of change in digital media. Common categorisation systems should be used, and older tools and information that are seldom used or have outlived their usefulness should be removed.
- In a data-intensive business, process knowledge, standards and integrity of business records are very important. Considerable effort and resources should be devoted to knowledge and information management needs in such contexts.
- KM projects should be aligned to the organisation's business strategy, with good cooperation between the KM team, KM representatives and the people doing the groundwork.

9.2.6. *Ministry of Finance (MOF)*

MOF has three key recommendations for KM practitioners beginning their KM journey as follows:

- Do engage the staff and key stakeholders early in the journey.
- Listen to the views of the staff and try to incorporate their requirements where possible.

- The KM team needs to maintain good relationships with all staff so that when they are engaged, they will contribute voluntarily to the initiatives.

9.2.7. National Library Board (NLB)

NLB provided several valuable lessons from their KM journey as follows:

- *Strong management support* — Like all projects, the KM project team also faced some initial barriers and hurdles, but with strong management support, the team was able to overcome them. For instance, with a management briefing as well as providing general directions on how the success of the initiative would impact the organisation, the staff were able to take on their roles in making the initiative a success.
- *Adopting a personalised approach* — Project team members also made efforts to talk to each staff individually. Each staff was approached whenever opportunities arose, and through informal chats it was possible to glean plenty of hidden thoughts about the system that were not raised in official meetings.
- *Changing conservative mindsets* — In general, librarians are open to sharing and not afraid to ask for contributions/assistance via the collaborative platform. However, there are some who are not accustomed to sharing on an open online discussion platform. These librarians are usually those who are not in the habit of blogging or participating in online forums, Yahoo/Google groups or Wikipedia. In order to help librarians change their mindset and the working behaviour that they have been accustomed to, the project team conducted regular communication sessions and involved most of them in the project planning stage. This is to make them feel that they are part of the initiative and hence developed a certain degree of responsibility to make it work.
- *Gathering feedback* — Two separate surveys and focus group discussions were conducted with participants of the system to ascertain their satisfaction and reception rate for the product as well as to address the staff's concerns. Measures were implemented promptly to address concerns raised during these sessions. For instance, the staff mentioned that they would be more eager to participate if their contributions are acknowledged and linked back to their work

performance. As such the project team ensured that the system tracks individual contributions and used it to provide statistical data of individual staff performance.

- *Improving user acceptability* — Due to the relative complexity of the system, the staff's feedback was that they could not remember how to use certain functions. The project team took the initiative to send weekly tips of key functions within the system to the staff via email. The logic behind the exercise was to break down the tools into digestible portions so the staff would not find it too overwhelming when they were taught how to use the system.

- *Buy-in from senior staff* — Despite the continuing efforts to encourage usage, there are still librarians who have yet to use the system in their reference work. It is hoped that as more people join the collaborative platform, their interest would be aroused by the vibrant discussions as they see the benefits of the system through testimonies from other librarians. On hindsight, the team realises that obtaining earlier buy-ins from librarians who are more senior could have helped garner more staff support and participation as these staff are regarded as 'leaders' among the librarians.

9.2.8. *Singapore Armed Forces (SAF)*

Among the broader learning from the SAF are some insights on the Asian culture that contributed to the successful implementation of KM strategies and initiatives. For example, a core element of the culture is the collaboration mindset, which is paramount to the formation of the communities of practice and interest groups. With the added element of the new generation who is capable of doing complex tasks with higher expectations of how much their time is worth, and who thrive on connectedness, there is a continuous flow of information across the SAF organisation. The negative side of this flow is that often 'dis-information' arises, which may be difficult to identify especially in the changing environment. It was then recognised that organisational learning was essential, and that each and every soldier, sailor and airman must have the thinking skills to make decisions and take actions quickly that are consistent with their commander's intent.

A lesser known fact is that the Asian culture is well endowed with the culture of storytelling as a way of knowledge transfer. This is demonstrated in the works of Sun Tzu and in many of the Chinese proverbs where meaning and context are encapsulated in short verses. However, the modesty and humbleness that are the strengths of the Asian culture can in some ways limit individuals in making forceful articulations, i.e. not voicing concerns and falling into a groupthink situation. This is increasingly changing with the emergence of the digital natives, people who blog more often and are not afraid to voice their opinions. These NetGeners are the people who are regularly joining SAF both as regulars and under the National Service program.

An important success factor in the SAF's KM journey has been the phased approaches for its tool and content implementation, the importance of an intuitive user interface, document life cycle management, the need for anywhere and anytime learning resources, identifying high pay-off areas for learning efficiency and mission effectiveness, improved access control for security considerations, the value of storytelling in effective knowledge capture (beyond informal 'mess stories'), and aligning organisational learning and KM to core processes.

Thus, the 'Learning Army' should be linked directly to the 'Thinking Soldiers'. SAF has five key recommendations for organisations planning to launch or re-position their KM initiatives as follows:

- *Alignment with mission and purpose* — Having KM clearly aligned with the SAF's mission and purpose is not pure rhetoric. The key challenge is for KM advocates to find alignment and to take advantage of the potential synergy across the entire enterprise.
- *Culture change before implementation* — A mix of knowledge with innovative thinking is necessary to create the future. SAF's separate experimentations in Learning Organisations and KM were complementary and dovetailed nicely in the plans to transform into the 3rd Generation SAF. The Learning Organisation principle created a rich culture in learning, which in turn paved a strong foundation for KM adoption. It also meant that unlike most KM implementations which typically began with infrastructure investment, SAF's journey began with a culture change.
- *KM Office under CIO* — Having the KM office under the Chief Information Officer (CIO) has proven to be an advantage for its successful implementation. As illustrated by the US Department of the Navy, which had effectively placed their KM program under the department-wide CIO office, and its Chief Knowledge Officer also served as the Deputy CIO for Enterprise Integration. SAF's CIO was

given full accountability for regular IT services and KM outcomes. This has proven to be a more integrated approach towards putting SAF's capital and human resources into implementing KM.

- *'Think big — Start small — Scale fast'* — Such an approach has proven to be an advantage in the early years of its KM journey. For instance, when the pilot was implemented, only 5,000 user accounts were created on the system. However, with growth in generating the content and in the number of communities, inclusive of the creation of blogs and wikis, the requests for entry in the system have increased, resulting in eSILK having about 15,000 users towards the end of its implementation.

- *Identify, build on, and utilise KM advocates* — Identify those individuals across the organisations who have a strong commitment to KM and related activities. In the early initiation, build on their expertise, making their successes highly visible across the organisation. Simultaneously, take every opportunity to 'inform' and 'grow' new advocates through speaking, co-editing, and educational opportunities around the world.

9.2.9. Singapore Police Force: Police Technology Department (SPF-PTD)

A key lesson learned in SPF-PTD's KM journey was that KM initiatives must be aligned to the organisation's strategic objectives so that KM would not be perceived as unnecessary additional work. Indeed, it faced a challenge with the middle management; there was not a 100 percent buy-in and there were perceptions that KM was a fad; worst, some felt KM meant additional work due to the existing heavy workload of their primary duties. PTD's approach to overcoming these challenges was to engage the middle management by gathering their feedback on the existing KM initiatives, identifying their needs and assessing how KM could assist in their work. Over time, they became more open to sharing knowledge and information, and are beginning to share without being told to do so. The organisation is comparatively more open when it comes to after-action reviews (AARs) as mistakes made were then shared so that they would not be repeated.

On hindsight, SPF felt that if they could start again from scratch, they would start off with the knowledge audit and alignment of KM strategy to business strategy. In fact, SPF-PTD's advice for KM practitioners is to begin their knowledge journey as follows: start small, aim high, look for low-hanging fruits, and secure the top management's support. Culture is more important than technology. Quality of the core KM team is important relative to the selection of the ones with the keenest interest in KM, and considering that KM can be a long journey, the management needs to be patient and learn to persevere.

9.2.10. Singapore Youth Olympic Games Organising Committee (SYOGOC)

Based on its successful KM journey, SYOGOC provided the following recommendations for knowledge practitioners:

- *Begin with the end in mind* — In other words, the management should be clear from the start what the organisation would like to achieve in terms of specific goals and objectives so that planning would be focused on the activities to support the achievement of that end objective. Indeed, a clear objective will help to avoid a losing of focus and keep key priorities in mind.
- *Design a balanced KM framework* — Keep in mind the challenges that the organisation would face during the design. Thus, it is important to have a KM framework or work plan that not only enables the capture of knowledge for future generations, but also helps to improve the operational efficiency of the current staff. There should be long-term knowledge benefits as well as practical benefits for day-to-day activities.
- *Have senior management walk the talk* — An activity or event is normally perceived as important when the senior management supports and participates in it. Therefore, involve the senior management in demonstrating that they are walking the talk. For instance, when the staff participates in AARs facilitated by the KM team after each major phase of work, learning points are captured from the senior management via the interviews conducted by the KM team.

9.2.11. Supreme Court of Singapore (SC)

At the Supreme Court, four key lessons learned from its journey are as follows:

- Employee buy-in and support for the KM initiative is needed to succeed. It is therefore important for KM practitioners to begin work with people who are positive and accept the premises of knowledge sharing whilst others who are not so keen can be engaged later, via a change management initiative.

- Support from the top management is also needed for long-term success; full commitment and support are needed so that KM is seen as not just another product but an initiative that has the brand support right from the top.
- Design components — such as assets and processes — in an easy and accessible manner so that they can be easily understood and utilised. KM problems and solutions need to be easy and user-friendly, so that people will come forward, learn about it, adopt it, make it a habit, and share their experiences about it.
- Align KM needs to business or organisational objectives, its aims should include improving productivity, quality, reliability and innovation. In other words, the KM team should drive a clear message why the KM programs are required to meet such goals within the overall organisational context.

9.2.12. *Urban Redevelopment Authority (URA)*

URA has acquired a number of useful lessons from implementing its KM framework and projects. KM is a journey rather than a destination. Not every KM project will be smooth-sailing, and practitioners should be prepared for some failures and obstacles along the way. Implementing pilot projects is one way to mitigate the risk.

Like other organisations, it is important to align KM efforts with the business goals, and communicate KM in business terms as end users are not interested in jargons (e.g. taxonomy, communities of practice). It might be more relevant to provide an explanation of how a KM project could make their work better. During deployment, it is crucial to use various communication approaches to cater for different groups of users.

It is natural to associate KM with IT implementation (which may require high investment in technology). In reality, the success of KM depends more on people and processes than on technology.

9.3. Discussion and Insights

Several interesting and useful observations and KM recommendations have emerged from the profiles of the case studies, in line with the research frameworks outlined in Section 9.2. Most KM practitioners in the case studies strongly recommended that a KM launch be preceded by a thorough understanding of the organisation's culture, strategy and context as this affects everything from process design to incentive mechanisms. The details are shown in Table 9.2.

Support from the top management is particularly critical at the early stages, followed by buy-in from mid-level managers for sustaining and

Table 9.2   KM Initiatives: Learnings and Recommendations.

Organisation	Lessons Learned and Recommendations
AGC	Gain a thorough understanding of strategy and culture; senior management support is critical for success; impacts must be on core functions; users must experience benefits.
DSTA	Make competency management framework accessible to all; adapt Web 2.0 to meet requirements; create framework for staff engagement; streamline for search; review Knowledge Hubs.
IPOS	Personalised approach is more effective; gain buy-in from management; change resistance arises from a lack of understanding; conduct training; understand processes, culture, and business needs.
IRAS	Keep targets flexible so learning and sharing culture happens willingly; encourage branches to share; record the sharing session; gain management support; articulate clear knowledge strategy and goals.
JTC	Four key pillars are content, process, technology and culture/people; centralised views of knowledge workspaces increases usage.
MOF	Support from top management is key; establish a network to reach out; comprehensive and effective communication is crucial; day-to-day work and operations should not be disrupted; involve staff via hands-on training.
NLB	Strong management support; regular communication for change management; gather feedback; adopt a personalised approach; improve user acceptability of system via regular tips; get buy-in from senior staff.
SAF	Collaborativeness and storytelling are strengths of the Asian culture; there are challenges of modesty and humbleness; use phased approaches; ensure alignment with the mission, 'Think Big — Start Small — Scale Fast'; utilise KM advocates.

(Continued)

Table 9.2 (*Continued*)

Organisation	Lessons Learned and Recommendations
SPF-PTD	Pull the right lever (not just rewards or disincentives); align KM with strategic objectives; engage middle management to gather feedback; start small, aim high, look for low-hanging fruits; choose keen members for the KM Team.
SYOGOC	Formalise the learning culture; shorten the learning curves of venue planning teams; capture and transfer knowledge during operations.
SC	Collective effort and communication are needed; cross-collaboration with various stakeholders is called for, within the organisation as well as externally.
URA	KM is a journey and not a destination, prepare for some failures and hiccups along the way; pilot projects can mitigate risk; align KM efforts with business goals; do not focus excessively on technology.

propagating the KM initiative. Phased rollouts and pilot projects can also help increase KM adoption over a period of time. Some KM practitioners also recommended that users must start seeing at least some benefits from the knowledge initiative early enough; hence it is important to aim for 'low-hanging fruits' in addition to harder, longer-term goals. The targets and goals should also be kept flexible.

Other KM leaders suggested that a personalised approach to KM is better than a uniformed approach. It is important for knowledge practitioners to clearly articulate the KM strategy without using too much jargon and buzzwords. Though some resistance to KM can be overcome with training, regular informed communication, feedback mechanisms, and improving overall awareness and understanding, it may be necessary to live with some insurmountable issues.

On social media, some KM practitioners are reporting successes with using social networking tools, particularly with the younger workforce. It appears that 'digital natives', especially those in the world of mobile and social media, exhibit very different knowledge sharing behaviours from 'digital immigrants'. For instance, the older generation used to differentiate between task-related aspects and personal aspects — the younger generation, however, integrates everything naturally and even employs a different language. Organisations used to drive KM, but now younger tech-savvy individuals using web tools are placing demands on their organisations for better KM, thus bringing fresh blood into the field. For instance, the Asian Development-ment Bank is turning to its younger generation of employees in their 30s to embark on knowledge activities without inherited silo mindsets of the past.

In Dave Snowden's keynote speech at KM Asia in 2009, the two key issues faced by knowledge managers currently are how to work across silos, and how to create a knowledge-sharing culture. It is impor-tant to focus not just on knowledge stocks but knowledge flows; as human knowledge is inherently messy, it would be difficult to find the relevant knowledge without a proper coherent structure. Knowledge managers need to think of themselves as ecologists, not just as engi-neers. Knowledge sharing is a gift and not just a ritual or transaction, and needs to be approached in a way other than the anthropological perspective. Human knowledge is contextual; it is only when you are asked a question that one knows what one knows. The size of teams affects knowledge dynamics. A big mistake people tend to make is not to understand the scale in communications activities and groups. Dave Snowden also cautioned that there are natural physiological limits to knowledge-sharing groups.

In conclusion, KM will succeed if it incorporates vision, top-level sponsorship, alignment with business objectives, and clarity of scope. The focus of the initiative could be on the entire corporate culture, or just simply introducing a new business or organisational restructuring. The balance between innovation and reuse is a critical success factor for any KM effort. Indeed, a KM initiative, if successful, never ends.

CHAPTER TEN

The Road Ahead

"Imagination is more important than knowledge. Knowledge is limited. Imagination encircles the world."

— Albert Einstein

In the course of the book, we have examined the 'why,' 'how,' 'who,' 'what' and 'so what' aspects of the KM initiatives within the profiled organisations in Singapore. This concluding chapter focuses on the 'what next' perspective, that is, what should be the next step after the KM initiatives. It re-assesses the initiatives and explores some emerging directions in the KM practices. Depending on the phase of the organisation's knowledge journeys, we have classified them into three stages — the mature, intermediate, and early stages — as each of these phases has different implications and outcomes with respect to building the knowledge culture, establishing the structures or even responding to the external environments.

Decades ago, Drucker (1988) predicted that the organisation of the future would be knowledge-based and, thus businesses need to turn themselves into "organisations of knowledge specialists". Knowledge has since become the primary ingredient of what organisations produce and trade with. As a result, creating it, managing it, sharing it, diffusing it, and growing it in terms of intellectual capital has become an important economic task of individuals, societies, corporations and nations (Stewart, 1997).

Organisations must be built to be robust, that is, the management should have well-thought out plans for backups, alternatives and/or contingencies. Thus, organisations need to be resilient so as to be able to bounce back with sound courses of action even during completely unanticipated scenarios; knowledge should also be accessible not just for those who are looking for it, but it should also emerge to members in unexpected ways. Such an approach therefore requires organisations to consciously build their KM platform and infrastructure to ensure flexibility and connectedness in the knowledge workflows, so that such serendipitous emergence of knowledge is possible. In this context, KM practices should not lead to organisational rigidities as it is not static; rather, according to O'Dell and Hubert (2011), "What keeps KM exciting and fresh is the way KM professionals respond to the forces swirling around."

10.1. KM's Evolution and Direction

A number of practitioners have described how they assessed their KM initiatives and how they calibrated the next steps, identifying emerging trends and leadership issues in their KM journeys.

10.1.1. *Recalibration of KM Initiatives*

KM is not just an operational fix but a strategic investment. Knowledge cannot remain delegated to a single or separate unit; it must eventually be an integral part of the way everyone in the organisation thinks and acts (Kluge *et al.*, 2001). It is therefore essential to calibrate the knowledge (which includes intellectual capital as well as social capital) in the organisation so as to instil in each member a sense that knowledge creation, sharing and transfer becomes a part of everyday life; rather than something that ebbs and flows as the mood suits. Indeed, every worker should be a knowledge worker.

Various scholars have urged knowledge managers to think of knowledge not just as stocks and flows but also as energy which drives the success of individuals, organisations and societies. Drawing on Einstein's '$e = mc^2$' equation, KM involves meaning, communication and content, as 'knowledge shared is knowledge squared'; and organisations should be structured like a 'holarchy' (where the value of individuals derives not just from their position in the hierarchy but also from their contributions and interactions with each other).

It is interesting to note that organisations are slowly moving with the wave of social media. For instance, Shell took a couple of years to embrace and adopt the wiki model of intranet collaboration. This is because wikis occupy the 'middle ground' between a website and a document management system. However, the challenges that Shell faces in implementing KM remained, in terms of dealing with expired content, as developing content for information such as news requires constant updating of technology tools and platforms.

In another context, the Knowledge Management Advisor of Shell Global Solutions, Aw Siew Hoong, observed that the 'knowledge as stocks' model also faces challenges, in particular, during exit interviews when employees leave the organisation or transfer to another role or department. Indeed, it is suggested that exit interviews should include a good facilitator, focusing on logic and not just checklists; it should also incorporate the usage of tools like mindmaps, as well as involve experts in the interview process so as to map the context and content of the interviews for learning in the organisations.

10.1.2. Knowledge Leadership

The growing role of leadership in KM has been addressed as a key success factor for knowledge initiatives in organisations with established and mature KM practices. It is known that exemplary knowledge leaders tend to inspire their organisations to develop and share a vision of increased knowledge acquisition and usage as knowledge workers; indeed, they also tend to challenge the way in which the organisation functions and approaches value creation (Kouzes & Posner, 1996). Good knowledge leaders often motivate their subordinates to become domain experts as they delegate authority and responsibilities to them, trusting their ability to accomplish goals.

Knowledge leaders are lifelong learners and possess a keen awareness of business and knowledge ecosystems (McFarlane, 2008). They understand the knowledge economy and the broad ramifications of increasing global interconnectedness and competitiveness. They devote their efforts to build such systems to ensure continuous performance improvement and to draw on different socio-cultural and technical knowledge fields. Such efforts will be needed right through an organisation's KM journey.

10.1.3. Beyond Organisational Boundaries

KM innovations need to operate across four dimensions: communication, collaboration, processes, and integration. In their knowledge journeys, organisations should move from episodic mainstream KM to innovation and creativity. As the challenge of organisations in this century is to improve the productivity of knowledge workers fifty-fold, just like the transformation for factory workers in the last century, knowledge is considered the 'electrical current' that runs among intangible assets to grow the human, structural and relational capital in the organisations (Saint-Onge & Wallace, 2002). In other words, organisations should move away from mere human resources configuration but towards strategic capabilities, thus advocating a shift away from an entitlement culture characterised by dependence, but rather, towards a culture based on self-initiative and an ability to collaborate and cooperate with another partner.

In addition, organisations of the future need to tap value from inter-related networks of employees, partners and the society at large for creating prosperity (Allee, 2003). The focus is moving toward a more participative than controlling stance, incorporating elements of sustainability, global citizenship, governance, modelling of living systems, and creation of value through democratic, adaptive and emergent means. In other words, 'value network modelling' draws out the web of relationships that generates both tangible and intangible value through complex dynamic exchanges between two or more individuals, groups or organisations. The modelling can be used for exchange analysis (unearthing coherent patterns, imbalances, and optimal flows), impact analysis (creation of benefits) and value creation analysis (creation and extension of value).

10.1.4. New Contexts for KM

KM is not just about content and tools but also context and interpretation. Holsapple (2004b) rightly identified that KM is viewed differently by social anthropologists as compared to software applications analysts. He traces the evolution of information technology (IT) tools over the decades from data and decision support systems to enterprise systems and ubiquitous computing. Knowledge has a wide range of attributes, which therefore makes it challenging yet rewarding to manage; it has different applications, orientation, utility, validity, sources, perishability, resolution, and measurability, hence there is no one-size-fits-all approach to managing the different kinds of organisational knowledge. The investigation of the nature of knowledge has

Table 10.1   Successive Business Paradigms.

Paradigm	Systems	Objective	Success Factors
Scientific Management (Taylor, Drucker)	Simple	Mass production	Control of function
Systems Thinking (Kaplan, Senge, Nonaka)	Complicated	Mass customisation	Control of information
Social Computing, Pervasive Technology Environments	Complex	Mass collaboration	Ability to situate in a network; distributed cognition

Source: Adapted from Dave Snowden's speech at the 2009 KM Asia Conference.

occupied mankind for thousands of years and will likely continue to do so for thousands more (Holsapple, 2004a/b).

In the 2009 KM Asia Conference, Dave Snowden sketches the role of knowledge in three successive business paradigms over the past hundred years, each marked by new disruptive technologies in the backdrop of an economic recession. Each paradigm follows a 'S curve' of increasing adoption and then fading relevance, as presented in Table 10.1.

KM requires social computing tools to achieve optimal mass collaboration, especially in the era of social computing, KM tools should facilitate workers to compete as networks rather than just as organisations. This is because the technology for KM is largely available for free or at a low cost. Indeed, Snowden identifies the following seven principles for KM in today's world of ubiquitous social computing tools:

- Knowledge can only be volunteered, not conscripted. Social computing works because everyone is a volunteer. Knowledge sharing takes place as a natural social activity in such environments.
- We only know what we know when we need to know it. Human thinking is centred on pattern-based intelligence and not information processors. The practice of sleeping on a decision is a good example of letting subconscious memories and past experiences work on the decision, hence letting patterns emerge.

- In the context of real need, few people will refuse to share their knowledge.
- Tolerated failure imprints learning better than success. For example, it can be illustrated by the way people learn from practice; apprentices learn from masters via their mistakes as well.
- The way we know is not the way we say we know.
- We always know more than we can say and say more than we can write. Narrative is a very important form of KM.
- Everything is fragmented; humans seek messy coherence. There will therefore be limits to tools like the semantic web. Context is everything, even in the case of explicit content.

10.2. Perspectives from the Case Studies

This section explores the future KM commitments and developments of the organisations in the case studies. Based on the study interviews, each profile covers the management priorities, emerging developments and the next steps to be taken, of which some are operational whilst others are strategic.

10.2.1. *Attorney-General's Chambers (AGC)*

At the AGC, KM is being increasingly integrated with work processes, and there are plans to engage professional KM practitioners to drive future KM projects. Under the KM Next Phase projects, the following initiatives are planned to ensure there is progress in its KM journey: implementation of the Enterprise Search Engine, the Automatic Taxonomy Classifier, the taxonomy review, and the KM portal upgrade.

The AGC currently has a 3–5 year IT Plan which outlines the development efforts for key projects like ELMS, Legislation Editing and Authentic Publishing (LEAP) project and the KM Next Phase. As the AGC has to work within the government's security procedures for handling and custody of classified information that adopts a need-to-know policy, ELMS is designed to allow selective access to documents based on an officer's security clearance level. In addition, the AGC has also migrated to a Standard information communication technology Operating Environment, SOEasy, which is a government platform providing a common desktop, messaging and network environment to over

60,000 public officers. The LEAP project will be the online platform for Singapore's legislation, developed with improved search features and functions.

In sum, the AGC will continue to streamline and integrate the collection, storage, sharing and reuse of information through its work processes. Its KM Central will continue to assist divisions to develop reference materials and guides to disseminate to officers through the KM Portal, which will be streamlined to incorporate work processes.

10.2.2. Defence Science and Technology Agency (DSTA)

As a long-term effort, DSTA will continue to nurture the culture of 'learn as we work, and share as we learn'. Looking at the future evolution of its KM initiative, a comprehensive competency management framework has been developed as part of its Competence Centre (CC) business. The next step is to extend the relevant information for specific staff competency to the respective MyHomepage and CC Portals for all to share and connect readily the expertise within the organisation. As an early adopter of Web 2.0, the staff are given the tools to update and share content, thus avoiding the need for webmasters as both the community and personal MyHomepage are integrated. Through the positive experience from its Directorate of Organisation Capability and CC applications, the management and staff are now more confident and ready for further KM implementations.

While keeping in mind the fundamentals of KM and what works best on the current eHabitat, the team is now embarking on eWorkplace as a step towards the next 'S curve'. Although the information is organised, it requires further streamlining to improve the search functions. Hence, its eWorkplace aims to put in place a simple, secure, and effective system where all staff can be connected to one another, share information more readily and be able to search easily for the needed information.

10.2.3. Intellectual Property Office of Singapore (IPOS)

Although the first knowledge audit was conducted in 2010 to ensure all documents migrated from the Lotus intranet are up-to-date on KENNY (Knowledge ENterprise 'N You), IPOS realised that there were inconsistencies in the creation and categorisation in KENNY compared to its Lotus Notes intranet soon after launching its KM Portal. Thus, it plans to have a half-yearly audit with a different objective and scope to ensure that there is compliance of its KM policy.

IPOS proceeded to rectify its problem in KENNY as it faced some resistance and scepticism in the new system. However, over time it appeared that the staff is adapting to the new technology with ease, and the resistance has reduced considerably. The real measurement of its long-term KM success will be in the form of stories shared by knowledge champions. In fact, as part of the initiative to connect people to people in knowledge sharing, it is thinking of developing its own communities of practice (CoPs) as well.

IPOS' activities were earlier tailored around KM technology; however, it has since expanded the scope to include the context of culture. Two activities to jumpstart this initiative are the continuation of the KM e-bulletin on a new and improved platform, i.e. in a comic storytelling format to encourage interaction, as well as Knowledge Café sessions. IPOS is also planning to enhance the capturing of knowledge assets, specifically via email, as email has evolved as a major communication tool in the organisation.

10.2.4. *Inland Revenue Authority of Singapore (IRAS)*

The focused KM approach systematically developed so far is built into the way IRAS develops its staff. It is following up on various action plans following the completion of the KM Strategy Review Project, e.g. implementation of Knowledge Maps and a project to develop knowledge and information management policies and information architecture. For instance, it will continue to build on the shared knowledge maps that function as a visual inventory of knowledge assets — both tacit and explicit (e.g. skills, experiences as well as documents) which are organised around the core business activities of the branches and divisions.

In terms of enhancing the knowledge and information management policies and information architecture, ensuring a more consistent way of managing information, as well as creating a more user-friendly intranet for the staff to contribute and locate documents and expertise, IRAS is concentrating on building an expertise audit for a greater focus on the areas of knowledge that have high strategic impacts or are vulnerable to loss. In brief, it is important to enhance the overall availability of information and knowledge to the staff.

IRAS has also introduced a new process to invite suitable retirees to share their work experience at IRAS sharing sessions. The staff would be able to obtain insights on some of the projects from the past. It is a meaningful platform for the retirees to reflect on their life in IRAS and pass on knowledge to the next generation of staff. A series of 'Learning Bites' is also being launched — brown bag lunches and informal discussions on a specific article or tax journal.

10.2.5. Jurong Town Corporation (JTC)

JTC continues to view KM as a core element of its business and organisational excellence efforts. It plans to continually renew and upgrade its systems to support KM so as to keep them relevant. Moving forward, the Corporate Reporting Information Services Portal (CRISP) would be further enhanced to provide automated notification using the push technology for targeting users whenever new reports are published on the portal. JTC will continue its focus on knowledge standards and integrity of business records.

KM projects will be aligned to JTC's business strategy, and more cooperation will be promoted between the KM team and the people doing the groundwork. On the inter-organisational front, JTC will share its extensive expertise in the application of platforms (such as Share-Point) with other government agencies.

10.2.6. Ministry of Finance (MOF)

MOF is looking at revamping its corporate intranet and Corporate Document Repository so as to integrate it with the existing Email Repository. The KM team is also looking for a more powerful search engine across all the various repositories as well as to incorporate various customisations to navigate the taxonomy within the Third Sight system.

With the implementation of the Civil Service's SOEasy platform, there are plans to migrate the repositories into the new platform. The KM team plans to migrate the existing MOF intranet, file management system, and other Lotus Notes applications onto the new platform. With customised advancements, the next step is to study ways to cultivate the KM culture so as to ensure that learning progresses along with the enhanced technology.

10.2.7. *National Library Board (NLB)*

It is foreseen that there should be an improved collaborative culture in NLB, thus measuring its collaborative culture forms part of its balanced scorecard. The measures include surveys, online contribution and usage of platforms, which are proxy indicators of its knowledge-sharing culture. Apart from the statistics, the KM team will focus on collecting and showcasing success through stories and anecdotes that will emphasize on how the K Champions influence culture by demonstrating the behaviours in their daily work. In fact, the K Champions are already actively involved in the CoPs such as the Knowledge Management CoP, U Group (a social media CoP); they are also starting to plan for upcoming Trainers CoP and Project Management CoP.

NLB has identified two other steps, in terms of internal self-service and external collaboration.

- *Self-service enquiry database of past enquiries.* This project looks into packaging reference enquiries and answers into a self-service enquiry database for both librarians and customers to access. As a searchable database, it will reduce the time taken by librarians to identify and select resources for similar enquiries that they receive.
- *External collaboration.* As the NOS collaborative platform can be extended to librarians and subject experts from anywhere, plans are well underway to extend it to the staff of other divisions in NLB as well as external parties. Furthermore, by tapping on the collective wisdom of librarians and subject experts both locally and overseas, it is hoped that the library brings the best resources to the users.

10.2.8. *Singapore Armed Forces (SAF)*

Overall, the 'One Objective', 'Three Imperatives' and 'Five Initiatives'[1] have shaped SAF's journey towards a knowledge-based organisation. SAF is not at the end of this journey; many of the initiatives are ongoing and a lot of work is still required. It is certain that with strong leadership support and enduring implementation of a unified IT system, SAF will continue to grow its knowledge tree and reap the knowledge fruits.

---

[1]The one objective was to build a knowledge-based SAF, driven by three imperatives: operational complexity, system complexity and quick turnover. This was to be achieved via five initiatives: building a knowledge-based organisation, building knowledge capital, unifying IT systems, creating knowledge hubs, and innovating new processes.

Current challenges faced by SAF lie in sustaining education and communication, meeting the demand for a more intuitive system, that is, the need for more focused engagements, and more tacit know-hows. Thus, its next major undertaking will incorporate leadership development and the creation of the knowledge portal. It will develop a knowledge portal for each of the networks to syndicate and provide access to various sources of information and databases, search engines, emails, news and so on, somewhat like that of a 'Commander Dashboard' with analytic tools to facilitate situation awareness and decision-making in the domain under one's charge.

Indeed, SAF has a greater need to engage the future generation of soldiers, sailors and airmen with more exciting challenges that make them think and value the SAF systems highly. The ability to think and act adaptively — to be comfortable with ambiguity and to know that one will never know all and must thus be ready to react — is a growing prerequisite of the future operating environment. This ability will require SAF to research and adapt or grow its own methodologies for thinking, planning, acting and reacting.

10.2.9. *Singapore Police Force: Police Technology Department (SPF-PTD)*

SPF-PTD has recognised that further success in KM will require refining its broad framework to align its KM plan with the organisational objectives. It also recognises that to continue to deliver on the KM promise, it needs strong continuous commitment from its senior management as well as a passionate core KM team. In fact, its next major task is to build capabilities amongst its officers, including nurturing open-minded officers who are willing to try new ideas and concepts.

SPF-PTD has progressed well along the early stages of its KM awareness, strategy formulation and planning. It had, indeed, executed a rather extensive and comprehensive range of activities and techniques to inculcate a KM culture amongst its officers. Its KM implementation was also noted by other government agencies; and it is thus looking forward to further enhancement and expansion of its KM implementations especially to integrate the enterprise systems. As KM implementation and adoption is akin to a journey, SPF-PTD will no doubt continue moving forward towards Stage 5, the highest level of achievement of the APQC KM Roadmap.

10.2.10. *Singapore Youth Olympic Games Organising Committee (SYOGOC)*

In the post-Games dissolution phase, SYOGOC conducted a knowledge transfer exercise for post-Games reports. During the dissolution phase, all functional areas produced a report on the organisation of the Games, and each of these reports contained the output of all pre-Games and Games-time KM activities. The various reports were consolidated into a single volume and presented to the IOC as part of the overall Youth Olympic Games KM programme, which in turn was uploaded onto an extranet for reference by future Youth Olympic Games organising committees.

Besides the post-Games reports, the experience and lessons learned from Singapore 2010 were conveyed via the debrief sessions. The KM Group conducted the Observers Programme during which the next organising committees were invited to attend seminars and venue tours to learn about SYOGOC's planning considerations and operational lessons. Programme participants included the 2012, 2014 and 2016 Youth Olympic Games host and candidate cities, as well as the 2012, 2014 and 2016 Olympic host cities.

In Singapore, besides the return of more than 100 assigned staff to the Singapore Sports Council, the knowledge that was captured during the planning and operations phases has been handed over to the Singapore Sports Council and the Ministry of Community Development, Youth and Sport as legacy documents. These documents will be used as references for future sport event bids, and organisation of sport events in Singapore.

In summary, not all organisations start with such a sense of urgency about the criticality of KM. Although it had to deliver extraordinary results with limited resources and simple technology, the true test of SYOGOC's KM was the successful completion of its post-Games knowledge transfer to the IOC and to the assigned Singapore government agencies, and the impact this knowledge would have.

10.2.11. *Supreme Court of Singapore (SC)*

According to the Chief Justice, creativity and continual improvements help the Supreme Court make a quantum leap and prepare for the challenges ahead. Therefore, for it to become a thought leader in judicial administration and court technologies, cross collaboration with stakeholders is called for within the organisation as well as externally. In this context, KM is exploited to transfer institutional knowledge through and across technology platforms.

Thus, its KM thrust is to ensure that institutional knowledge and memory are preserved and shared, so that such knowledge is not lost and unnecessary duplication of information is avoided. Coupled with constant upgrades for the portal which began as a one-page portal, it has evolved into a multi-page portal catering to the growing needs of the organisation. When the organisation re-organised itself from departments into specific directorates, the portal was likewise revamped to allow for one homepage per directorate/functional group, so as to cater for the growing need to capture, categorise and share information. To standardise the directorate pages for uniformity and ease of navigation, the KM team is in the midst of converting all homepages to wiki-style pages to encourage sharing.

Another plan is to design a taxonomy that is flexible enough to have a generic structure to cater for all directorates as well as having specific branches catered for each directorate's requirements. Ultimately, a common taxonomy may not be possible for all directorates/functional groups because of the delineation between administrative work and legal work, which has its own specialised taxonomy. Moving forward, with a full-time Knowledge Manager, the KM Steering Committee will be able to put in place strategic programmes and initiatives that will combine the people, process and technology aspects of a successful KM programme.

10.2.12. *Urban Redevelopment Authority (URA)*

URA will continue to leverage its KM framework to formulate a more focused roadmap to identify, consolidate and formalise all the KM-related projects. KM efforts will be increasingly aligned with corporate business objectives, which include transforming Singapore into a liveable, vibrant and world-class city.

Judicious land use planning and good urban design will be powered by strategic plans and informed decisions; approaches ranging from geographic knowledge systems and social media to organisational development will play crucial roles. URA will continue to deploy KM in a significant manner as it is through KM that URA was able to demonstrate its award-winning performance and service excellence.

Further, it was KM that helped URA attract, develop and retain a team of passionate and motivated staff that include mentoring and scholarship programmes. URA's core values of Spirit, Passion, Integrity, Respect, Innovation and Teamwork (the URA SPIRIT) will continue to drive it in becoming a successful learning organisation.

10.3. Discussion and Insights

Although successful KM leaders have evangelised the knowledge movement and draw on different socio-cultural and technical knowledge fields, in the road ahead, organisations should focus not just on past knowledge practices but also emerging innovations. In fact, organisations of the future need to tap value from various interrelated social networks and not just knowledge networks. As KM is not just an operational fix but a strategic investment, it must therefore be an integral part of the entire enterprise-wide network incorporating both internal and external stakeholders.

In brief, the next steps for some of the KM initiatives of the organisations profiled are summarised in Table 10.2. Many organisations are in the midst of upgrading to more integrated IT platforms (e.g. MOF) and advanced KM portal features (e.g. AGC, SC), or improving processes like knowledge mapping (e.g. IRAS). Not surprisingly, social media features high on the agendas of many organisations, a feature which barely existed five years ago (e.g. SC, URA). Audit cycles, incentive schemes and metrics are constantly being refined (e.g. IRAS), with some organisations adding emphasis to qualitative approaches like storytelling and anecdotes, with discussion and brainstorming formats such as knowledge cafés and informal lunch sessions also being examined (e.g. IPOS).

The KM directions of the organisations can also be analysed into the following categories: those which have had KM for more than ten years as being considered in the 'mature stage', those which have KM around 5–9 years can be considered in the 'intermediate stage', and those which have KM around 2–4 years can be considered in the 'early stage'. Table 10.3 shows the three stages of KM developments. Depending on the duration of the KM initiatives, the organisations would have different scopes and scales for the projects, with differing levels of complexities, natures of incentives, types of metrics (internal versus external), and types of thought leadership (national versus global).

Table 10.2   The Next Steps in KM Initiatives.

Organisation	Next Steps
AGC	Sharing more from senior officers, more e-gov services, new legislation database, search upgrade
DSTA	Competency management framework, streamlining workplace — eWorkplace
IPOS	Knowledge café, CoPs, sharing of success stories, a half-yearly knowledge audit, focus on culture
IRAS	Recognition to those who share, build on knowledge maps and expertise audit, subscribe to knowledge maps from other departments, sharing by retirees
JTC	Enhanced portal to provide automated notification when new reports are published, share expertise with other agencies, build technology and infrastructure
MOF	More customisation of system, investigate the Software as a Service (SaaS) model, search engine, migration to a new linked platform
NLB	Improve collaborative culture, collect more anecdotes via quarterly gatherings of K Champions, database of past enquiries, collaborate with external libraries
SAF	More intuitive tools, leadership competency, dashboard analytics, adaptive thinking
SPF-PTD	More KM capability development, evolution along APQC's KM Roadmap to Stage 5
SC	Portal upgrade, converting homepages to wiki-pages, flexible taxonomy, ensure institutional knowledge is shared, regular knowledge audits
SYOGOC	Post-Games Reports, a legacy for Singapore and international sporting organisations
URA	Embrace Web 2.0 technology for even better collaboration and sharing, innovative culture

Accordingly, as the KM projects mature over the time, some organisations are hiring more KM professionals to handle the complexities of the enterprise-wide implementation, or moving more people into KM roles (e.g. AGC), whilst others are extending their KM footprints to ex-employees (e.g. IRAS), partners in other parts of Singapore, and to counterparts in other countries (e.g. SYOGOC); indeed, the more

Table 10.3   KM Issues at Different Phases of Maturity.

Duration	Issues
Mature Stage (10 years)	— Benchmarking at regional/global levels — Driving KM across organisations and sectors — Winning global awards — Thought leadership: books, case studies
Intermediate Stage (5+ years)	— Phasing out incentives as culture is established — Assessing social media (internal and external) — External metrics for assessing KM effectiveness — Competing for national/regional/global awards
Early Stage (1–3 years)	— Scaling KM footprints: horizontal or vertical — Identifying incentives for knowledge behaviours — Evolution of KM metrics (largely internal) — Organisation-spanning initiatives

advanced organisations are taking part in global thought forums on KM or benchmarking their KM maturity paths (e.g. SAF).

KM is no longer the sole preserve of MNCs as it was in the 1990s — NGOs, SMEs, and government agencies are also getting on board. This knowledge movement continues to grow in strength and is fuelled by grassroots communities of KM professionals, events, national initiatives, cross-cultural collaboration, professional acceptance and awards.

Further, the field of KM continues to draw from other disciplines ranging from quantum science to cognitive theory. Some researchers liken the duality between tacit and explicit knowledge to the duality between matter and energy in quantum science; other researchers draw extensively on cognitive complexity, the scientific paradigm and systems dynamics. Perhaps more than ever before, it is important for KM practitioners and academics to cooperate in research and brainstorming. Each group often dismisses the other as fuddy duddies, ivory towerheads, moneygrubbers, shallow managers, and so on! But thought leaders from each sector have a lot to learn from each other and even more so in the co-creation of frameworks and opportunities. This could include joint research, internships and guest lectures.

KM should focus not just on best practices and scenarios but also on building organisational agility and resilience, which needs renewal and re-creation of socio-technical systems which go beyond mere replication of social media sites like Facebook on corporate intranets. Designs for knowledge sharing in an organisation should be conceptualised from the ground up, and not just as social layers. The use of social media will lead to the creation of 'digital breadcrumbs' or useful knowledge nuggets scattered in real-time micro-narrative streams (e.g. Twitter/Yammer). Federated search tools can be used to unearth these nuggets and trace valuable experts and volunteers. The web and social media are now emerging as examples of cognitive augmentation and distributed cognition on a global scale, almost like a 'Mind Machine Matrix'. While social media are more than the flavour of the month and are here to stay, optimal use of social media for knowledge flow requires more than just allowing employees to blog and tweet; they should also address rules, policies and culture.

While much KM focuses on content management, the essence is context. Processes for codification, editing and distilling knowledge assets will still be useful as what may be data to an organisation today may be knowledge tomorrow. Thus, organisations should be able to weave different views and interpretations on top of existing assets. There is no fixed end state for successful KM — knowledge is dynamic and horizons will continue to change. Hierarchies and flat networks will co-exist; the classic and the new must synergise. Organisational hierarchies will co-exist with flatter social networks; top-down taxonomies will co-exist with bottom-up folksonomies. Again social media is to be promoted, but investments in earlier KM infrastructure should also be harnessed and blended.

A number of areas are emerging for such research focus, addressing knowledge skills and interpretations. For example, as effective personal KM is a critical skill of the 21st century, it is also vital for managers to closely observe how employees work socially, and model knowledge cultures around it. The user's experience should incorporate core cultural values, such as respect, humility, passion, and being comfortable with ambiguity, for successful KM. As digital natives tend to naturally gravitate towards social media, and indeed one may have the opposite of the knowledge hoarding problem: Some members of Generation V (virtual) almost share too much information. Concurrently, digital immigrants can bring other valuable perspectives to the table. A good example is the 'work casting' or 'mind casting' use of Twitter by employees as opposed to the 'life casting' approach of teenagers.

At the KM Asia 2010 conference, Ron Young calls for collaboration between Asian and Western thinking in the area of KM, describing it as the 'need of the hour' whilst Dave Snowden, drawing on philosophical roots, acknowledges that there are attributes of Hinduism and Taosim in the realm of causality and nature that do not exist in common Western thinking, and a blend of both approaches is called for. Knowledge is not either explicit or tacit. Knowledge is both explicit and tacit (Takeuchi & Nonaka, 2004). Organisations need to embrace dialectical thinking, which calls for a synthesis of body and mind, individual (knowledge creator) and organisation (knowledge amplifier), top-down/bottom-up/middle-out flow, hierarchy and task force, global and local focus, and Western and Eastern thinking. The future belongs to organisations that can synthesise the best of the East and the West and construct a universal model of knowledge creation and sharing (Takeuchi & Nonaka, ibid).

References

Ahmed, P., Lim, KK. and Loh, AYE. (2002) *Learning through Knowledge Management*. Boston: Butterworth Heinemann.

Akhavan, P., Jafari, M. and Fathian, M. (2005) Exploring Failure-Factors of Implementing Knowledge Management Systems in Organisations. *Journal of Knowledge Management Practice*, 6.

Alfs, S. (2003) Accenture's New Operating Model: Meeting the Needs of the Knowledge Worker. In A. Beerli, S. Falk and D. Diemers (eds), *Knowledge Management and Networked Environments: Leveraging Intellectual Capital in Virtual Business Communities*. New York: Accenture/AMACOM Books. pp. 181–194.

Allee, V. (2003) *The Future of Knowledge: Increasing Prosperity through Value Networks*. Boston: Butterworth-Heinemann.

Alstete, JW. and Halpern, D. (2008) Aligning Knowledge Management Drivers with Business Strategy Implications. *Journal of Knowledge Management Practice*, 9(3).

Al-Ali, N. (2003) *Comprehensive Intellectual Capital Management*. New York: John Wiley.

Al-Hawamdeh, S. (2002) Knowledge Management: Re-Thinking Information Management and Facing the Challenge of Managing Tacit Knowledge. *Information Research*, 8(1), Retrieved January 7, 2013 from http://informationr.net/ir/8-1/paper143.html.

American Productivity and Quality Center. (2012) *Knowledge Management Frameworks*. Retrieved April 2, 2012 from http://www.apqc.org/knowledge-management-frameworks.

Amidon, D. and Macnamara, D. (2004) The 7 Cs of Knowledge Leadership: Qualification, Roles and Responsibilities. In C. Holsapple (ed), *Handbook on Knowledge Management*. New York: Springer. pp. 539–552.

Anumba, CJ., Ugwu, OO., Newnham, L. and Thorpe, A. (2001) A Multi-Agent System for Distributed Collaborative Design. *Logistics Information Management*, 14(5), 355–367.

Applehans, W., Globe, A. and Laugero, G. (1999). *Managing Knowledge: A Practical Web-Based Approach*. New York: Addison-Wesley.

Ashkenas, R., Ulrich, D., Jick, T. and Kerr, S. (2002) *The Boundaryless Organization: Breaking the Chains of Organizational Structure*. San Francisco, CA: Jossey-Bass.

Balfanz, D., Grimm, M. and Tazari, MR. (2005) A Reference Architecture for Mobile Knowledge Management. *Proceedings of Mobile Computing and Ambient Intelligence*. Germany: Schloss Dagstuhl.

Beerli, A., Falk, S. and Diemers, D. (2003) *Knowledge Management and Networked Environments: Leveraging Intellectual Capital in Virtual Business Communities*. New York: Accenture/AMACOM Books.

Bennet, A. and Neilsen, R. (2004) The Leaders of Knowledge Initiatives: Qualifications, Roles and Responsibilities. In C. Holsapple (ed), *Handbook on Knowledge Management: Volume 1 Knowledge Matters*. New York: Springer-Verlag. pp. 523–538.

Blair, BT. (2004) An Enterprise Content Management Primer. *The Information Management Journal*, September/October, 64–66.

Boisot, M. (1995). *Information Space: A Framework for Learning in Organizations, Institutions and Culture*. London: Cengage Learning Business Pr.

Boisot, M. (1998). *Knowledge Assets: Securing Competitive Advantage in the Information Economy*. USA: Oxford University Press.

Boland, RJ. Jr. and Yoo, Y. (2004) Sense-making Processes in Knowledge Management. In C. Holsapple (ed), *Handbook on Knowledge Management: Volume 1 Knowledge Matters*. New York: Springer-Verlag. pp. 381–392.

Carr, N. (2003) IT Doesn't Matter. *Harvard Business Review*, 81(5), 41–49.

Chatzkel, JL. (2002) Conversation with Alex Bennet, Former Deputy CIO for Enterprise Integration at the US Department of Navy. *Journal of Knowledge Management*, 6(5), 434–444.

Chatzkel, JL. (2003) *Knowledge Capital: How Knowledge-Based Enterprises Really Get Built*. New York: Oxford University Press.

Chin, BC. (2002) *Heart Work*. Singapore: Singapore Economic Development Board and EDB Society.

Chong, SC. and Choi, YS. (2005) Critical Factors in the Successful Implementation of Knowledge Management. *Journal of Knowledge Management*, 6.

CIO Council. (2001) Managing Knowledge@Work: An Overview of Knowledge Management. Knowledge Management Working Group of the US Federal Chief Information Officers Council. August, 2001.

Collins, H. (2003) *Enterprise Knowledge Portals: Next Generation Portal Solutions for Dynamic Information Access, Better Decision Making and Maximum Results*. New York: AMACOM.

Cong, X. and Pandya, K. (2003) Issues of Knowledge Management in the Public Sector. *Electronic Journal of Knowledge Management*, 1(2), 25–33.

Conway, S. and Sligar, C. (2002) *Unlocking Knowledge Assets*. New Jersey: Prentice Hall.

Cortada, JW., Hargraves, TS. and Wakin, E. (1999) *Into the Networked Age: How IBM and Other Firms are Getting There*. USA: Oxford University Press.

Davenport, T. and Probst, G. (2002) *Knowledge Management Case Book: Siemens Best Practices*. Germany: John Wiley/Publicus Corporate Publishing.

Davenport, T. and Prusak, L. (1998) *Working Knowledge: How Organisations Manage What They Know.* Boston: Harvard Business School Publishing.

Davenport, T. and Prusak, L. (2003) *What's the Big Idea? Creating and Capitalising on the Best Management Thinking.* Boston: Harvard Business School Publishing.

Denning, S. (2001) *The Springboard: How Storytelling Ignites Action in Knowledge-Era Organisations.* Boston: Butterworth-Heinemann.

Dewett, T. and Jones, GR. (2001) The Role of Information Technology in the Organization: A Review, Model, and Assessment. *Journal of Management*, 27(3), 313–346.

Dinca, M. (2011) Organisational Knowledge Development. *Journal of Knowledge Management Practice*, 12(3).

Dixon, N. (2000) *Common Knowledge: How Companies Thrive By Sharing What They Know.* Boston: Harvard Business School Publishing.

Donoghue, LP., Harris, JG. and Weitzman, B.A. (1999) Knowledge Management Strategies that Create Value. *Outlook*, 1, 48–53.

Drew, S. (1999) Building Knowledge Management into Strategy: Making Sense of a New Perspective. *Long Range Planning*, 32(1), 130–136.

Drucker, PF. (1988) The Coming of the New Organization. In *Harvard Business Review on Knowledge Management*. Boston: Harvard Business School Press, pp. 1–19.

Edvinsson, L. (2004) The Intellectual Capital of Nations. In C. Holsapple (ed) *Handbook on Knowledge Management: Volume 1 Knowledge Directions.* New York: Springer-Verlag. pp. 153–164.

Ekbia, HR. and Hara, N. (2006) Incentive Structures in Knowledge Management. In D. Schwartz and D. Te'eni (eds) *Encyclopedia of Knowledge Management.* Hershey: IGI Group, pp. 237–247.

Figallo, C. and Rhine, N. (2002) *Building the Knowledge Management Network: Best Practices, Tools and Techniques for Putting Conversations to Work.* New York: John Wiley.

Fontain, M. and Lesser, E. (2002) *Challenges in Managing Organisational Knowledge.* USA: IBM Institute for Knowledge-Based Organization Publication.

Ford, D. (2004) Trust and Knowledge Management: The Seeds of Success. In C. Holsapple (ed) *Handbook on Knowledge Management: Volume 1 Knowledge Matters.* New York: Springer-Verlag. pp. 553–576.

Gamble, P. and Blackwell, J. (2001) *Knowledge Management: A State of the Art Guide.* New York: Kogan Page Limited.

Garvin, DA. (1993) Building a Learning Organization. *Harvard Business Review*, 71(4), 78–91.

Gold, AH., Malhotra, A. and Segars, AH. (2001) Knowledge Management: An Organizational Capabilities Perspective. *Journal of Management Information Systems*, 18(1), 185–214.

Hanley, S. and Malafsky, G. (2004) A Guide for Measuring the Value of KM Investments. In C. Holsapple (ed) *Handbook on Knowledge Management: Volume 2 Knowledge Directions.* New York: Springer. pp. 369–394.

Hansen, MT., Nohria, N. and Tierney, T. (1999) What's Your Strategy for Managing Knowledge? *Harvard Business Review*, 77, 106–116.

Hasanali, F. and Leavitt, P. (2003) *Content Management: A Guide for Your Journey to Knowledge Management Best Practices*. Houston: American Productivity and Quality Center.

Hickman, RC. and Silva, AM. (1988) *The Future 500: Creating Tomorrow's Organizations Today*. London: Unwin Hyman.

Hicks, CR., Dattero, R. and Galup, DS. (2006) The Five-Tier Knowledge Management Hierarchy, *Journal of Knowledge Management*, 10(1), 19–31.

Ho, P. (2009) Speech at the *Interdisciplinary Conference on Adaptation, Order and Emergence*, Nanyang Technological University, February 12, 2009.

Holden, N. (2002) *Cross-Cultural Management: A Knowledge Management Perspective*. London: FT/Prentice-Hall, Pearson Education.

Holsapple, CW. (2004a) *Handbook on Knowledge Management: Volume 1 Knowledge Matters*. New York: Springer-Verlag.

Holsapple, CW. (2004b) *Handbook on Knowledge Management: Volume 2 Knowledge Directions*. New York: Springer-Verlag.

Holsapple, C. and Singh, M. (2004) The Convergence of Electronic Business and Knowledge Management. In CW. Holsapple (ed), *Handbook on Knowledge Management: Volume 2 Knowledge Directions*. New York: Springer-Verlag. pp. 657–678.

Honeycutt, J. (2000) *Knowledge Management Strategies*. Seattle: Microsoft Press.

Ives, W., Torrey, B. and Gordon, C. (2000) Knowledge Sharing is a Human Behaviour. In D. Morey, M. Maybury and B. Thuraisingham (eds), *Knowledge Management: Classic and Contemporary Works*. London: MIT Press. pp. 99–138.

Jain, P. (2009) Knowledge Management in e-Government. *Journal of Knowledge Management Practice*, 10(4).

Kaplan, RS. and Norton, DP. (2004) *Strategy Maps: Converting Intangible Assets into Tangible Outcomes*. Boston: Harvard Business School Press.

Kayworth, T. and Leidner, D. (2004) Organisational Culture as a Knowledge Resource. In C. Holsapple (ed), *Handbook on Knowledge Management: Volume 1 Knowledge Directions*. New York: Springer-Verlag. pp. 235–252.

Keen, P. and Mackintosh, R. (2001) *The Freedom Economy: Gaining the m-Commerce Edge in the Era of the Wireless Internet*. New York: McGraw-Hill.

Kluge, J., Stein, W. and Licht, T. (2001) *Knowledge Unplugged: The McKinsey & Company Global Survey on Knowledge Management*. New York: Palgrave.

Koulopoulos, T. and Frappaolo, C. (1999) *Smart Things to Know about Knowledge Management*. New York: Capstone Publishing.

Kouzes, JM. and Posner, BZ. (1996) *The Leadership Challenge: How to Get Extraordinary Things Done in Organisations*. San Francisco: Jossey-Bass.

Kuriakose, KK., Raj, B., Murty, S. and Swaminathan, P. (2011) Knowledge Management Maturity Model: An Engineering Approach. *Journal of Knowledge Management Practice*, 12(2).

Lambe, P. (2007) *Organising Knowledge. Taxonomies, Knowledge and Organisational Effectiveness*. Oxford: Chandos Publishing.

Lesser, EL. and Storck, J. (2001) Communities of Practice and Organizational Performance. *IBM Systems Journal*, 40(4), 831–841.

Lengnick-Hall, M. and Lengnick-Hall, C. (2003) *Human Resource Management in the Knowledge Economy: New Challenges, New Roles, New Capabilities*. San Francisco: Berrett-Koehler Publishers.

Liebowitz, J. (1999) Knowledge Management: Fact or Fiction? In J. Liebowitz (ed), *Knowledge Management Handbook*. Boca Raton, FL: CRC Press. pp. iii–v.

Liebowitz, J. and Chen, Y. (2004) Knowledge Sharing Proficiencies: The Key to Knowledge Management. In C. Holsapple (ed), *Handbook on Knowledge Management: Volume 1 Knowledge Matters*. New York: Springer-Verlag. pp. 409–424.

Malhotra, Y. (2001) *Knowledge Management and Business Model Innovation*. Hershey, PA: Idea Group Publishing.

Marks, J. (1983) *Science and the Making of the Modern World*. London: Heinemann.

Marwick, AD. (2001) Knowledge Management Technology. *IBM Systems Journal*, 40(4), 814.

Mathew, V. (2011) KM Strategies: Key to Change and Development in Business. *Journal of Knowledge Management Practice*, 12(1).

McAdam, R. and McCreedy, S. (2000) A Critique of Knowledge Management: Using a Social Constructionist Model. *New Technology, Work and Employment*, 15(2), 155–168.

McFarlane, DA. (2008) Toward a Knowledge Management Body of Knowledge (KMBOK): A Philosophical Discourse in KM Concepts and Ideas. *Journal of Knowledge Management Practice*, 9(4).

McKeen, J. and Staples, S. (2004) Knowledge Managers: Who Are They and What Do They Do? In C. Holsapple (ed), *Handbook on Knowledge Management: Volume 1 Knowledge Matters*. New York: Springer-Verlag. pp. 21–42.

Mertins, K., Heisig, P. and Vorbeck, J. (2003) *Knowledge Management: Concepts and Best Practices*. New York: Springer-Verlag.

Nair, S. (2010) Drivers of Knowledge Management. Retrieved April 2, 2012 from http://knowall2009.blogspot.in/2010/01/drivers-of-knowledge-management.html.

Natarajan, G. and Shekhar, S. (2000) *Knowledge Management: Enabling Business Growth*. New Delhi: Tata McGraw-Hill Publishing Company.

Newell, S., Robertson, M. and Swan, J. (2002) *Managing Knowledge Work*. New York: Palgrave.

Nonaka, I. and Takeuchi, H. (1995) *The Knowledge-Creating Company: How Japanese Companies Create the Dynamics of Innovation*. New York: Oxford University Press.

Nonaka, I. and Nishiguchi, T. (2001) *Knowledge Emergence: Social, Technical, and Evolutionary Dimensions of Knowledge Creation*. New York: Oxford University Press.

Norris, D., Mason, J. and Lefrere, P. (2003) *Transforming e-Knowledge: A Revolution in the Sharing of Knowledge*. Michigan: Society for College and University Planning.

O'Dell, C. (2004) *The Executive's Role in Knowledge Management*. Houston: APQC.

O'Dell, C. and Grayson, J. (1998) *If Only We Knew What We Know: The Transfer of Internal Knowledge and Best Practice*. New York: Free Press.

O'Dell, C. and Grayson, J. (2004) Identifying and Transferring Internal Best Practices. In C. Holsapple (ed), *Handbook on Knowledge Management: Volume 1 Knowledge Matters*. New York: Springer-Verlag. pp. 601–622.

O'Dell, C. and Hubert, C. (2011) *The New Edge in Knowledge: How Knowledge Management is Changing the Way We Do Business*. New York: John Wiley.

O'Dell, C., Elliott, S. and Hubert, C. (2004) Achieving Knowledge Management Outcomes. In C. Holsapple (ed), *Handbook on Knowledge Management: Volume 2 Knowledge Directions*. New York: Springer-Verlag. pp. 253–288.

OECD. (2003) Conclusions from the Results of the *Survey of Knowledge Management Practices for Ministries/Departments/Agencies of Central Government in OECD Member Countries*. February 3–4, 2003. GOV/PUMA/HRM (2003)2.

O'Sullivan, K. (2011) Synergy: Mobile Devices and Knowledge Management. Retrieved April 2012 from http://knowledgecompass.wordpress.com/2011/06/04/synergy-mobile-devices-and-knowledge-management/.

Owen, JM. (1999) Knowledge Management and the Information Professional. *Information Services and Use*, 19(1), 7–16.

Pentland, BT. (1995) Information Systems and Organisational Learning: The Social Epistemology of Organisational Knowledge Systems. *Accounting, Management and Information Technologies*, 5(1), 1–21.

Plessis, MA. (2005) Drivers of Knowledge Management in the Corporate Environment. *International Journal of Information Management*, 25(3), 193–202.

Powell, WW. and Snellman, K. (2004) The Knowledge Economy. *Annual Review of Sociology*, 30, 199–220.

Rao, M. (2005) *Knowledge Management Tools and Techniques: Practitioners and Experts Evaluate KM Solutions*. Boston: Elsevier.

Rosenberg, D. (2002) *Cloning Silicon Valley: The Next Generation High-Tech Hotspots*. London: Financial Times.

Rumizen, MC. (2002) *The Complete Idiot's Guide to Knowledge Management*. Wisconsin: Alpha Books.

Ruth, S., Shaw, N. and Frizzell, V. (2004) Knowledge Management Education: An Overview of Programs and Instruction. In C. Holsapple (ed), *Handbook on Knowledge Management: Volume 2 Knowledge Directions*. New York: Springer-Verlag.

Saint-Onge, H. and Wallace, D. (2002) *Leveraging Communities of Practice for Strategic Advantage*. Boston: Butterworth-Heinemann.

Schwartz, DG. (2007) Integrating Knowledge Transfer and Computer-Mediated Communication: Categorizing Barriers and Possible Responses. *Knowledge Management Research and Practice*, 5(4), 249–260.

Shekawat, U. (2002) Five Mistakes CKOs Must Avoid. Retrieved May 2012 from http://www.providersedge.com/docs/leadership_articles/Five_Mistakes_CKOs_Must_Avoid.pdf.

Shen, J. (2003) Utilising Mobile Devices to Capture Case Stories for Knowledge Management. In CHI '03 *Proceedings of the Human Factors in Computing Systems*. New York: ACM, pp. 688–689.

Smith, H. and McKeen, J. (2004) Valuing the Knowledge Management Function. In C. Holsapple (ed), *Handbook on Knowledge Management: Volume 2 Knowledge Matters*. New York: Springer-Verlag. pp. 353–368.

Srikantaiah, K., Koenig, M. and Hawamdeh, S. (2010). *Convergence of Project Management and Knowledge Management*. Maryland: Scarecrow Press.

Stewart, T. (1997). *Intellectual Capital: The New Wealth of Organisations*. London: Nicholas Brealy Publishing.

Taipei Times (Staff writer with CNA). (2009) *Education, Up to 60 colleges may close*, October 16, 2009, page 4. Retrieved 30 June, 2012 from http://www.taipeitimes.com/News/taiwan/archives/2009/10/16/2003456103.

Takeuchi, H. and Nonaka, I. (2004) *Hitotusbashi on Knowledge Management*. Singapore: John Wiley & Sons.

Terra, JC. and Gordon, C. (2003) *Realising the Promise of Corporate Portals: Leveraging Knowledge for Business Success*. Amsterdam: Butterworth-Heinemann.

Thompson, M. and Walsham, G. (2004) Placing Knowledge Management in Context. *Journal of Management Studies*, 41(5), 725–747.

Tiwana, A. (2002) *The Knowledge Management Toolkit: Orchestrating IT, Strategy and Knowledge Platforms*. New Jersey: Prentice Hall.

Tyndale, P. (2002) A Taxonomy of Knowledge Management Software Tools. Origins and Applications. *Evaluation and Program Planning*, 25(2), 183–190.

Wenger, E. (2006). Communities of Practice. A Brief Introduction. Retrieved May 22, 2008 from http://www.ewenger.com/theory/index.htm.

Wenger, E., McDermott, R. and Snyder, W. (2002) *Cultivating Communities of Practice: A Guide to Managing Knowledge*. Boston: Harvard Business School Press.

Wiig, KM. (1999) Introducing KM into the Enterprise. In J. Liebowitz (ed), *Knowledge Management Handbook*. Boca Raton: CRC Press. pp. 3–41.

Wimmer, MA. (2002) A European Perspective towards Online One-Stop Government: The eGOV Project. *Electronic Commerce Research and Applications*, 1(1), 92–103.

Zhou, Z. and Gao, F. (2007) E-government and Knowledge Management. *International Journal of Computer Science and Network Security*, 7(6), 285–289.

Zoppè A. (2002) Patent Activities in the EU: Towards High Tech Patenting 1990 to 2000. *Statistics in Focus, Science and Technology*, No. 112002. Luxembourg: Eurostat.

Index